WAYS OF THE ANT

Also by John Crompton

A HIVE OF BEES
THE HUNTING WASP
THE SEA
THE SNAKE
THE SPIDER

To
Rowdy FitzGerald
co-workers friend
whose love of all
creatures is an
inspiration to me.

John J. Reid
1/8/93

WAYS OF THE ANT

BY JOHN CROMPTON

*with eight drawings
by J. Yunge-Bateman*

NLB

Nick Lyons Books

Copyright © 1954 by J. B. C. Lamburn.
Introduction copyright © 1988 by Paul Schullery

ALL RIGHTS RESERVED. No part of this book may be reproduced in
any manner without the express written consent of the
publisher, except in the case of brief excerpts in critical
reviews and articles. All inquiries should be addressed
to: Nick Lyons Books, 31 West 21 Street, New York, NY 10010.

Printed in the United States of America

10 9 8 7 6 5 4 3 2 1

Published by arrangement with William Collins Sons & Co., Ltd.

Library of Congress Cataloging-in-Publication Data

Crompton, John, 1893–1972
    Ways of the ant.

    Reprint. Originally published: Boston : Houghton
Mifflin, 1954.
    Bibliography: p.
    Includes index.
    1. Ants I. Title.
QL568.F7C85 1988   595.79′6   88-2682
ISBN 0-941130-84-3 (pbk.)

CONTENTS

ILLUSTRATIONS

THE MANY KINGDOMS OF JOHN CROMPTON

ABOUT fifteen years ago, a friend and I drove to Panama. It's a long story—it's a long drive—but one brief part of it came to mind when I was asked to write an introduction for this book about ants.

We were in Guatemala, having entered it from Belize across a frontier best called "uneasy." I was driving our Volkswagen down a jungle road, humming along with the washboard rhythms, when I slammed on the brakes and started to back up. I remember that my pal was a little annoyed—we were making bad enough time as it was—but as soon as he saw what I had seen, he was with me again.

There was a double line of large ants crossing the road, most of them carrying things. We watched them for a few minutes, wondered what they were going to and coming from in the jungle, decided not to look, took some pictures, and drove the car over them once more as we left. Ohio, I thought at the time, had nothing like this.

I was wrong, of course; Ohio had just the same thing. The difference—what Ohio *didn't* have—was the setting. Seeing a little line of ants crossing a dusty spot in the lawn under the maples had nowhere near the romance of seeing that same line passing between two wildly tangled walls of jungle. It was the stage, not the players, that made the drama so exciting.

Which brings me around to John Crompton, who, whatever else he may or may not have been (he wasn't even John Crompton, that apparently being a pen name), was a superb stage-setter. He understood, as few nature writers and interpreters do, the importance of scale. In only a few words, he can get you into his subject's world (whether ants, or bees, or spiders, or some other popularly alien creature) and make it *matter* to you. His characters were really that: *personnae* that must be evaluated, then disliked or sympathized with. Reading Crompton reminds me, repeatedly, of a statement by Louis Agassiz that Charles Fergus quotes in his engaging little book of essays, *The Wingless Crow*: "I spent the summer traveling. I got halfway across my back yard." Crompton understood the dimensional richness of local geography.

But he understood much more than that. It would hardly be enough just to get us to an interesting world; he had to make great things happen there. He did. Verlyn Klinkenborg, who wrote the introduction to the new (1987) edition of another Crompton book, *A Hive of Bees,* likened Crompton's narrative sweep to "Prescott on Peru or Parkman on Quebec." That's fair enough, but that's not how I see things in *Ways of the Ant*.

In ant land, at least in Crompton's ant land, there is an exoticness that transcends historical narrative. I see, instead of historical scenes, grandly fictional ones. When Crompton takes me into a nest of warrior ants, with slaves annointing them and preparing them for their next battle; when he introduces his Amazons, and his Pharoahs, and his Soldiers; when he describes the hesitation of an army at siege or a Queen occupying a new home; when he does all these things I am reminded, not of great history, but of great saga, whether it be some ancient tale of northern kings or the epic adventures of H. Rider Haggard. These scenes of Crompton's are only marginally real landscapes; I don't lose sight of that, even as I am wrapped up in the tale. But the grand stakes, and the tragedy, and the glory, of the events being described are real in the best sense of the word. Kingdoms are won and lost, heroes die foolishly and are avenged magnificently, royalty is betrayed by selfish heirs.

But how are we, here in the late twentieth century, to deal with such egregious anthropomorphism? Ants aren't little people; people aren't big ants. Why should I get such a big kick out of stories written more than thirty years ago, when not only is his perspective fairy-tale-like, but also his scientific reliability is diminishing with the years? Most of what's in this book isn't even firsthand observation; it's culled from scientific texts Crompton read. Why not just read the books he lists in his bibliography and hear the story from the real experts?

I've probably already answered that, at least partly: the magic's in the telling, not in the tale. If readers just wanted scientific data on wildlife, the *Journal of Wildlife Management* would have a million-and-a-half circulation. But I think there's also magic in the man doing the telling. I and the others who have written introductions for these new editions of his books (Verlyn, Klinkenborg, Stephen Bodio, David Quammen, Robert F. Jones) are all intrigued by this little-known British gent Crompton, or J.B.C. Lamburn, which might have been his real name. He was something of an adventurer—a traveler, soldier, and sportsman in Africa and Asia in the years before World War II—who settled down to write these books and some others, based in part on his own experiences in the odd places of the world, in part on his fresh readings of other people's knowledge.

He seems to me a late model of a notable British "type," those marvelous creatures who dashed off to the wild corners of the empire, did amazing, daring, outrageous things, came back (or stayed), and wrote charming books about it. Burton, Selous . . . how long is the list of names, men (mostly) who alternately surrounded themselves with the comforts of the club, and exposed themselves to unspeakable hardships, always reporting on it with that detached whimsy now more often poked fun at than admired. Had a bit of a row one night with a pair of tigers; nasty chaps, they were, came into camp and carried off the cook. Spilled my cocoa.

Crompton is a spiritual descendant of those better-known writers. He seems to have had his share of rows, too, but it's more for his commitment to the job at hand—telling a good tale—that he reminds me of the famous old adventurers.

It's also for his eye to detail. Some of the best of the African big-game hunters of the nineteenth and early twentieth centuries, right in the middle of some gripping account of a lion stalk, would launch into a "by-the-way" sort of digression on just what those little beetles were that had such pretty wings, or what they noticed about the directional orientation of the den openings of this local badger species, or how often that bird seems to sing just before a storm, or some such other charming irrelevancy that makes their books so much more than mere sporting narratives. Crompton was simply carrying that digressive skill (call it a skill, call it an obsession, it was a hallmark of the best of those writers) to some sort of extreme, where the little asides became the story, and took on the tension and thrill of the lion hunt.

You'll want to read this book to learn about ants. Don't get me wrong; I'm not saying it isn't full of amazing stuff about ants. It is, and you'll never again see an ant without wondering what it would have to show you if only Crompton were its agent.

You'll want to read this book to learn about nature—wild animal nature, human nature (many of his little anecdotes about ant life, when they don't seem like sagas, seem like parables), evolving nature, nature as a cultural force.

But mostly you'll want to read this book for the fun of good story telling. Most people who want to learn about wild things are capable of wading through the technical journals, but for them nature is a pastime, not a profession, and they don't really care to work that hard, or learn quite that much. They want translators, people who can do more than read the news to them; they want people who can interpret, editorialize, and tell them what it might mean. And they want people who can entertain them. If asked, they would insist on accuracy and current information, but most nature readers don't bother to worry about the accuracy of something they read, much less go check on the author in some scientific journal. That would not be fun, however much fun it was for Crompton, or is for any of the rest of us who write.

So here's John Crompton on ants. I hope it's your first, so that when you finish it, you will still have all his other books to look forward to. But don't worry about those others now. You're traveling with the ants here, and long before you're halfway across the yard you'll be in a different world.

—PAUL SCHULLERY
January 1988

PREFACE

A BOOKSELLER told me that a lady came into his shop once and asked him if he had a book on ants. He had only two and she asked him which was the better. He suggested Maeterlinck's *Life of the Ant*, and she bought it. As she left, carrying the small book neatly wrapped up, she said brightly that her house was full of ants and she wanted to know how to get rid of them. Before the bookseller could speak, the door had closed and she was gone. Had that lady merely glanced at the preface to the book she bought she would have known that it was extremely unlikely that it would give her instructions on the extermination of ants.

For it is one of the duties of a preface to set out the scope treatment and limitations of what follows. In any bookshop, any library, any second-hand bookstall, you will see men and women earnestly engaged picking up books and looking at the beginning pages. Eventually they will select the book that, from what they can gather, is most likely to appeal to them, and the selections of erudite scientists will be different from the selections of laymen, who, unlike the scientists, have not been over that ground before.

This book then is a book written for laymen. Such a book must obviously differ from a book written for students or teachers or biologists. It must assume that the reader knows little or nothing about the subject, and it must present ants not as biological specimens but as interesting beings leading their lives just as we lead ours—but in a different way and under different impulses.

Quite what these impulses are we do not know. As I say, they are certainly not like ours. Nevertheless, we who view ants do so through our own senses and intelligence. A book written about ants by an ant would be incomprehensible to us. So to make ants comprehensible to ourselves we have to endow them to a certain extent with attributes that we possess but that they probably do not, having others of their own. This sort of interpretation can be carried too far, but when it helps to make the subject clearer its use is legitimate. The reader must not be too literal-minded—that is all.

Apart from an explanation of the treatment, a preface ought perhaps to offer some justification for the book itself. Is a popular book on ants "necessary"? Nearly all the known facts about ants have been dealt with in other books—not to mention magazines. My answer (after some exploration) is that I do not think too many popular books *can* be written about ants. I may be thought to be biased, so before giving reasons for my opinion, I will quote an expert, Professor Alexander Petrunkovitch, the leading arachnologist of America, who did me the honour of writing an introduction to my book on spiders. Spiders are not ants, but what he says about spiders holds good also for ants.

" . . It is true that many careful observations and painstaking studies have been made by specialists, dealing with all phases of structure, development and life of spiders, so that our knowledge of this interesting group of creatures is now quite extensive. But the average man still lives in ignorance. . . . The reason for this attitude is quite simple and is not entirely the fault of the average man himself. What causes it is the scarcity of good popular books. There are some good books of great merit in several languages, serious accounts from which one can learn a great deal without a prerequisite knowledge of natural sciences, and large treatises for specialists. But there are very few books on spiders written not only with a knowledge of the subject, but in a manner to make it fascinating to the lay reader. The interest of such a reader is quite different from that of a student of nature, so that a book written for the latter may be tiresome to the former. . . ."

The average man is aware that ants are "interesting." He will also often say that they are the most advanced of the insects. But I do not think he is particularly well informed about them. There is no reason, of course, why he should be. A knowledge of ants will not help him in his business. But a thirst for knowledge is one of the characteristics that distinguish man from the other animals. The Scaly Ant-Eater possibly knows several things about ants and termites that human experts do not. The Green Woodpecker, too, knows where new nests have started just under the surface far better than we do. But this is their "career," and by this expert knowledge they sustain themselves and their families. One could never get *them* interested in butterflies or fishes or in the origin of species.

It would be tedious, and uncalled-for, to cite the instances of ignorance about ants that I have met amongst my acquaintances. As I have said, there is no reason why they should know about ants. But I will give one example merely because it happened last week (at the time of writing) and because in another couple of weeks I will probably have forgotten it. Held up for transport, I dined at a country hotel some fifty miles from London. Three men came in and sat at the table next to me. I judged them to be city men who had their homes in the country. I heard, of course, all their conversation. Amongst other subjects they spoke about gardening, politics, books, and the theatre. I learnt a lot from them. I jotted down the name of a recent rose which is apparently well worth growing, and I heard some ins and outs about politicians and actors. Indeed, I take this opportunity of thanking those three men for making my solitary meal so interesting and instructive. Then—it was in connection with gardens—the subject turned to ants. They spoke for quite ten minutes about ants and their ways. Knowledgeable as they had been about all their other subjects, they failed on ants. One said that ants, unlike bees, had a king as well as a queen. Another mentioned the swarms of flying ants that had issued recently from nests in his garden. Those flying ants, said the third, were the old ants who, when they got too old for work, developed wings and flew off and founded new colonies before they died. And so on; some information right, most wrong. These were intelligent men with an interest in the things around them, including ants. Why were they so ignorant about ants? Obviously because they had not taken the trouble to read about them. Will they read this or any other popular book on ants? Not perhaps those particular three, but some will, and of these some may pursue the study further.

The last thing I wish to do, however, is to pose as a self-appointed teacher, for, although several readers of previous books wrote asking for a book on ants, I wrote this one chiefly because I wanted to write it.

I wish to thank James Fisher for his kindness in going over my manuscript and for his very helpful criticisms and suggestions. I also wish to thank J. Yunge-Bateman for his striking drawings, and Miss Chloë Talbot-Kelly for the sketches that appear on pages 82, 149, and 210.

CHAPTER I

THE BEGINNING

GRANULAR craters all over the lawn and flower-beds and between the stones of the crazy paving do not endear ants to gardeners. Nor do any of us welcome the straggly processions that invade our larder and eat our food and expose the inadequacy of almost every known brand of ant-killer. I respect ants, indeed I am awed by them, but I hold no brief for them. Whether the nests in the flower and vegetable plots etc. do any harm I cannot say. By undermining they certainly kill off some of the young roots, but do they not make up for this by aerating the soil? I asked a knowledgeable modern-trained farmer about this. He said no. He said they brought up the sub-soil and did more harm than good. This may be true but he forgot one thing: ants have been working on the soil for countless ages. That same farmer possesses some very fertile fields and that fertility is mostly due to the labour of by-gone ants and earthworms who put in about fifty million years' work " double-trenching" his property for him.

Returning to the present, I do not, as I say, know whether the nests in the garden do much harm, but, personally, I am all for getting rid of them. The difficulty is to do so. I had some melons once growing in a frame and the conditions in that frame were just right for ants. They love heat, but moisture must be available. They got both, also the light, friable, stony soil they adore. I tried a large number of preparations. These upset the ants and killed some of them, but next day the little craters would reappear.

Then I came upon a preparation which not only the label but friends of mine said was sure to kill. The smell of it made one gasp. I poured it over the ant holes and, to help it in its task, shut the frame. It must have done tremendous damage to the ants for they did not recover until a fortnight later. The melons never recovered.

Harmless or not as the *nests* may be, the occupants must be looked upon with grave suspicion. I do not think that all their activities are yet known, but when you see ants very busy about a tree or a plant, that tree or plant is not, or very shortly will not be, healthy. It is, of course, greenfly that they chiefly plant out, but they plant out other pests as well.

There are many species of out-door ants that never go near a garden or cultivated land. Ants also nest in a variety of places as well as in the ground: in tree-stumps, hollow trees, stone foundations, and the rest. We will touch on some of these nests later on; for the time being we are going to be fully occupied tracing the life-cycle of the ant itself, and for that purpose we will select one of the common species and one that nests in the ground.

If you turn over a flat stone you may find a number of shallow channels just underneath filled with greatly alarmed ants and one or two patches of cocoons. This is the roof of the nest, also the exit and entry. The nest itself will probably extend deep below and may contain as many storeys and rooms as an American sky-scraper. In this underground nest are corridors, chambers, galleries, shafts, pillars. If it could be fossilised and dug out it would look rather like a large sponge.

Inhabiting this complicated maze are, in the simplest cases, a queen (two or three perhaps) and a large number of diminutive but very busy workers. In the summer months other types appear; winged, fully-sexed male and female ants that soon fill the place with a multitudinous and eager throng. Incidentally they have little reason for this exuberance for most of them are about to die.

Looking more closely, we see in some chambers eggs, in others grubs, in others cocoons, the progeny of the queen mother in their various stages of development. The eggs are very small and often need a lens to see them. They are tended with great care by the workers, who nevertheless, unlike bees, do not regard them as sacred. They believe that eggs were made for ants and not ants for eggs, and will eat them when hungry without hesitation. So will the mother, who, at this stage of her existence, views her whole brood—eggs, grubs, cocoons, callows and the rest—with complete indifference.

In a few days—or weeks, according to several controlling factors—the eggs hatch out into the minutest grubs, white and legless. They are then called *larvae*, though grubs is just as good a word. The workers feed them assiduously and they wax big and fat. They are fed mostly with liquid food regurgitated into their mouths, though sometimes they are given a bit of solid food—a dead insect perhaps—which is held close to their mouths so that they can nibble at it.

In three weeks or longer (sometimes very much longer, a year or even more than a year), the workers shovel earth over them, or make pits and bury them alive. The grub now, unaided, has to spin a silk bag all round itself, and to do this it must have some purchase—some solid surrounding to spin against. Having buried the grub, the workers throw the last soil over the grave, clean their feet, and appear to forget about it. But they do not forget. At the right time they dis-inter it and find that it has made a coffin for itself and lies apparently dead and disintegrating inside. In other words, it has made itself into a parcel, a neat, cylindrical, white or yellowish-white silk parcel, the "Ant's Egg" that goldfish like so much.

This parcel is the cocoon, or *pupa*, and from it, in about three weeks, will emerge the fully developed ant, male, female or worker as the case may be.

The ant, however, cannot get out of its coffin by itself. At (again) the right time the workers break the coffin open and help out the resurrected one. As a matter of fact, it is not really quite an ant just yet. It is flabby, colourless, and it will be some days before its outside skeleton (and the skeletons of insects are outside and not in) hardens and takes on the black, red or yellow or mixed colouring of the adult. In this in-between stage it is called a *Callow*.

Not all grubs spin cocoons. In point of fact there seems no necessity for any of them to do so. So if the grub belongs to a species that does not spin a cocoon, its soft, arched figure will straighten out and gradually become stiff as if in death. The skin will shrivel and become translucent, and underneath another mummified form of a different shape will begin to appear. This is called a *semipupa*.

In due course, like an over-tight silk dress, the skin of the semipupa (which was once the skin of the grub) splits down the back and the callow emerges.

All these forms, eggs, grubs, pupa and semipupa, require attention and varying degrees of temperature and moisture. That is why ants are always carrying them about and laying them in heaps in different rooms. For certain rooms in the nest are hotter than others but the temperature is always changing. By day the hottest rooms are near the surface where the sun has warmed them; at night they are in the basement. Unlike bees, ants have no means of regulating the temperature artificially, so they get over the difficulty by moving their various forms of young from place to place, which involves a lot of work. Hard-worked housewives who cry plaintively, " Up and down! Up and down!" might well go to the ant to see what "Up and down" really means!

Barring accident or deliberate abandonment, the ants' nest is permanent. There is no reason why it should not endure for ever. They have not the same control over their affairs that bees have; to a certain extent and in certain directions they trust to luck, but luck often serves them better than the elaborate and theoretically foolproof system of the bees. The snag to ants is that most of them cannot make a new queen to replace a failing one. They can make new queens, but not one that will with certainty replace the old one. For the virgin female ant, like the virgin female bee, must fly away to mate, but the female bee, when fertilised, will come back to her own nest, the female ant will not—at least, not deliberately.

To replace a queen, bees raise about half a dozen new ones, release the first, send her out to get mated, and wait anxiously for her return. When she sails back (providing she is dragging behind her the bloody entrails of her husband—proof of her union) joy is registered, the old queen and the one or two reserve new ones are killed, and the newly mated queen installed. Ants merely send out thousands of virgin queens every year and trust to luck that one or more of them, after mating, will chance to fall near the nest, and out of so many this is almost bound to happen. The drawback is, one would imagine, that these thousands of males and females need a lot of feeding before they depart, and the return for all this feeding is practically negligible. Wasps, of course, and bumble bees

Newly-emerged Minims come to the rescue of their exhausted Mother

raise queens in the same extravagant way, but with them it does not matter. The parent nest is an annual affair and is doomed in any case: as well let virgin males and females eat what food there is as leave it for rats and mice and beetles later on.

With bees colonisation and the renewing of queens are two quite different and distinct operations. With ants, the "swarm" fulfils both purposes, though it is chiefly a colonising affair.

Ants really, although they leave it to chance, have no occasion to be concerned about the renewal of their queens. For one thing, their queen lives longer than the honey-bee queen (ten years or more against five years or less), for another, she does not suffer from the hysterical jealousy of the bee queen, who will suffer no rivals. So the ants can keep a number of queens reigning in harmony in their nest, and often do so, especially when the old queen's span of life is drawing to a close.

However, we are not concerned here with the renewal of queens or even with old nests, we wish to start at the beginning, and the beginning is the swarm, or "marriage flight"—the issue of winged male and female ants in summer from the nest, which can be observed in almost any garden.

The ant workers decide the day and hour of departure but have much difficulty in restraining their young charges. Excited by sex and the knowledge of coming liberty, these impatient creatures have to be pulled back and kept in by force until the time is ripe. We do not know what influences the workers in deciding when that time is; weather conditions perhaps, though these (to us) do not always seem ideal. Almost invariably a large number of nests of the same species, scattered all over the place, swarm at the same time. It is almost as if arrangements had been made between them beforehand. One cannot seriously think that this is so, and therefore it must be the weather. Whatever the reason, since all mate in the air together, it certainly prevents inbreeding.

Released at last, the eager young things pour out. They have never flown before and never will again, and for all their excitement they find they cannot rise up into the air as they wish. They have to run about on hillocks, pebbles, grass stems, filling their breathing tubes with air and exercising the muscles of their gauzy wings. Then at last the wings can bite the air and they are off.

Mating (with most species) takes place in the air, and the two partners fall to earth, often *in copula*. With so many thousands at large, some of the females may fail to be over-taken by a male. These are given no second chance, but have to descend to the ground and die.

The male ant escapes the savage mutilation that is the drone's reward for obeying Nature's edict. After the act of mating he can leave his partner whenever he chooses to do so, and depart uninjured. But he is a spent force; he is like the chaff that blows away after the wheat has been extracted. He has given the female enough sperm to fertilise millions of her eggs. This treasure has been placed into her purse, or spermatheca, to draw on whenever needed. It must last her for ten years or so. She will get nothing more from him, nor will any other female. Nature has no use for poverty of this kind; she withdraws her patronage and he soon perishes. He may last a few days, even a few weeks—fed and kept under artificial conditions he has been known to last a year—nor-mally, however, he lives very little longer than the disem-bowelled drone.

The fertile female now rubs herself against a stone or piece of grass, and in this deliberate manner rids herself of her wings. Wings that can operate are not just appendages attached to the back like the wings of cherubs depicted on stained glass windows; they need large and powerful muscles. The female ant possesses these great wing-operating muscles. What a waste, then, to rub off her wings after only one short flight! Actually it is not so extravagant as it sounds. The wings were needed for emigration and, since after landing they will not be required again, it is good policy to get rid of them as quickly as possible, just as we hurry from a plane after it has taken us to some destination. As for the wing muscles, they are even more important as reservoirs of food than they were as wing propellers.

For the young queen will get no food for many months, she must live on her own fat and these same muscles. Not only this, she will have to lay eggs and feed grubs on the same material. No, the extravagance lies not in giving these creatures temporary wings but in raising so many of them.

After getting rid of her wings the queen looks around and then begins to dig a little burrow in the soil, in the open or under a stone. At the end of this burrow she makes a small chamber and then closes up the aperture, immuring herself. She uses her jaws and teeth for digging, and if the ground is stony loses all her teeth.

Until the eggs come there is little to do. She knows nothing of the ceaseless labour of the queen wasp or bumble bee at this stage. Finally a little clutch is laid and the queen broods over them. They hatch, and the queen feeds them from her mouth with a secretion she manufactures in her body. The grubs grow, and the more they grow the more food they need.

This is the time of the most frenzied and exhausting activity with queen wasps and bumble bees, of journeys to and fro collecting food, of building inside the burrow, of further egg-laying and incubating. The queen ant does nothing. But her stocks are low. There is nothing much left in her of fat and wing muscle, yet, though herself starving, her only hope of survival lies in feeding others. It is going to be a close thing. Luckily, nature helps her to a certain extent by making the grubs form cocoons, or pupate, as it is called, long before what is the normal time in established nests. This saves the queen from having to provide any more infant nourishment from her exhausted frame, but it is at the expense of the grubs —or rather of the adult forms into which the grubs eventually develop—for the first workers that emerge are stunted little things, hardly fitted, one would think, to cope with the herculean labour that awaits them. They rise, however, to the occasion.

Wheeler tells us that with some species it is fully ten months before the first workers appear—ten months without food or water for the queen. Undoubtedly there are many, many cases when, almost within sight of salvation, the queen dies of hunger and her little brood perish with her.

There are many other hazards. Statistics are impossible so, one cannot say how many females that fly from the old nest survive. Probably not one in a thousand. The first hazard is the worst.   Swarms of flying ants attract attention.   Birds, frogs, toads, mice, lizards, etc., go after them in a big way, both in the air and on the ground.   Indeed birds not infrequently become unable to fly from a sheer surfeit of flying ants.   Even afterwards, when the surviving queens have dug their burrows, things are not much better.   Other insects kill them, mice dig them out, mould and fungus smother them, flood, cold, drought, exterminate them, and hunger, as we have pointed out, must do away with a number of the remainder.

And all this, I think, is just as well: ants are sufficiently numerous already.

But to return to our particular queen, who is one of those that survive.   The little stunted workers (they are called *minims*, by the way) emerge from their coverings and get to work.   First, they open the aperture, closed so long ago by their mother, and hasten out in search of food.   Almost anything will do, minute insects dead or alive, refuse, anything—their mother is not likely to be finicky by this time.   They hurry back and give her what they have found.   She must be pleased: she has cast her bread upon the water, and it has returned to her after many days.

From now on the mother's troubles are over.   She "hands over" to her stunted daughters.   Out of the food they give her she lays more eggs, and these develop into normal-sized workers.

In human circles opulent mothers not infrequently employ nannies and Froebel-trained nurses, and thereafter pay little further attention to their young, being, in fact, almost forbidden to do so.   It is the same with the young ant mother. She lays the eggs, and the more-than-Froebel-trained workers do everything else, including feeding and looking after *her*. So the mother, once so devoted and efficient in difficult circumstances, now takes no part in the upbringing of her young.   She just lays eggs.

Which brings us to the end of the cycle.   And again it must be stressed that the above is an account of the life of a large number of ants.   But not of all: in the following pages we shall meet many queens and many workers with very different habits and very different lives.

CHAPTER 2

THE NEST

THE ant is a diligent builder, but that, in most cases, is as far as it goes. Its work, though adequate, is crude—chambers, pillars, corridors, put in with no real plan. The nest compares with the bees' nest as the catacombs compare with a modern block of flats. And it possesses no furniture; no cradles for the young, no storage bins for food. The bees' home contains three different types of cradles—worker, male and queen cradles—and storage cells for solid and liquid food: not rough affairs, but made with precision and delicacy. The rough and ready (though laborious) way of building practised by the ants means that no two nests are ever the same, and I should imagine that the ants themselves sometimes get a bit confused and take the wrong corridor. Nor have the ants in their homes any real control over that important matter, temperature, which, together with ventilation and moisture, has been completely mastered by the bees. And yet temperature is almost as vital a factor in the upbringing of ant babies as of bee babies. What the ants do we have seen already; they carry their young to whatever chamber in the nest happens to be of the required heat, and when that heat begins to fail they carry them somewhere else. The ant baby knows little rest. Ants are not hot-blooded like we are: bed-clothes would be no use to them. It is as if we carried a naked baby about the house into whatever room was being warmed by the sun; then at night down into the kitchen.

But to compare the ants' nest to that of the bees is a little unkind. If a man has built a house which, though unpretentious, fulfils his requirements, there is no need to sneer at him because he has not erected a Buckingham Palace. And ants—at least most of them—are very fond of their homes. There *are* ants of certain species, however, that can never settle down, that have the urge always to be moving somewhere else, and there are those who do not want to move but are *made* to do so by restless companions.

The general conception of a nest of social insects is of a large body of creatures acting in complete uniformity. How they achieve that uniformity of purpose and action has long been a subject of debate and disagreement. As a matter of fact, in certain respects a community of ants has often as little uniformity of purpose as a collection of human beings. Like ourselves, ants have their radicals, who are always wanting change, and their conservatives. When the radicals propose a removal to a new place, the conservative ants are solidly against it and, being in the majority, out-vote, as it were, the restless radicals. But the radicals care nothing for votes. They are determined to "remove," and start doing it straight away. They seize the young in their various stages, the queen, and even some of the conservatives themselves, and march off in file with these burdens to the proposed new home, hoping to present their opponents with a *fait accompli*. But the conservatives have no intention of letting them get away with that sort of thing. They run after them, enter the new nest, pick up the larvae, etc., that the radicals have just deposited and go back with them to the old home. Very soon one sees the ridiculous sight of a double procession going opposite ways, and composed on the one side of ants bearing the contents of the old nest to the new, and on the other of ants carrying those contents back again.

There is no quarrelling, no fighting, just grim determination. It resolves itself merely into a question of who tires first. The double procession goes on often for days, and then one side weakens, its members fall out, or join the other procession and their fellows accept defeat though one or two diehards struggle on for a long time. The desire for change indicates a more active spirit, so it is generally the removalists that win, in spite of the fact that they start as a minority.

A new underground nest is but a small affair and is only just under the surface. It is thus in very real danger. There are a *few* creatures who eat the small, brittle, stinging worker ant, but there are many who relish the succulent grubs and cocoons. Later on, as the nest gets deeper, the risk is not so great. For the time being, however, camouflage is necessary. A flat stone is best—it protects *and* hides—but flat stones over suitable material are not always available. So in the initial stages of a nest we find deliberate and clever camouflage. Leaves, grasses, even rabbit dung, skilfully used. At this stage, too, the betraying pellets of earth brought up by the diggers are not thrown into mounds or craters just over the nest but carried far away and scattered inconspicuously.

Later on some species, particularly *Formica rufa*, the well-known "Horse Ant" of the pine forests, throw up huge mounds several feet high and broad at the base. But when they make these mounds they are well established deep below and have little to fear from enemies. Even man would be well advised to leave heir fortress undisturbed. Yet in spite of this, these ants are careful to close all their doors at night, covering them with whatever is available or suits their fancy—cut grass, pine needles, leaves, twigs, and so on. These are removed early in the morning and replaced at dusk. Some completely thatch the outside mounds.

These mounds are not just earth thrown up from the excavations below, they are an important part of the internal economy of the great colony that lives in and far below them. A mound presents a greater surface to be warmed by the sun than does a portion of level earth. *And* it gets much hotter than the surface earth. In a way it is a moderate oven, possessing not only high temperature but more space at high temperature. The temperature inside is often 10° C. higher than that of the surrounding air. So its advantages as an incubator for the large number of eggs and larvae being dealt with by a colony that may number 150,000 inhabitants are obvious.

Many species clear the ground for several feet from the nest, make long roads by cutting down the vegetation, and erect earthen "rest-houses." Arboreal species also make out-houses of leaves at some distance from their nest, in which they keep their livestock.

The nests of ants are of all sizes and are found in almost every conceivable place from branch stems and oak-galls to the foundations of our houses. Furthermore, the same species may nest in different places; tree-stumps, earth, crevices in walls, etc. Probably the most intricate nest is that made by

Œcophylla, an ant that lives mostly in the tropics. Its nest is in the interior of large leaves sewn together and situated in some tree or bush. The workers are reddish, the females green, the males black. Natives treat their nests with great respect. Unknowingly I have camped near one or brushed by one when stalking with a camera, and in an incredibly short time have been covered with red ants all biting and stinging furiously, and their sting is something quite out of the ordinary.

This ant sews together the outside leaves of its nest with the finest silk and how it manages to do so used to be a mystery. Where did it get the silk in the first place?—for no ant can manufacture silk.

Doflein first discovered the *modus operandi*. He found a nest and cut a rent in one of the outside leaves. Evidently he did not stay after that for he escaped the punitive expedition that immediately poured out. When he came back he saw that a row of ants had ranged themselves in a perfectly straight line along the bottom edge of the cut. He waited. They reached up on their hind legs and grasped with their jaws the upper edge of the rent. Then, holding on to the lower edge by the claws of their feet they began slowly to drag the two edges together.

The rent had been made across a portion previously sewn with silk and the broken threads hung disorderly from the edges. Other ants came running out whose job it was to clear these threads away, just as a tailor removes the old thread before sewing on a new button. They bit and pulled them off, and when they had got a mouthful of them hurried off to the other side of the nest where they stood in the open waiting for a gust of wind. When a gust came they released their burden and it floated away. One large lot of matted silk came away all of a piece and a number of ants combined to hold it. Then, walking all together to the other side, they stood waiting for the puff of wind. When the wind came, as if on a word of command, all opened their mandibles together, and the unweildy webbing eddied off.

All this time the line of ants stood waiting, still holding on to the lower and upper edges of the rent.

When the old thread had been removed they drew the two edges completely together. Eagerly Doflein waited to see

what was to happen. Alas, a sudden and strong gust came.
The straining creatures could not hold on. The rent flew
apart.

It takes a lot to discourage an "insect." If they can teach us
nothing else, spiders, ants, bees, and many more can teach
us patience. The ants, sent tumbling, lined up again, and in
half an hour had brought the edges close together once more.
Fortunately, this time, no gust came. Had a hundred gusts
come the patience of the ants would have survived them, but
not, I imagine, that of the observer.

The ants stood motionless holding the rent together, and
seemed content to stand motionless. Doflein almost gave
up and went away (he had been there nearly two hours).
Then, as if on some stage cue, there emerged from the
wings a number of workers carrying white maggots in their
jaws.

These maggots belonged to the nest and must have objected
strongly to the treatment they received, for apart from being
brought out into the open they were being pinched about
their middles.

Now the plot became apparent, for ant maggots *do* produce
silk to make their cocoons. And even if they make no cocoons
they can still produce silk.

The silk comes out in a fine thread, which is glutinous at
first and then hardens. The ants were carrying living shuttles.

These new arrivals got to work immediately. Each
sempstress jammed the hinder end of the maggot against the
leaf, thus forcibly attaching its thread, then, carrying the
creature to the adjoining leaf, banged its posterior down again,
and rammed home the sticky thread firmly with her head.
Upways and downways and crossways went these unfortunate
babes, the silk being squeezed out of them by their busy
carriers. The rent was repaired, held firmly and securely by
a "thin, fine, silken web."

So fine is the thread emitted by the maggot (which is
always only a half-grown maggot) that it is invisible to the
naked eye. Naturally, Doflein wanted to see it. So he produced
a strong lens and bent forward to see the sempstresses at their
work.

I can testify that he must have been very quiet and careful

before. For two hours he had escaped notice. Now his eagerness got the better of him. "In a twinkling," he says, dozens
of ants covered his eyes. He did not stay, and considers, with
reason, that he was lucky to have preserved his sight.

When the gap between leaves is very wide it is obvious that
a single ant's body cannot bridge the distance. In such case
they form a number of chains composed of ants linked together.
Some of these chains are four inches long. As the topmost
ant drags down the leaf she hands the edge to the ant beneath
her, and so on.

The viciousness of this little ant raises a sort of general
knowledge question. Do ants sting, or bite? They do both.
Some just bite, the severity of the pain varying with the size
and power of the mandibles. Some bite and, almost at the
same moment, arch their bellies and squirt formic acid into
the wound. Some squirt formic acid with a force to carry
it six inches to two feet. (If one is bending over a nest and
gets a dose of this from several hundred ants the effect is
similar to ammonia—contraction of the throat and coughing.)
If the acid touches the skin, pustules are raised like those caused
by nettles, while the vapour alone is sufficient to make the
skin peel. Some (and these are generally regarded as the more
primitive types) sting with a sting situated at the tips of the
abdomen like that of the bee or wasp. These stings are always
unpleasant and some are extremely painful, but it is to be
doubted if any are as severe as that of the honey bee.

Although many ants seem to choose their nesting-sites
haphazardly, it is remarkable what discrimination they possess.
For instance, there are ants which will never be found in
cultivated land, others must have open spaces, others forests.
Yet most of these nests were founded through the agency of
the mating flight, which is completely haphazard. The flying
females have no control over their destinations: they are little
more than so many dandelion seeds and must at times—under
the agency of winds as well as their own motive power—
travel long distances. (Little is known about this for we cannot
ring ants as we can ring birds.) Finally they drift to earth,
where they immediately get rid of their wings and thus more
or less immobilise themselves. A female then can walk or
run but she certainly cannot travel far; so how can she select

cultivated or non-cultivated land, forests or plains? Possibly conditions in uncongenial places prove fatal, but it is difficult to think why or how.

That, however, is enough of nests for the time being. We shall now study the ways of certain groups of ants that have been sorted out according to their mode of life and their ways of obtaining food.

CHAPTER 3

THE HOUSE ANT

WHEN man built a house, heated it, and put food in it, he must surely have known that others would wish to share it with him.   Warm, wind-proof, rain-proof, enemy-proof residences, stocked with food, are not easy to find in nature. So, since building that house he has had many callers, to all of which he has given a cold reception. The callers swallowed any indignation they may have felt and, being denied entry at the front door, went round to the back. To do them justice, none of them knew that this was the man's house, made by himself, and *had* they known, it would not have made the slightest difference; he was in a place that suited them, and there was room and food for both—especially since most of them proposed to live with him on a sort of Box and Cox arrangement, they to operate at night and he to go about his business by day. So they went in by the back door to share his dwelling with him, and have been there, on and off, ever since—a motley crew of rats, mice, cockroaches, spiders, beetles, flies, mosquitoes—and ants.

There are two sorts of ants in houses; the first have found the larder or some place they like and merely trickle in from a nest outside, the other *lives* in the house, in the foundations. The first is comparatively easy to deal with, the second is not. To get rid of the second a major operation often is called for, a digging up of part of the foundations. People often go to entomologists and say that ants have invaded their place and what can they do about it? What they want is something they can put down to kill the ants. They do not want any nonsense or talk of foundations.

Well, there *are* preparations you can put down to kill ants. There are proprietary preparations and mixtures you make yourself, and by them you can reduce the invasions and even, for a time, stop them. The trouble is that you are attacking the wrong end. You do not permanently get rid of the hair on your face by shaving, nor do you exterminate docks by cutting their leaves off. You have to attack the root. And the root, with ants, is the nest, together with the queen, or queens.

The manufacturers of many ant-killing powders have realised this, for in their instructions they say, "First trace the ants to their nest . . ." It is excellent advice, but how to do it is a different matter and the instructions do not carry one that far. It is indeed rather similar to Mrs. Beeton's instructions on how to cook a hare—"First catch your hare . . ." Unless one is an ant oneself one cannot go through crevices between bricks into some spot underneath a cellar. One may perhaps track the ants to an outside crevice in the wall and stop it up, but stone walls do not a prison make, for ants; they are probably deep in the foundations and can only be got at by pulling half the house down. Indeed I know of someone who did this. He did not pull half the house down but he had the bottom floor up and workmen went down into the foundations and demolished part of them. They found the nest and destroyed it and put everything back, including the floor. Either they missed a queen or there was another nest close by, for the ants were soon back again in full force.

In ancient Egypt there was a small inconspicuous yellow ant that nested only in the ground under little stones and went about its affairs without harming anyone. With the possible exception of Brazil, it was found nowhere else, but in that small body dwelt a great spirit: it had the pioneering urge: it embarked on ships and spread itself over the whole world. Now, denizens of hot countries, if they wish to live in cold countries, have to take precautions. They cannot live in the open as they used to. So this Egyptian ant that once nested on the surface of the soil now lives only in houses. It is called Pharaoh's Ant (*Monomorium pharaonis*). It arrived in Britain about 200 years ago and heads the list as the worst of ant pests in houses.

In his book, *British Ants*, the late H. St. J. K. Donisthorpe says: "When once *Monomorium pharaonis* has become established anywhere it is almost impossible to get rid of it." He goes on to mention a certain Dr. Bostock, who took similar steps to the man who had his floor pulled up. "Dr. Bostock," he says, "had the whole of his kitchen floor taken up, the grate, and part of the walls and woodwork removed, and new tiles, set in cement, fixed on the walls and floor, and even then this pest was not eradicated."

Donisthorpe collected a lot of information about the activities of this ant. We give, shortly, three examples. In 1834 several houses in London and Brighton had to be vacated, so intolerable had the swarms of ants become. They over-ran in thousands a hotel in Winchester in 1846. Robert Service saw a house in Dumfries literally "taken over" by these ants from cellar to attic, covering the white walls and turning them yellow. Like the cricket the Pharaoh ant flourishes in bakeries, but (except that such places are warm) one would hardly expect to find it in Corporation Baths; yet in 1926 it became well established in the Corporation Baths of a town in Scotland—and to find one's clothes, after a bath, infested by ants is not pleasant.

House-hunters are beset with various problems. I do not wish to add to their many difficulties, but I advise them to make quite sure that there are no Pharaoh ants in any house they propose to purchase.

Courage and hardiness help in the preservation of species, but I am inclined to think that an omnivorous diet helps even more. Man, the most successful animal, eats almost anything. Ants vary, but the Pharaoh ant (except for vegetables) has almost as catholic a diet as man. It eats sugar, sweets, cakes, pastry, butter, bread, lard, fat, meat—anything, as those who have it in their houses know. It enjoys its food too, and eats a lot. We could put up with this perhaps—after all, the actual loss of food is not very great and ants are not germ-carriers like flies—what we really object to is finding our eatables covered with dense masses of ants.

These ants have a remarkable sense of smell—or whatever sense serves them for smell. They seem to appear from nowhere whenever even a very small bit of food is left lying about. Their sense of smell must be keener even than that of a mouse —which is exceptionally keen. I had a mouse in a Nissen hut in Iceland; shall I digress and tell the story?

This hut was only a sleeping hut; no food was kept there, except from time to time a piece of chocolate on a bookshelf or some place that ought to have been inaccessible to the mouse. But during the night, the mouse always found the chocolate and nibbled it, making a great deal of noise doing so. Every night I put that chocolate somewhere else, but it hardly ever failed to get it—put it where I liked.

This mouse became, not tame, for I had no dealings with it, but contemptuous of me. I soon found that it would operate with the light full on. This was a pity for the light had been left on in the first instance in order to keep the mouse away. So now I had no option but to study its methods. I never saw it sniffing the air or moving its head about like a dog to try and catch the scent. It would run about and climb a bit, and then stand motionless. After that it seemed to know where the chocolate was and would make straight for it, often doing the most amazing climbing feats before it reached it.

Things, however, could not go on like this. I am allergic to mice and could not sleep in the dark for fear of the mouse, and I could not sleep in the light because of the light. There was a lot to do on that Iceland aerodrome and I needed my rest. Then why, you may ask, take chocolate into your room? Because things were worse without chocolate. Without chocolate that mouse was a rover, an examiner of every nook, cranny, shelf, cupboard . . . or bed. I got a small break-back trap and baited it with that mouse's favourite food, chocolate.

The last thing I wanted to see was the execution, but I *had* to keep my light on. Inconsequently, I rather hoped the mouse would not come, but it did, from its usual corner, and it had not got a foot into the room before it halted and turned its beady little eyes towards the trap. It seemed pleased and ran to it but, just outside the danger area, halted, stared at the chocolate (whose fumes must have been tantalising almost beyond resistance) and stayed motionless. What thoughts ran through its little head? Did it wonder why the inevitable piece of chocolate had suddenly become so accessible? It did not examine the trap or move round it; it just stood. Then it turned and ran back scared to its corner.

In ten minutes it returned. This time it went backwards and forwards in a semi-circle in front of the trap, its nose held up. It reminded me of those children in the advertisements of a well-known gravy compound. Then, putting temptation behind it, it streaked back to the corner.

From now on, at roughly two-minute intervals, the mouse came out, went back, came out, went back—often getting so dangerously close that my heart was in my mouth. This went on for the surprising time of an hour and a half; an hour and a half of the tortures of Tantalus for the mouse. Then it decided to have one little nibble and see what happened. What happened did not interest it much: the trap caught it fair and square on the neck and after a short flurry it was dead.

The Pharaoh ant has changed its habits in many ways, and luckily for those whose houses it infests it no longer engages in wedding flights. It is almost intolerable as it is, but were several hundred thousand winged ants to invade our rooms at certain periods evacuation would be necessary until the orgy was over and the mess cleaned up. The true females still grow wings but never use them. Fertilisation probably occurs in the nest. After that the females lose their wings and run about inside the house and out. Each one of them can found another nest. No wonder they are hard to get rid of.

Can anything good be said of the Pharaoh ant ? From our point of view I do not think so. At one time they were supposed to destroy bed-bugs; but a naturalist travelling on a ship had both bed-bugs and Pharaoh ants to contend with, and says the two got on perfectly well together.

The Pharaoh ant is the pioneer in large-scale house invasion, but others are following in its footsteps, and the prospects for householders in another thousand years or so are none too good. People domiciled in temperate regions are, so far, comparatively little affected; the bulk of ant house-invaders are confined to hot countries, but the history of the Pharaoh ant makes us doubt whether they will always remain there.

In nature the majority of ant species nest in stony soil, tree stumps or logs. Amongst the latter is the North American Carpenter Ant (*Camponotus pennsylvanicus*), and this ant is amongst those that have decided to share houses with man. Now whereas the ants (including the Pharaohs) that nest in stone or brick foundations do no harm to the house itself, the Carpenter ant *does* do harm. It still regards wood as the only thing to nest in. It can riddle and almost hollow out the woodwork of a house (in addition to robbing the larder and covering the food with their biggish black bodies). The damage it causes to wood approaches at times even that of termites.

The Carpenter ant visits Britain fairly frequently. Nests come over in timber (pine, ash, etc.) imported from America, but strangely enough it cannot settle down in British houses. Donisthorpe thought that our wet winters discouraged it. I confess I cannot follow this; once it is in a house rain can mean nothing to it.

Continuing with America, there is another ant trying hard to qualify for a position amongst the big house pests. It is known as the Argentine ant (*Iridomyrmex humilis*). It is in the changing-over process and some nest in the foundations of houses and some out-of-doors in fields, etc. In winter, however, all the country ants go to town and join their house cousins, who apparently welcome them with open arms. Then all nest together in somebody's basement, so that during this annual reunion there may be (according to Newell) 1,000 fertile queens in one community in one nest. In spring the guests leave in their masses for their country homes. They have probably outworn their welcome, but it is a safe bet that some time in the future they will *not* return to their country homes.

To give a list of house ants is impossible. Many are casual invaders. Of the rest, there is a list for one country and another list for another, together with a long list for tropical countries. The one or two examples we have given must suffice.

CHAPTER 4

MISTRESSES AND SLAVES

IN the East—at any rate until comparatively recent times—
"Foreigners" possessed many servants. It was the normal
thing to do. I knew one Customs official on the Yangtse (a
Portuguese) who lived alone and had nine servants. He had
his own personal servant, a house-boy, a cook, two engineers
to run the lighting plant of the house, a groom and a stable
boy for his ponies, a private rickshaw boy, and an amah to
do his washing and mending. This particular man was certainly somewhat ostentatious, but the rest of us were not in
a position to sneer; our own servants were sufficiently
numerous.

Now these servants of ours took pride in their work. The
"boy" liked to see his master turned out smartly, and the
cook took pride in making appetising meals. And so on. What
did they get in return? They got payment, prestige, the protection of a foreign settlement (no small item in those often
disordered times), and, doubtless, rake-offs from grocers,
bakers, butchers and the rest. They *liked* being servants. In
fact, they went to a lot of trouble to *be* servants, and the
competition was tremendous.

This was not slavery: any servant could leave when he
wished: but in some respects it was very like the slavery
practised by one or two species of ants. In Britain there is
only one slave-making ant. America has more. The name
of the British slaver is *Formica sanguinea*, sometimes called the
Blood Red Ant in translation of the Latin, though there is
little that is blood red or any red about it—a touch here and
there in the thorax and legs, that is all. An older and simpler
name is the Sanguin or Sanguine Ant: let us use it. By our
standards in this country it is a large ant (5-9 mm. long) and
is quite common. It is fierce and brave when need be and

possesses large fighting forces, but these forces rarely attack until they have ascertained beforehand that the enemy can be overwhelmed without too much difficulty. And this goes to their credit. It indicates good generalship.

We associate slavery with cruelty. Human slaves used to be, and still are in certain places, made to work under the lash of the whip. The slaves of the Sanguin ants work equally hard but not under the lash of the whip. They, too, like being servants.

And what do *they* get in return? They get the peace and security that a powerful army gives, plenty of food, and plenty of hard work—all things that make for happiness. And no doubt the Sanguin ants would pay them were currency in use amongst them, for the Sanguins like their slaves in a vague, careless way.

So far, slavery as practised by the Sanguin ants sounds idyllic—lenient mistresses, contented slaves. But the question arises, how do the mistresses *get* those slaves? And here the scene changes.

Dr. Livingstone and others have described the methods of the Arab slavers in Africa in the previous century. Villages were surprised, old people and children put to death, and the rest led away under conditions that resulted in only some ten per cent surviving. The slaving raids of the Sanguins are similar in the initial butchery, but not afterwards, for the ant method of coming to maturity makes things much simpler for raiding parties. All they have to do is to capture and carry off what one might perhaps describe as the babes-in-arms. These are already conveniently packed in cylinders ready for transport. In the new nest to which they are taken the children emerge from the cocoons and grow up with no memories of slaughtered parents and kinsfolk. There are no mournful "Darkie" songs amongst the slaves of the Sanguins.

Human slavers were not in such a happy position. They *could* take babes-in-arms and sometimes did, but these were hardly an asset. Few survived and those that did were little use for about fifteen years. Even then they had to be trained; and to train them to reach the competence of the Sanguin slaves would, if it were possible at all, take another long period.

When an ant nest is turned over there is obvious panic, but

that panic does not prevent the inhabitants from trying to carry away the cocoons to safety. They must think the cocoons very valuable. And they *are* valuable, for inside each is a fully trained and efficient servant. It is these cocoons, and only these cocoons, that the slavers are after. They will carry off larvae also, but probably only for food.

In a few days young ants emerge from the cocoons. They are in an alien nest but they do not know it. Not far away is a ravished home strewn with the corpses of their family, but they do not know that either. Their bodies harden and they get down to work. They tend the children of their mistresses and help their own sisters to emerge from *their* silken prisons. They are contented in their work. There is only one thing that might be expected to surprise and worry them—though it does not seem to do so—and that is that every male and true female that emerges from a captured cocoon is killed. Only workers are allowed to live, and this for obvious reasons.

The Sanguin ants differ from other slave-making ants in that they are perfectly well able to get on without any slaves at all. They can do the work; the nursing, foraging, cleaning, digging, just as well as their slaves. But they prefer not to, and most of the Sanguin nests we examine *do* possess slaves, but not all.

In the old days Arab and European slavers selected the unfortunate Negro for the bulk of their depradations. Curiously enough, ant slavers also go in for a certain dark victim which was called the Negro ant long before it was known that ants made slaves at all. They *do* take others at times, but only when the Negro ant is not available.

The scientific name of the Negro ant is *Formica fusca*, and it is smaller than Sanguinea. It is a common ant and its nests are sometimes found in the garden, generally near walls. It is a dark brown ant.

And now, I think, it is time to witness an actual raid by Sanguin ants on Negro ants. If you are lucky you *may* see one for yourselves, but in lieu of that the best thing is to go to Huber.

Pierre Huber (the son of the famous blind Francois Huber, who so greatly advanced our knowledge of bees), was a pioneer amongst ant observers and we owe much of what we know, even to-day, to him. Here is part of an account of a Sanguin raid, taken from his *Natural History of Ants*:

". . . On the 15th July, at ten in the morning, a small division of Sanguin Ants was despatched from the garrison and arrived in quick march near a nest of Negro Ants situated twenty paces distant, around which they took their station. The inhabitants, on perceiving these strangers, rushed forth in a body to attack them, and led back several prisoners. The Sanguin Ants made no further advance; they appeared to be waiting some reinforcements. From time to time little companies of these insects came from the garrison to strengthen the brigade. They now advanced a little nearer and seemed more willing to run the risk of a general engagement; but in proportion as they approached the Negro dwelling, the more solicitous did they seem to dispatch couriers to the garrison, who arriving in great haste produced considerable alarm, when another division was immediately appointed to join the army. The Sanguin Ants, although thus reinforced, evinced little or no eagerness for combat, and only alarmed the Negro Ants by their presence."

(Evidently the Sanguin Ant has nothing to learn about a "Cold War"—or a "War of Nerves.")

"The latter" (the Negroes) "took up a position in front of their nest of about two feet square, where nearly their whole force was assembled to await the enemy.

"Frequent skirmishes take place all around the camp, the besieged always attacking the besiegers. The Negro Ants, judging from their number, announce a vigorous resistance; but distrusting their own strength" (the War of Nerves has beaten them already) "they look to the safety of the little ones confided to their care, and in this respect show us one of the most singular traits of prudence of which the history of insects can furnish an example. Even long before success is in any way dubious, they bring the pupae (cocoons) from the subterranean chambers and heap them up on the side of their nest opposed to that where the Sanguin army is stationed, in order to carry them off with the greater readiness should the fate of arms be against them. Their young females escape on the same side.

"The danger becomes more imminent; the Sanguin Ants, sufficiently reinforced, throw themselves in the midst of the Negroes, attack them on all points, and arrive to the very gates of their city. The latter, after a brisk resistance, renounce its defence, seize upon the pupae deposited on the outside, and convey them to a place of safety. The Sanguin Ants pursue and endeavour to steal from them their treasure.

"The whole body of Negro Ants are in flight; some few pass through the enemy's rank and at the hazard of their lives enter once more their habitation and expeditiously carry off the larvae, that would otherwise remain devoted to pillage.

"The Sanguin Ants descend into the interior, take possession of the avenues, and appear to establish themselves in the devastated city. Little bands of troops continually pour in from the garrison, and begin taking away the remainder of the larvae and pupae, establishing an uninterrupted chain from one ant-hill to the other: thus the day passes and night comes on before they have transported all their booty.

"A considerable number of Sanguin Ants still remain in the Negro residence and on the following morning, at break of day, recommence the transfer of the rest of its contents. When they have taken away all the pupae and larvae they then carry each other to the garrison, a few only remaining behind." (Ants frequently "carry each other." To an ant, with its strength, the weight of another ant is very small. It amounts, with us, to you or I giving a friend a lift behind on a bicycle.)

The above is an account of one particular raid. No two raids are quite the same. Although Sanguins often do indulge in wars of nerves, it is not their invariable method. They often aim at a surprise attack with superior numbers, and before a Negro nest is assailed considerable work has been put in by scouts. The exact route to the nest is known and the various apertures of the selected city have been studied, also the strength of its garrison. In ideal circumstances delay would only make their work more difficult, nevertheless they often do delay when there seems no reason for it. The Sanguins are brave, but they regard a raid as a raid and not war (we shall see their conduct in war later) and if, after launching an

attack they find the resistance so hot that there is a likelihood
of high mortality, the troops are quickly called off and the
attack postponed until sufficient reinforcements have been
sent. Sometimes they may even call the whole thing off and
march home.

In these slave raids Negroes are often massacred in large
numbers, but the Sanguins never seem to get possessed by
mere blood lust. They will kill all who put up a strong resistance and all who try to restrain them, but if a raid meets with
no resistance and they get what they want, the affair may be
conducted without any loss of life on either side.

A Frederick Smith is supposed to have been the first man
in England to witness a Sanguin raid. By that, of course, is
meant to witness it intelligently. To most people ants, whatever they are doing, are not worth a second glance. Let us
listen to Smith's account, for to get a true picture one raid is
not enough.

"It was in the summer of 1843 I discovered a colony of this
slave-making ant, and very closely I watched it, in the hope
of witnessing what others had described. Three successive
years passed without any satisfactory result."

One morning Smith found this colony assembled in
numbers outside their nest apparently keyed up for something,
the larger soldiers constantly jumping up and "assuming the
most threatening attitudes." It all came to nothing. Eventually
they went back to their nest. Evidently this was a preliminary
mustering, a sort of roll call for the raid that had been planned,
for:

"Again, in the evening, I visited the spot and to my delight
I found the army again in battle array. Numbers of the
largest ants at length separated from the rest and formed an
advance guard, and the whole body was in motion. At a
distance of about twenty yards was a nest of *Formica fusca*"
(Negro Ant). "This was the object of their attack. Without
the slightest pause the advanced warriors boldly entered the
nest, and in poured swarms after them. After a few moments
had elapsed numbers issued forth, each carrying their slaves
in their jaws. Occasionally a number of black ants rushed
out of the nest and gallantly attacked their invaders, but they
were quickly overcome and carried off to the nest of the

victors. Frequently, however, they were torn limb from limb, in which case their mangled bodies were borne off, no doubt as food, to the nest."

This was a very unusual raid for Sanguins in that they entered the nest so promptly. Donisthorpe indeed suggests that the writer wrote it up some time after the event and did not get all the details quite right. For, although everything is mapped out beforehand, the canny Sanguins do not usually act with such precipitation.

Finally let me quote Darwin. His account is of no value really for he only saw the end of a raid. But it paints a picture.

"One evening I visited another community of *Formica sanguinea* and found a number of these ants returning home and entering their nest, carrying the dead bodies of *F. fusca* and numerous pupae. I traced a long file of ants burdened with booty for about forty yards back to a very thick clump of heath, whence I saw the last individual of *F. sanguinea* emerge, carrying a pupa; but I was not able to find the desolated nest in the thick heath. The nest, however, must have been close at hand, for two or three individuals of *F. fusca* were rushing about in the greatest agitation, and one was perched motionless with its own pupa in its mouth on the top of a spray of heath, an image of despair over its ravaged home."

That ants think (in their own way), come to decisions (not always unanimous), and act according to those decisions is so obvious that there is no need to labour the matter. Nevertheless it is interesting to give examples from time to time. Here is one in connection with a Sanguin slave raid. An observer witnessed the raid which took its usual grim course until by evening the last Sanguin ant had staggered home with the last pillaged cocoon, and the Negro city, littered with dead, was left bare and desolate.

Quietness fell on the Sanguin nest, but things were happening inside, for after a while the whole populace came pouring out once more. It was no raid this time, for all, or nearly all, carried cocoons. Moreover, they carried their own cocoons as

" An Image of Despair ". (page 40)

well as the captured Negro cocoons which they had been at such pains to transport and store only a short time ago. In addition they carried their queen, eggs, grubs, and all their food, and the whole lot marched back to and entered the now empty Negro city and made it their permanent abode—or at least as permanent as any Sanguin abode ever is.

Now in this case three more or less mental processes must have taken place. First, certain of the attacking army, even in the heat of battle and murder, must have noticed that the city they were despoiling was better than their own and must have borne this in their minds. Second, they must have communicated this impression of theirs to the others. Third, a a decision must have been made, followed by immediate action on a wholesale scale.

Doubtless a number of the stay-at-home faction were against the idea, but the bulk must have been in favour, for the exodus was complete.

Barring accidents, there is no reason why a Sanguinea community should not be permanent. I do not refer to the actual nest (which they like to change from time to time) but to the community itself. The slaves die off, of course, in time, but they can make another raid if another Negro nest is within reasonable distance. And if not, they can get along without them and do the work themselves. (And in this they are unique amongst slave-possessing ants.) They have their queen and their marriage flights so that a failing queen can always be replaced.

But species do not survive by keeping to one family and one place. How do the Sanguins found *new* colonies? Obviously, you may say, by the normal method: i.e. the marriage flight, the coming down to earth of the newly fertilised female, then the hole in the ground in which this same female raises her first bevy of young. You get two out of three marks only for this because the third link in the chain is missing; the pregnant Sanguin queen cannot by herself raise a family as her distant female ancestors did. She must have servants to help her— her own sterile sisters, or slaves.

Leaving out the hazards of all migrating queens—birds, frogs, toads, mice, lizards, etc.—four things may happen to a newly descended, newly fertilised Sanguin queen. (1) She may wander about and die of hunger; (2) She may descend near her own home and either enter it herself or be escorted there by workers and become a reserve or a co-reigning queen; (3) She may find workers of her own blood who agree to go down some hole with her and raise her children.

Otherwise (4) she must perish or go on a slave raid by herself—a one-woman raid, a very different matter from an attack by thousands.

The Negro ants are not a warlike people, but when in numbers are formidable enough, formidable enough, as we have seen, to make whole Sanguin armies think twice, and more, before attacking. A Sanguin queen is larger than a soldier and possesses a terrible pair of serrated pincers. Nevertheless, she *is* but one; one against a multitude, and a multitude that bear her race as much affection as Central African natives bore the Arabs in the old days!

The young Sanguin queen has first to *find* a Negro nest. So she roams about and eventually finds one. (If she does not she dies and is of no more interest to us.) Let us suppose it is a strong, that is to say thickly populated, nest. In this case (and with every reason) she seems diffident about going any further in the matter. When females in general are doubtful about the reception they may get they try to be ingratiating. The Sanguin queen accosts two hurrying Negro workers.

Ants do not smile, but if they did, the queen's face at this moment would be almost split in half. It is wasted effort; one horrified glance is enough for the two workers; they make off at full speed. The queen smothers the annoyance she feels and accosts other workers with almost as broad a smile and with the same result.

Most queens realise after a while that there is no profit in dealing further with this particular type of nest and go off in search of another. But the Sanguin queen is her own worst enemy; she has a wicked temper and nothing brings it out more than having her advances repulsed (a trait not confined to female ants, as Shakespeare has observed), and the queen may get so annoyed at seeing nothing but the rear ends of fleeing workers that she marches straight into the Negro nest. In this case she will come out more quickly than she went in. When she collects herself outside she will find herself badly buffeted and bruised and bitten. If she tries to force her way in a second time she will probably be killed.

The wise queen, however, goes away and searches for another and a weaker nest of Negro ants. What happens when she finds it?

Here I will break off for a moment to answer the inevitable question: "How do we *know* what happens when she finds it?" Well—queens can be deliberately placed outside these various nests and the reactions of the parties noted, but in nature we certainly cannot follow the queen after she has *entered* the nest. We can, however, do so in artificial nests containing light and dark chambers. And this is what has been done, and a very large number of observations have been made. It is not quite the same as doing the impossible and finding out what happens under natural conditions, but it is the next best thing. It is the only way, and surely if enough experiments are made we cannot be very far out. Later, I will describe a few of these experiments; for the time being I will resume the story of the hypothetical queen we have been watching.

The queen, then, wanders away from the strong Negro colony and finds a weaker one. She approaches it, again putting on the ingratiating smile. Probably this is not hypocrisy on her part. It may be she really does think these Negroes will fall for her. After all, she knew them in the old home and they were amiable enough then. As we have said, her trouble is her short temper. She cannot bear being thwarted and is aware that she is armed with very punishing pincers.

At the entrance of the nest she again meets two workers, puts on her "meek and mild" act, and, brushing by them, tries to go inside. The horrified couple fasten on to her legs and the metaphorical smile fades from the queen's face. Her innate irritability comes to the surface and she kills them and marches into one of the galleries of the nest. Here she simmers down and tries to look pleasant, but she still feels upset. She rounds a corner and the terrified and precipitate flight of a number of Negroes almost brings on another attack of tantrums. But she controls herself, for she honestly regards herself as an apostle of peace and goodwill, and does not realise that she is as dangerous as a stoat in a rabbit warren.

In a chamber she comes upon some cocoons that the owners in their fright have temporarily abandoned. Does she see into the future? Does she realise that these globules will later hatch into ants that will attend to her and love her?—ministrations she is far from getting at the moment. She gathers these cocoons into a pile of her own careful arranging and gloats over them.

Meanwhile small frightened ants are hovering ghost-like in corners. They see this intruder in possession of some of their cocoons! It is as if human parents, flying from an ogre, turned to see the ogre grabbing their children. Brave deeds would happen then. Brave deeds happen now. Two Negro ants rush up and carry off two cocoons before the queen realises what they are about. She dashes after them, recovers the cocoons, and leaves two bodies writhing on the ground.

She steals more cocoons, and there are more attempts to take them from her—and more deaths. But the queen has had a tiring day—several tiring days probably, especially if she has tried to visit other nests. She goes to sleep. The little workers take immediate advantage of this and get all their cocoons back. They stack them in the farthest corner and mount guard over them.

The queen wakes, gazes unbelievingly at the emptiness once occupied by "her" cocoons, sees them in the far corner, and, enraged by the theft, charges forward. She gets them all back. The Negroes defy her and fight her whilst she is doing it. A nasty business this, with much slaughter.

All hope of an armistice, such as the queen thought she wanted, is at an end now. Were the remaining workers never so subservient, did they fawn and grovel—which they do not —they would get no mercy. The young, excitable queen is in a hysterical state. She prances[1] over the pilfered cocoons, screaming abuse and defiance at the Negroes. (*Need* I point out that "screaming" is a figure of speech?—though ants do pipe and make various noises. They may make louder and

---

[1] " Prancing " is a high-stepping dance of defiance which has been frequently observed in artificial nests.

higher ones not attuned to human ears.) Woe betide the worker that approaches her store now. But they do, and in one or two days not one of them is left alive.

So we have the Sanguin queen in sole possession of a mass of cocoons which she has won at the cost of much Negro blood and, usually, of some injury to herself. The cocoons begin to hatch, and the queen's blood-stained pincers have to be employed on a more delicate task than slaughter. The young ants cannot emerge without a kind of Caesarian operation. The covering skin has to be cut in a circle, and the top part removed. This the queen does, and very delicately. She is as good a surgeon as she is a butcher. The young emerge, and in a few days harden, and begin to make themselves useful. They take over the midwifery for the rest of the cocoons and, assuming the Sanguin queen to be their mother, give a good deal of attention to her also, and feed and wash her.

The queen can relax now. She gets stout, placid, and uninteresting. The new Sanguin nest has started.

But the Negroes had a queen. What of her? Alas, she is eliminated. If not found and destroyed by the Sanguin queen in the intitial stages of the "dispute," she is murdered by her own children, who, brought up by her rival, never realise that they are committing matricide.

Forgetting the initial murders, everything is perfect now. The queen gives birth to her own daughters and they become the mistresses. The slaves have to do the same work that they would have had to do amongst their own people had the Sanguin queen never intruded, but they are much more secure now than they would have been then. The army that comes into being, with its large soldiers and its workers armed with pincers and lethal sprays of formic acid, is an efficient one. Sanguin nests *are* occasionally raided by other ants, but it is usually an unprofitable undertaking for the attackers.

When things seem to be going smoothly that is the time to be on one's guard. An insinuative, quietly-spoken serpent once entered the Garden of Eden. How it got there we do not know. Nor do we know how the Golden Haired Beetle, in other words, *Lomechusa strumosa*, gets into a nest of Sanguin ants, but, occasionally, it does.

One of the many faults of ants is that they are gourmets. They have a gastronomic discrimination and appreciation that probably exceeds that of any human *bon viveur*. Their normal diet is plain, often to the point of austerity, but they love unusual and exotic tit-bits and will go to any length to satisfy this craving. This beetle exudes from the base of its golden hairs some secretion which the ants find irresistible. So it is not only allowed to enter their nest but is fawned on and courted. In almost no time it becomes an honoured guest and is allowed to do anything it likes, even to lay its own eggs, which soon turn into grubs. So besotted do the workers become that they feed the beetle with food intended for their own infants, and even with food reserved for the queen. Worse, much worse, they allow the beetle to kill their infants and eat them: they even kill their own infants themselves and feed them to this stranger. For which the beetle responds with a generous allowance of the secretion they crave. When the Beetle's eggs hatch they are cared for by the ants and fed, and always the Beetle and her brood come first in the workers' attentions.

Soon we find a half-starved queen, and children that are not getting the attention they should, and workers that are to all intents and purposes drug-adicts. This under-feeding of the queen, or the inattention of the workers to her young, or both, result in a strange thing. Instead of workers, pale-coloured hunchbacks emerge from the cocoons, distorted objects, half male, half female, mongolians, idiots incapable of work, mere encumbrances.

The Siren has done her business. The end is not immediate. The colony *may* last two years more, but the end is certain: unless the Beetle and her brood die out and the dope-adicts come back to their senses, the colony will perish.[1]

I forgot to mention that the Sanguin slaving raids usually take place in July and August, and that not more than three raids are ever made in one year. This ought to be borne in mind when we go on to deal with other slaving species.

I promised to mention the experiments that give us our

[1] The abnormal workers are called *pseudogynes*, and not all authorities are agreed that *Lomechusa strumosa* is the cause of their occurrence in Sanguinea nests, but the bulk of the evidence goes to show that this beetle *is* the cause.

data as to how a lone Sanguin queen takes over a (weak) Negro nest. Here they are, and as I have said these experiments are not *entirely* reliable. For one thing, the ants are not in a natural environment. For another, neither the queen nor the workers can leave an artificial nest: they have to fight it out in a closed-up prison. But it is as near as we can get, and there is no reason to think that things are much different in the hidden chambers of a real Negro city.

A large number of the experiments I am about to cite were made by Donisthorpe, and they do not show the whole thing from beginning to end. They are more like short, one-act plays. Let us produce them.

(1) It is June the twenty-fourth. A Sanguin female is introduced to a small colony of Negroes consisting of workers and grubs. There are *no* cocoons.

Immediately the queen appeared the workers ran away in terror. The queen ignored the grubs they had deserted, but eyed them speculatively. The workers huddled together and appeared to be trying to screw up their courage. Each tried to push one of the others forward, evidently urging the other to *do* something about it. Finally they decided to take the plunge, and all of them advanced on the queen. A rousing fight took place, and by the evening they were still hard at it, with the queen giving ground and often running away—only to have to turn and fight again.

The next day it was found that a half-hearted truce had been arranged and the Negroes had collected all their grubs in the passage-way between the two compartments. Five of the workers had been killed.

The truce was soon broken by the Negroes by other attacks on the queen, and this continued for two days, with much loss of life to the Negroes.

The armistice proper came on June twenty-eighth, and as soon as it had, so to speak, been signed, workers and Sanguin queen snuggled down together for a much needed rest, the workers cleaning the queen and licking her wounds.

Alas, the cessation of hostilities came too late. The queen was already mortally hurt and died on July 2nd.

(In natural conditions the queen would undoubtedly have

left, or been thrown out of this nest and gone in search of one with less aggressive workers.)

(2) Two days later. There is exactly the same set-up, except that this time the Negro colony (another one of course) possesses cocoons.

The newly introduced Sanguin queen appeared to be a much more amiable creature than the other. She took no notice at all of the workers, but was evidently greatly interested in the cocoons, which she tapped and studied.

The workers viewed this dubiously. They felt, no doubt, much as we would feel if a complete stranger paid us an apparently friendly visit but showed more interest in the silver spoons on the sideboard than in ourselves. And they did what we would do in such circumstances, though not, perhaps, so tactfully: they removed their valuables to a safer place and set a guard over them.

There was friction over the removal. Not much, just a vague unpleasantness: a pushing aside of the other by both parties; a sort of "I say! Dash it! What *do* you think you're doing?" attitude.

The experimenter then poured in a little honey, and all unfriendliness was swallowed in it, stranger queen and Negroes drinking together.

But next day the queen had stolen all the cocoons and was sitting watch-dog fashion over them, and there were many dead Negroes lying about, and many badly hurt. Worse was to come. By the next day all but three of the Negroes had been killed.

It is the usual thing to call the Negro ants cowardly, yet these three, the last survivors of the colony, never faltered in what they thought their duty: they kept dodging in and taking the cocoons away one by one. Each cocoon taken was immediately retrieved by the queen. I give these three little Negroes full marks for courage of a high order.

The experimenter then, for some reason and as if there was not already trouble enough, threw in some cocoons and grubs from another Negro nest, and the queen took the whole lot into her corner.

This particular play has a very unsatisfactory ending, for

all we hear now is that on July 15th (ten days later!) the queen was there with the cocoons and two workers. Still, it is satisfactory to know that two of that gallant band survived.

(3) The scene for the next play is the same artificial nest, nine days later, and the actors are a small Negro colony and many cocoons.

Enter the Sanguin queen.

Action is quick in this play. Two Negroes attack at once, and meeting those efficient pincers immediately fall writhing to the ground. The queen goes straight to the cocoons, removes as many as she can and sits on top of them. The Negroes collect the rest and take them into another corner, as far from her as they can get.

There they sit facing each other. A tense moment. Obviously things cannot remain like this. There will be murder soon. There is. The queen advances, steals more cocoons, kills one worker and grievously injures another.

By next day all but one of the Negroes have been killed and the queen has all the cocoons under her in her own corner. She is beginning to carry these cocoons about and arrange them when: *The Curtain Falls.*

Poor Negroes! When tackling a Sanguin queen in defence of their young they do so against heavy odds. But, as we have seen, the queen is not always the victor—and not always the aggressor either. Anyway, our experimenter (Donisthorpe) had a young Sanguin queen which he proposed to use for a similar experiment to those above. It was three years later. He had a strong Negro colony in his artificial nest, but he had to go away for two days. So, pending his return, he put this queen into a partition and blocked this partition up with cotton wool.

One would have thought that the Negroes would have been only too glad to have this dangerous interloper thus fenced off. But no; they forced a way through the cotton wool and killed her. From their point of view it must have been like going into a tiger's cage. When Donisthorpe returned he found fifteen dead Negroes lying beside the body of the queen.

(4) The next experiment is made, not with a Negro colony, but with a curious assortment, to wit: seven Negro females, three Negro workers, a few grubs and one cocoon. Note the *one* cocoon. There is going to be trouble here.

Enter once more the Sanguin queen. Negro females and workers run away and hide in corners.

A few hours later the Negroes had got the grubs into a corner, but the queen was in possession of the cocoon, which she held in her mouth as a dog holds a bone, daring anyone to take it from her.

By the next day the three workers had been killed, and the seven females were huddled trembling in a corner with the grubs.

They cower still closer against the wall as the Sanguin queen goes up to them, kills one of them, and picks out the two largest grubs.

At this juncture, when the play has become like one of those recent ones of unrelieved brutality and terror, the experimenter takes four Negro females away. Lucky for them perhaps, but since we are told that they were required for other experiments it is probable that their fate was merely postponed.

This left two Negro females only, and the outlook for them was grim. Actually the queen did not kill them outright but, what was worse, savaged them to such an extent that they died of their injuries in two days.

Crawley introduced a Sanguin queen to two Negro workers only and a number of cocoons. The two workers each seized a cocoon and fled to the top of the box, where they remained, holding their cocoons, completely motionless for *two days*. Both the wretched creatures were found later killed by the queen.

Similar experiments were made by Wheeler in America, using a species closely allied to Sanguinea, and Negroes "even more cowardly" than their European cousins.

It depends, of course, on what you call "cowardly." In most of the experiments we have seen, the Negroes die in defending their young from an interloper. True, they were frightened when they did so, but to be daring when afraid demands more courage than to be daring when not afraid. In short, the experimenters have got hold of the wrong word. The word they want is "unaggressive."

These experiments of Wheeler, now that we have mentioned the others, provide us with no really new data. In one of them thirty-three Negro workers (the total number) were killed by the Sanguin queen in one day for daring to guard their own property.

2

The Sanguin ants cannot be called very thorough-going slavers. At the most, as we have said, they make only three raids a year. They do not all go slave-raiding, and they do not all have slaves, and even when they do have slaves they work quite hard themselves. They do not force their slaves, like the ancient Romans and Egyptians, to carry them about. Indeed when they move from one city to another they themselves carry the slaves.

I remember hearing in my youth a woman say of some rich folk she evidently did not like, "I wonder what they'd do without all their servants!" We know the answer now. They "do" quite well so far as servants are concerned. Indeed, many like the possession of a privacy they never got before. The Sanguin ants are rather like that. I do not say they prefer to be without servants, because they don't, but they *can* get on without them. It is a sort of half-and-half slavery. We come now to those whose slavery is *not* half-and-half, whose lot without servants *would* be like the lot fondly imagined by the woman I heard speaking when she referred to the rich family she disliked. I speak of the Amazons, whose scientific name is *Polyergus rufescens*.

The Amazons are large and clad in shining copper-coloured armour which they spend all their spare time (and they have a lot) burnishing. At home they are vain and indolent; in the field they are as formidable as their legendary namesakes.

Amazons are fairly common in America, where there are three sub-species that are almost identical. So we are justified in classing them together under the name *Polyergus*.

The Amazons enslave many tribes of ants, but the commonest is the same Negro ant (*Formica fusca*) that we have seen working for Sanguinea. Therefore we shall continue to refer to the slaves as Negroes, even though sometimes they may be paler, fiercer varieties.

Where shall we start? Not at the beginning, I think. We are a little tired for the time being of queens founding colonies. We will keep that till later, and start in the middle with a full and populous colony of Amazons and slaves.

The Sanguin ants, as we know, make no more than three raids in a year. The Amazons often make two raids a *day* in the summer, in spite of the fact that they are late risers and never bestir themselves much until four o'clock in the afternoon. A colony observed by Forel made forty-four raids in thirty afternoons. Scouts have to find the nest to be attacked and lead the army afterwards, and if there are sufficient of these nests in the vicinity doubtless a colony of Amazons *will* make two raids a day.

Let us look into a nest round about midday. All is activity. Mining is going on, and extra rooms and galleries are being made. Young are being carried here and there, and fed and cleaned and looked after. Activity, yes, but all the activity is by Negroes. Of those invincible warrior ladies there is no sign; indeed no one would ever suspect that this was anything other than a Negro nest pure and simple.

And then, in a large chamber, we spot them. They are reclining at their ease, though from time to time one or two raise the energy to get up and polish their already shining armour, and comb and beautify themselves. In a way they are justified in their vanity, for—as ants go—they are handsome creatures.

At times an overworked slave comes along and feeds them, because these great, well-developed females are incapable of feeding themselves, incapable, too, of digging or nursing or any honest work. They are good for one thing only—fighting and plundering.

The slaves that look after them and their mother and their immature sisters and brothers, and who make every inch of the nest, have been acquired by raids, often cruel raids. One irritated nip from a mistress would kill a slave. What is the relationship between them? Do we see a trembling slave grovelling in fear of her life before her mistress? Not at all. Indeed you would think that the slaves were the mistresses. Admittedly an Amazon does at times lose her temper and kill a slave, but not often. Mostly the Amazons submit to the bossiness of their slaves as a man might submit to the bossiness of an old family retainer.

And now one of the Amazons in our nest, feeling bored, gets up and lounges towards the entrance. She meets a slave. The slave bustles towards her like an indignant hen. I have been told again and again that I *must* not make insects talk. I do not, as a rule, but if talking happens to be the quickest way of conveying an attitude, then I do make them talk. "Now then," says the slave (though not, I hasten to say, vocally), "now then, what do you think you're doing! Go inside and don't get in my way when I'm busy. There's a raid on this afternoon and you'll need all your strength. Off you go!"

And "off" the powerful Amazon does go, helped by a shove and possibly (if she is lucky) a mouthful of sweet.

In short, the Amazons *like* being bullied by their slaves, and the slaves like bullying them and working themselves to skin and bone for them.

The amazing Huber has witnessed many raids. So have others since his time, particularly Wheeler in America. No two raids, of course, are quite the same, but they do not differ very much. Let us show what normally happens.

I presume the slaves go round about three o'clock amongst the warrior ladies still busy at their toilets, and tell them to get ready. The fall-in may go at any minute. The fall-in sounds. Who sounds it? Who knows? A definite signal of some sort, made somehow, is given, and concertedly the waiting Amazons, gleaming in burnished copper, jump to their feet and pour out of the nest.

Outside, some run about and some form into groups as if in animated discussion. A further signal comes: the groups break up and form into line. Then they march off in close column formation at great speed.

We have seen the cautious Sanguins investing a city,

hoping the inhabitants will flee at the sight of them, waiting, calling for reinforcements, waiting again, and then calling for more. The Amazons invariably pour straight into a city without any hesitation whatsoever. Inside, they take all the young, and slaughter the adolescents or not according to their whim. As Wheeler says, " When on one of their predatory expeditions the Amazons display a dazzling courage and capacity for concerted action compared with which the raids of Sanguinea resemble the clumsy efforts of a lot of untrained militia."

Very soon they come out, each warrior bearing a cocoon between her jaws, and leaving, as often as not, a complete shambles behind. Then they go home, but not in formation. Evidently the "Dismiss" has been given for they straggle back in ones or twos or threes, any old how. This, however, only applies to a raid on a *Negro* city. When they attack fiercer species they are not dismissed to go home as they like; they fall in and march in formation, harassed at the rear and flanks by the brave little inhabitants of the despoiled city, and fighting a ceaseless rearguard action, which is made difficult for them owing to the burden of the loot they are carrying.

At home the slaves are waiting outside. The sight of the cocoons, evidence of a ravaged city of their own people, does not distress them. They welcome the army back as human populaces welcome returning victorious troops. The slaves relieve the warriors of their burdens and place the cocoons in tidy heaps which, later, they take inside. They feed the warriors and clean and massage them, and then carry them inside to their sofas. They will need a rest, for probably another raid has been arranged to take place in an hour's time.

It was not always known that any ants enslaved any other ants. Ants of all kinds make raids frequently and carry away booty, including cocoons, to their nest. But this booty and these cocoons are used only as *food*. Everyone knew this, and in the main they were right. It was Huber who found out that the Amazon raids had an entirely different motive. He had seen many of these raids of theirs and had been interested in them, but he had never been able to follow an Amazon army back to its own nest. So, like everyone else, he took it for granted that what they bore away went straight into the larder.

Then, one day, he did manage to follow an Amazon army back. There had been a raid on a Negro colony and he had seen the whole of it, and when it was over he accompanied the straggling troops on their homeward journey. And then he saw that they were *not* going home : they were making for still another unfortunate Negro nest. The greedy creatures, already overburdened with loot, wanted more!

We know now that an Amazon nest looks exactly like a Negro nest. It is built by Negroes and apparently occupied only by Negroes. But Huber did not know this, so he looked forward with pleasurable anticipation to another scene of slaughter and pillage.

Now, on the approach of Amazons, there is invariably consternation and precipitate flight on the part of the Negro citizens who see them and can get away in time. Huber gasped with surprise: the Negroes of *this* nest were all running *towards* the Amazons!

His amazement increased: the two forces met, and not a single Amazon retaliated! Instead, they all gave in completely and allowed themselves to be seized by the Negro soldiers and carried like so many slaughtered carcasses into the nest. Huber had never seen anything like *this*. He probably felt he wanted to pinch himself to find out if he was awake.

And then he saw that certain Negroes were cleaning and feeding certain of the Amazons. "No enigma," he says, "ever raised my curiosity so high as this singular discovery."

I wonder if any *Amazons* ever make the same mistake as Huber. Do they ever attack a nest which is apparently Negro but really Amazon? What a fight there would be then! There are no records of such a thing, but Amazon nests are few and so are observers. It *may* occasionally happen—unless scent, or some allied sense, warns the scouts who first discover the nest.

We have seen the Amazon army returning after a successful raid bearing cocoons and grubs, and we have seen their enthusiastic reception by their slaves. What happens when things go wrong? I do not mean when they are defeated—

such a thing happens to Amazons very rarely indeed—I mean when they come home dejected and bootyless.

The indefatigible, invaluable Huber once witnessed such a return. He saw the Amazon army set off in the usual manner —strict formation, undeviating course, great speed. He followed it and after a while an unusual thing happened: the column veered off in a curve. Then it halted, went on, halted again, went on, halted. Formation was abandoned. The troops fell out and began searching all around. Some scout had blundered.

The result was that at long last they gave it up, got in formation again, and marched back home, and the nearer they got to home the slower their march became.

Their reception? . . . Let us ask Huber.

"Upon their return our Amazons met with no flattering reception from the Negroes, who individually assailed, buffeted and dragged them to the outside of the nest, where they even obliged them to act on the defensive. This hostile disposition, however, continued only a few moments, when the Amazons were allowed to re-enter their citadel."

Anxious as the slaves are that their mistresses should return bearing the spoils of victory, they are sometimes strangely reluctant to let them go off on a raid at all. Peculiar scenes have been witnessed at the outsides of Amazon nests when the warriors are about to march off: slaves in numbers rushing and seizing them, and trying to pull them back.

Why do the slaves do this? Why, indeed! Is their regard for their mistresses almost maternal? Do they suddenly think that their fierce charges may suffer some small hurt? Or is it, as some observers think, that the slaves have knowledge of weather conditions and have come to the conclusion that it may rain before long?

During raids there is often much slaughter, the Amazons ruthlessly piercing the heads or breasts of the whole crowd of the trapped garrison. But these warrior women are creatures of moods. Sometimes they sack a city from top to bottom without killing a single one of the helpless inhabitants. They may go even further, for Wheeler records one case when an army of Amazons flowed into the entrances of a Negro city like wine being poured through funnels and came out almost immediately bearing all the cocoons. The defenders remained, trapped and at their mercy. A thorough loot took place and then, nothing else being left inside, the Amazons began to come out carrying the bodies of the defenders between their jaws. These, completely unhurt, were gently deposited outside and allowed to run away. Not one Negro was killed or harmed in this affray. Evidently these Amazons have a code of chivalry —but they do not often practise it!

If we gently spread our fingers in the path of a Sanguin army on the march, those fingers will be pierced by dozens of pairs of pincers and injected with formic acid and will be of little use to us for some hours. But if we do the same to one of those swiftly-moving, more heavily armed columns of Amazons, the marchers will swarm over and past our fingers without giving one nip or sting.

We know well enough now that Amazons cannot feed themselves or look after their young or make a nest, but Huber did not know it. At least, he was not sure of it. So he took thirty Amazons and put them into a glass box with a deep layer of soil underneath. He gave them honey for food and put in a number of cocoons and grubs. One or two Amazons carried the grubs about in a vague way as if some long-disused instinct was trying to work, but they soon gave it up and put the grubs back where they had found them.

In less than two days more than half the Amazons were dead of hunger, and none had even begun to trace out a dwelling. The honey remained untouched. The rest were alive— but only just.

Then Huber, "commiserating" with them, took a single Negro from their former nest and put it in with them.

"This individual, unassisted, established order, formed a chamber in the earth, gathered together the larvae, extricated several young ants that were ready to quit the condition of pupae, and (by feeding them with the honey) preserved the life of the remaining Amazons."

Wheeler tried an experiment of a rather different kind. It was different in that the Negro ants introduced to the starving

Amazons were not from their nest. Moreover, they were "wild" ants, taken from a nest of their own and knowing nothing of slavery.

Here again thirty Amazons were put into an artificial nest and given water to drink and honey for food. They could not eat and, being famished, began piteously to beg each other for food. When all but sixteen of them were dead, six Negro ants were introduced, but, as I have said, unenslaved ants; ants, that is, having a horror and dread of Amazons.

These Negroes were terrified, and the Amazons, though starving, were irritated. Soon all but two of the Negroes had been killed, and these two ran about hiding in corners. Then one of them (whom we will call A) came out and protruded her tongue to one of the Amazons and fed her. After doing this she ran to the honey, filled herself, ran back again, and fed a large number of the others. Backwards and forwards she went, feeding the starving Amazons until all of them were fed and saved.

The next morning found the Amazons all asleep together, and, sleeping in their midst, was the little servant who had saved them. The other Negro (B) was still hiding in a corner.

Wheeler tapped the nest, and the ministering ant jumped up like some skivvy found oversleeping, rushed to the honey, filled up, and gave the whole lot of the Amazons their breakfast. She continued to feed them throughout the day, and the Amazons lounged contentedly where they were.

Next morning B was found killed in a corner, but A was bustling to and fro again getting breakfast, this time without being roused.

Alas for the ingratitude of ants and men—before noon A was found dragging herself painfully along trying valiantly to get food for her charges, but failing to do so. Her head had been pierced by one of the Amazons she had rescued, and she died in a few hours.

I am very keen on poetic justice. I believe in it too. It may take a long time coming, but in the end it does. It came quickly to those sixteen Amazons—though, to be sure, only one of them had sinned. That same afternoon Wheeler introduced twenty Negro workers, and as soon as the Amazons saw them they went for them in a sort of cavalry charge. To the utter amazement of the observer the Negroes held their ground. Nay, more—and still more inexplicable—they attacked in return and were soon driving the Amazons round and round like a flock of sheep. They "showered them with formic acid, mauled them about, gnawed off their legs, and left them in a pitiable plight." Doubtless the Amazons were weak with starvation and distracted by recent events, but the behaviour of the "cowardly" Negroes is worthy of note.

Poetic justice is all very well, but it is a pity that in this particular experiment one of the Amazons had lost her right antenna and her right leg (which carries the comb). She was, therefore, continually trying to comb a non-existent antenna with a non-existent hind leg and falling over sideways when doing so. This would irritate anyone, particularly a female, and perhaps it was she who bit into the head of the little voluntary servant.

And now for the beginning—the founding of a new nest.

Like the young Sanguin queen, the Amazon queen cannot found a new nest for herself. She, also, has to go off on a one-woman raid. But she has to be much more subtle than the Sanguin queen. She must not indulge in fits of temper or in *any* attrition of the Negro workers of the nest she enters. All the Sanguin queen *really* wants is cocoons. If she can steal enough of those and get away with it she is content. She can free the young herself, and look after them herself for the short period that passes before they begin to look after her. Not so the Amazon queen. *She* cannot free the young, nor look after them. The Sanguin queen regards cocoons as a miser regards gold pieces: she hoards them, arranges and rearranges them, and gloats over them. The Amazon queen, if she looks at cocoons at all, does so without the slightest interest or comprehension. In short, her technique has to be different.

The usual experiments in artificial nests give us our data. The young Amazon queen finds a *weak* Negro colony and enters and has a rough time. The workers go for her and drive her about and, although capable of killing them all, the queen puts up no resistance. She allows herself to be chased from pillar to post, and buffeted and bruised.

This meek attitude in due course has its reward. Sooner or later the attacks die down. For one thing, *this* queen never tries to steal the Negroes' cocoons. So *that* bone of contention is absent. For another, with iron self-restraint, this queen never gives a worker even a warning nip with her death-dealing pincers, so none of them feel any real grievance.

So far it would appear that all the queen wishes to do is to appease the workers. But that alone would not get her very far in founding a colony of her own. These Negroes have a queen and they are fond of her. The Sanguin interloper got round this difficulty by raising the Negro young herself so that, when fully grown, they thought *she* was their mother and that their real mother was the interloper. Then they either killed their real mother themselves or allowed the Sanguin to do so without protest. And by that time the Sanguin had seen to it that there were none of the original workers (who knew their queen) left alive—or very few of them.

Things are entirely different with the Amazon queen. By now she is an object of contempt, almost of ridicule in the Negro nest. Anyone who likes can bully her,—she never retaliates—and soon they come to ignore her and let her roam about. After all, they are busy creatures with little time for sport.

And the Amazon queen *does* roam about, *and* she has an object in this roaming. She wanders round the corridors and eventually finds the compartment of the Negro queen.

The Amazon must have charm of a sort; at any rate she makes up to the Negro queen and that placid, stupid, and probably bored personage accepts these advances at their face value. In a week the two are living together and are on friendly terms.

Those casual creatures, the Negro workers (most of them, not all), have by now accepted the situation, and since the two queens are always together, find it as easy to feed two as one. It becomes routine: the workers feed their queen and their queen's friend.

Then, out of the blue, comes tragedy. The Negro queen is found lying dead.

There are no post-mortems in Ant-Land so far as we know. If any such took place this would be a simple case: a wound would be found on each side of the Negro queen's head, caused by a pair of extremely powerful pincers that had bitten into the skull.

The unexpected loss of a queen is a very serious business in an ants' nest. They have had no time to make preparations. The workers of this particular nest are very disturbed. But by some instinct they know that their late queen's friend is a fertile female. It is possibly not the only way out, but it is certainly the easiest. She is known to all the workers. Why not make *her* the queen? and save a lot of trouble.

And so another Amazon colony comes into being.

Not all Amazon females have the restraint and fortitude to put up with the rough treatment they get from the workers before they make friends with their queen. Some of them ruin everything by letting their temper get the upper hand and turning on the Negroes and killing them. In the case of the Sanguin female this does not matter, in the case of the Amazon it is fatal—unless she starts the whole weary business over again and goes away and tries to find another Negro nest.

In the lifetime of this generation, just before Rhodesia was "opened up" (and indeed after), a very war-like race of natives, the Matabele, ruled by their king, Lobengula, used to make an almost bi-annual affair of raiding the kraals of a cowardly race called the Mashonas who lived to the north and east of them. They were murderous affairs, but the young and fit were spared and led away to act as slaves in the fields or (unconsciously following the Roman method) grafted into the army. Before very long a curious change came over these slaves. They adopted the characteristics of their masters: cowardly once, they became aggressive. The same thing has been noticed with Negro ants: those found in Amazon nests are always far fiercer than the normal Negroes.

I have called the Amazons lazy. And they certainly might do more than they do, but two raids a day is not real laziness. I think, to them, a raid corresponds to a game of golf by a man, and it is (to my mind) a more interesting game. What we really despise in them is their utter reliance on slaves. But . . . if we sneer at them because they cannot even eat without the help of slaves they are entitled to sneer back at us because *they* can get slaves, and *we* cannot.

There is a snag in this, of course. The Amazons destroy Negro (and other) nests and do not replace them. The more Amazon nests there are, the scarcer becomes the source of their life blood—the slaves. That is why Amazon nests are never over-numerous. The time comes when an Amazon colony must move on to other territory if it hopes to survive. And it often *does* move on, but—trust them!—the mistresses do it *en seigneure*, with their slaves carrying them.

But we, too, are more or less in the same position. We, too, have been moving on for generations, though not in the comfort of the Amazons, in search of ever dwindling food supplies (and slaves to Amazons spell food). All life is the same. There is always a limit of expansion.

Two raids a day (especially compared with the Sanguin three or so a year) seems rather much. Can the Amazons cope with that amount of slaves? The usual quota is six slaves to one Amazon, and yet every cocoon in every nest raided is always carried home. What happens to the booty after that the Amazons themselves never know. It is all under the control of the slaves. *They* decide how many cocoons and grubs to keep, and how many to eat. And the matter could not be in better hands.

3

We come now to a different type of slave-maker. There are two genera of this type and both are small, though their names are not. The first is called Strongylognathus and the second Harpagoxenus. and unfortunately they have no popular names like "Sanguins" or "Amazons." Some writers try to get over the difficulty of Latin, etc., names in general by translating them. This is a practice that should be used with restraint, for if every name is translated it makes matters more bewildering than before, and one translator may translate differently from another. Thus, in one book and in little more than one page, I once read of Fourfold-Turf Ants, Yellowish-Red-Scimitar Ants, Huber Scimitar Ants, The Dark-Grey-Cloaked Ones, The Black-Frocked Ones (the two latter, by the way, being the same ant), The Grass-Green Ones, The Co-Savers, The Narrow-Breasted Ones, The Tapestry-Hangers, The Tooth-Fighters, and so on. The writer was trying to be helpful but only succeeded in being confusing and irritating. Moreover, one misses the help of the first generic name. No, when there is no accepted common name one should use the Latin, even if this name is long and almost impossible to pronounce. Whether there is any real need for the Latin names to be long and unpronounceable does not concern us here, and it is too late to do anything about it in any case.

Strongylognathus enslaves an ant named *Tetramorium caespitum* (known to us as the Turf Ant), and Harpagoxenus enslaves Leptothorax.

Both of these slave ants abound in Britain, but will never there be found enslaved, for neither Strongylognathus nor Harpagoxenus live here, though they occur on the Continent.

We can dismiss Harpagoxenus, and that will ease the situation a little, for Harpagoxenus has only two species, both rare, and its methods are very like those of the Amazons, except that the enslaved queen and the enslaving queen live amicably in the same nest.

Strongylognathus has also two species, *testaceus* and *huberi*, of which by far the most common is *testaceus*, so we will confine ourselves to that one. Its slaves, the Tetramoria, though fairly small, are very much larger than Strongyloganthus. They are yellowish ants and exceedingly fierce and warlike—very different from the Negroes, so that one wonders how it ever comes about that they can be beaten in war and their cocoons taken by such diminutive and weak creatures as the Strongylognathi. Well, make no mistake, they never are beaten in war by the Strongylognathi, they are beaten (when they are beaten) by the *slaves* of the Strongylognathi—their own kind, and therefore as warlike as they themselves.

Actually, Strongylognathus is more like a character from comic opera than from real life. He is undoubtedly the bravest of all the ants but he has nothing to *go* with his bravery. He is like a human guardsman (a very small one) who goes into battle armed with a paper helmet and a cardboard sword. His method when the enemy is sighted is to shout to the others,

"Follow me, chaps!" charge down on the enemy, and get killed immediately.

Probably, long ago (very long ago), he *was* a great warrior, but a life of ease spread over numberless generations have so weakened him that though he still retains the spirit he does not retain the strength of his ancestors.

The trouble is he does not realise it. He thinks he is still the warrior he was.

Yet, in a raid, the Strongylognathi generally win the day, and what is more, nine times out of ten the victory is due to their matchless courage. It happens like this: the raiding party is composed largely of slaves, who move steadily along with a number of their small masters marching importantly in front. They approach a Tetramorium nest, whose army pours out, more than ready to give battle. Naturally, the slaves halt, to discuss the matter and make dispositions. But their masters do not halt at all: without hesitation they charge straight down on the foe.

I said they were killed immediately. As a matter of fact, I was not quite right. For the time being the Tetramoria are awed and disconcerted by this unexpected attack. They break up a little, and the gallant little Strongylognathi sweep into the thick of them, furiously biting into the heads and breasts of all they meet.

Or rather, *trying* to bite into the heads and breasts of those they meet, because their jaws are so weak now that they could not bite into a red-currant.

It does not take the Tetramoria long to realise this. They form up again—and that is the end of most of the Strongylognathi.

Meanwhile, however, the slaves have been watching from the hill above, and though doubting the wisdom of so precipitate an attack have been inspired by the courage shown. When they see their leaders being slaughtered like sheep in an abattoir, they hesitate no longer and rush down to the rescue.

The ensuing engagement is bloody, but, as I have said, more often than not it is the slaves that win. Then the army goes back, headed by a very reduced body of masters—if by any at all.

I must apologise for using the masculine gender in the above description. It is a mistake easy to make and I shall probably make it again. For "masters," therefore, read "mistresses," or workers. We will now deal with a real female Strongylognathus and study *her* method of founding a nest.

All slave-making ants, for some reason, are incapable of starting a nest of their own and have to take over a "wild" nest of their slave species. We have seen the Sanguin and Amazon queens trying to do this: carefully selecting a *weak* slave colony, and having a very rough time even then. The young Strongylognathus queen, in spite of the fact that she has a far fiercer ant to deal with than the Negro, selects the *strongest* colony she can find and enters without any qualms. And since her confidence is completely justified, it follows that there must be some inborn understanding between these two—the Strongylognathus queen and the Tetramorium workers—though how that understanding arose we do not know. Were they associated in some way in the past? You would not think so to look at them, though both come from the same sub-family, Myrmicinae, and the same tribe, Tetramorii. But you would not think that Pekinese dogs and wolves were descended from the same stock—an apt comparison in a way, for the Peke still imagines it is as fierce and formidable as a wolf, if not more so.

Certainly there is no understanding between the workers of the two parties when they meet in the field. Perhaps Strongylognathus is an older slave-maker than Sanguinea or Polyergus and acceptance of the queen is now in the germ plasm of the Tetramoria—even of those who for generations have never even seen her kind.

Whatever the reason, she has no trouble. She is accepted, and the two queens—the Tetramorium queen and the diminutive Strongylognathus queen—reign side by side, the Tetramorium workers bringing up her offspring as well as their own.

How can one understand these things? What goes on in the collective mind of the Tetramorium workers? For after this queen has taken office, together with their own, they kill off all the males and true females bred by their own queen but preserve those bred by the Strongylognathus queen. Is there some masochistic urge that prompts these normally fine and virile ants to mutilate and de-sex themselves, to renounce their hope of increase and permanence in order to concentrate on breeding slaves to serve a contemptible band of ridiculous mistresses?

Folly such as this, one would think, could go no further, but in the case of the Tetramoria it does, as we will see in the next section.

Either on account of the loss caused by the Don Quixote-like valour of the Strongylognathus workers, or because their decadent queen cannot breed like the queen of the Tetramoria, the amount of slaves in a Strongylognathus-Tetramorium nest greatly outnumbers that of the mistresses. Wasmann went to a lot of trouble to get an idea of the proportion. He estimated an average of 15,000 to 20,000 Tetramoria to some 1,000 Strongylognathi.

The Strongylognathus worker can excavate a little and can feed itself a little, but on the whole its efforts in the nest are about as useful as those of a very small child in a house—more of a nuisance than a help. In its own young—or rather in the young of its queen—it takes no interest at all.

4

The last of the slave-holders is a shocking creature with no redeeming features. Its name is Anergates (there are others with like habits, but the best known is *Anergates atratulus*) and it is the most degenerate of the ants, which, contrary to popular conception, is saying not a little. It is rare though widely distributed on the Continent. It is a small yellow ant.

In spite of its degeneracy it is still entitled to be called a slave-holder. Some prefer to call it a parasite because it is so helpless, but it is a mistake, I think, to stretch that elastic word too far. It loses its value then. Put yourself in the place of Anergates and decide. You are a cripple and a mental defective but, luckily for you, you have an attendant who carries you about, feeds you, washes you, and does everything else for you. You never asked him to do it—you are too stupid to think of that—he insisted. Furthermore, he killed off the family that were dependent on him in order to be able to devote all his time to you. Is that man your slave, or are you his parasite? Both, I suppose, but, on the whole, I class him as your slave.

It is again the warlike Tetramoria that sacrifice themselves, their mother, their city, their progeny, their lives, for this effete little ant.

It all starts with the flight of a large number of Anergates females from the nest. Note that there are no males: this is not a "mating flight," they have mated already and mated very thoroughly. Most of them perish, but one *may* fall near a Tetramorium colony. If Tetramorium workers are in the vicinity and see her, one or two of them will probably grab her by the legs or body and drag her into their nest. If she goes into the nest of her own accord (and she has not the sense to do this unless she alights almost immediately opposite an aperture), workers will meet her in the galleries and seize her there.

This seizure is not in anger at such unwarranted intrusion, but in joy. It is as if a couple of emotional women suddenly come upon a friend they have not seen for a long time, seize her with exuberant affection, and insist on her coming home with them and staying with them.

Long-staying visitors, often cause trouble, but few visitors in any circles cause more trouble than this one. And yet one cannot blame her. The Anergates female is quiet, unobtrusive, decorous, for the whole of her stay. Nor can one blame her children when they arrive; they, too, make no fuss or bother. No, the Tetramoria can only blame themselves. Queer things go on amongst ants; there is an undercurrent of vice, of strange, unnatural friendships. There *are* Tetramorium colonies (or at any rate individual workers) strong-minded enough to resist the charm or hereditary influence (whatever it is) of the Anergates female. These take hold of her also, but instead of carrying her into their nest, drag her to the top of some stone or other eminence and push her over, thus putting Satan behind them. Indeed, on occasion they will go further and calmly sever this female into two separate portions. But these strong-minded ants are few and far between.

Inside the nest the Anergates queen is cleaned and fed. She

is only a small female and has a nice, trim figure. It does not long remain so. As her pregnancy advances and her ovaries enlarge, she begins to swell until in a comparatively short time she is a helpless bladder. But the Tetramorium workers think none the less of her for this: indeed, they admire her so much that they put their own queen to death, together with her male and female children, and thereby turn themselves into the complete slaves of this swollen object and her brood.

Soon the Anergates queen is laying eggs, and these are carefully tended through their changing forms until the adults appear. All are either fully-sexed male or female. There are no workers. Anergates has lost the power of breeding workers. Hence its name, $\dot{a}$=no, $\epsilon\rho\gamma\dot{a}\tau\eta\varsigma$=worker.

The females are normal enough in appearance, but the males are not. It is a case of arrested development; as if a baby were born and kept through life its wrinkled face and toothless gums and inadequate legs. For the Anergates male is a flabby, distorted creature of a corpse-like yellow hue. He can walk a little in a halting way, but not much. Mentally he is completely deficient. And these monstrosities the Tetramorium workers carry about and feed and fondle and obviously love! For the more seemly young females they have little regard, pushing them out of the way, though they feed them from time to time in a grudging manner.

Normally, as we all know, at mating time, male and female ants fly forth in the splendour of their temporary wings and mate in the open. Moreover, ants time these affairs so that other nests are flying at the same time and inbreeding need not take place. This is impossible with Anergates, for the creeping, hunch-backed males never grow wings. And so, inside the nest, a scene of debauchery takes place. Like many of the mentally deformed, the Anergates male is over-sexed. And his sisters tend to be similar in their inclinations. Thus it happens that, more or less in the presence of their mother, brothers and sisters jam the corridors in solid incestuous lumps. So firmly joined are the couples that they can be taken up *in copulâ* and killed in spirit without separating them.

The workers (and by that, of course, we mean the Tetramoria), though normally used to a different and more decent mode, view the scene without apparent disapproval, and if the nest is opened at this time will hastily try to carry off the males to safety, leaving such females as are not united with their partners to their fate.

After the orgy the females fly away. Their brother husbands remain with the slaves, who still carry them about and pet them. But not for long. A temporary period of sanity comes over the workers and they wonder *why* they are carrying these things about and feeding them. Then they take them outside and throw the whole lot of them away.

When the Tetramorium colony, for the sake of Anergates, murdered their queen and destroyed her sexed young, that colony castrated itself. Its span of life became as long as the span of life of the individual workers—possibly three years. Populous at first, its numbers begin to dwindle. It must be a grim scene towards the end when only a few aged, worn-out workers remain and their expensive pet, the Anergates queen, lies dying of hunger.

Anergates is rare. It could hardly be anything else. Its preservation depends on one species of ant, and when the two meet they indulge in a mutual suicide pact. It is a state of affairs that cannot continue indefinitely. Anergates can send out pregnant females in quantity every year (by kind permission of *Tetramorium caespitum*) but these females now lack the initiative to hunt out a Tetramorium colony: they have to fall almost right on top of it. Furthermore, not for ever, one presumes, will Tetramorium recognise Anergates as a mistress. It must be an hereditary impulse, engendered when Anergates was strong and bred workers capable of making slaves. Indeed it would appear that this change is taking place now, for as we have seen, there *are* workers who refuse to bend the knee and who treat this interloping degenerate as she should be treated.

To get slaves in the first instance, species have to be warlike and hardy. Ease and luxurious living sap hardiness and mental vigour. Normally, with most forms of life, this is just a cycle; a hardier race or species then destroys the ease-loving species to be themselves destroyed when the fruits of conquest have enervated *them*. Ants that keep slaves, however, can put off the inevitable hour by letting the hardiness of their slaves protect them from the consequences of their own lack of hardiness. But it *is* only postponement. Even if their slaves do not desert them, mental and physical decay will in itself and in its own time exterminate them. There must be many species of slave-making ants that have died out for this reason. Strongylognathus and Anergates are on their way to join them. Will Sanguinea and Polyergus, the Amazon, follow in their footsteps? Probably.

CHAPTER 5

THE HOUSE NEXT DOOR

In ant-infested fields and gardens a congestion of nests will often be found. Though close together, however, these nests are probably nests of the same species, and the inhabitants will be found to have no dealings the one with the other; they may, in fact, be compared with houses in exclusive London squares where the occupants go about their business, ignoring entirely the occupants of the house next door.

But in some cases different colonies and different species of ants *will* share one nest—or at any rate will merge their two nests together, even if the junction is only at the edges—and live on terms varying from friendship to the bitterest enmity. These are called " Compound Nests," and there is an infinite variety of them, so many that we cannot hope to deal with them all here. We will, therefore, select two of the better-known examples and describe, firstly, a combination of enemies, and secondly, a combination of friends—friends, that is to say, of a sort.

The first is rather a nightmarish story and deals with a little yellow ant called Solenopsis—full name *Solenopsis fugax*. It is a tiny ant, hardly larger than a grain of sand, and it makes a compound nest with almost any *large* species, particularly with that splendid and useful creature, *Formica rufa*, the " Wood Ant" of the pine forests.

Solenopsis fugax makes up for its smallness by numbers; the inhabitants of a single colony are to be counted by hundreds of thousands, and as many as twenty breeding queens have been found in one nest. It is common on the Continent, and fairly common in Britain by now, but a hundred years ago it was unknown in this island. If you unearth a stone and see a number of minute yellow ants they may quite possibly be *Solenopsis fugax*. You will, however, rarely see them running

71

about on the ground, for they are an underground species, half blind, shunning the light of day.

Small as it is, this ant stings most wickedly. If cornered, it will also fight any other ant, regardless of size, but it prefers to run away, not from cowardice but because it is the simplest thing to do, especially when burdened with loot. Hence its name, "fugax," which might be translated "He Who Runs Away," but the running away is generally from the scene of some crime, a robbery perhaps, but more often a ghastly murder.

The generic name "Solenopsis" is derived from $\sigma\omega\lambda\acute{\eta}\nu$ "Channel," and $\check{o}\psi\iota\varsigma$ = "Face." For nature has given this genus a groove along its face—a cut or scar as it were. So a combined translation might read "Running Scar-Face." This sounds like the name of a Chicago gangster and is not inappropriate.

Things start by a nest of Solenopses coming into being some distance from a nest of (say) Wood ants. The Solenopses increase and soon the little tunnels of their nest are close to the great galleries and chambers of the Wood ants.

To get a proper view of what happens now it is necessary to be anthropomorphic and compare this particular nest of Wood ants with a family of human beings. The idea is not original, for the same comparison was made by Lord Avebury.

The family of human beings we picture is a large one, with many children, nurses and servants, and it lives in a huge rambling house. It has lived in this house for generations and nothing has ever gone wrong. Then, one day, holes about eighteen inches in diameter begin to appear in the walls and wainscoting of the various rooms and passage-ways. These are filled in by the servants, but others appear. Later on a nurse reports that one of the children is missing. A day later three more children have disappeared.

Let us keep watch over one of those holes. In the dead of night (for it is always dark in this house) a band of gnomes crawl out and tip-toe swiftly to a bedroom, where they steal up to one of the cots. Silently they pull the blankets back, draw little knives, and cut the living child into ragged hunks of meat. Then, each carrying a grisly joint, they hurry off and vanish into the hole.

The next night a nurse sees the last of a band of gnomes going back into the hole. She cries an alarm. Others hasten up. But what can they do? A human being cannot get into a hole eighteen inches in diameter and travel a hundred yards or more along a tunnel of the same width. They may try to enlarge the hole, but it avails them nothing. All they hear is the mocking laughter of the gnomes.

They watch the children very carefully after this, but there are many children and they cannot watch all of them all the time. Besides, they have their other work to do. The children continue to disappear. Sometimes the gnomes are caught in the middle of their horrid work, or intercepted as they are running away. They fight like fiends then, and, being armed with poisoned daggers, are dangerous creatures to tackle. Some are killed. It makes no difference: by now the house is surrounded on all sides by countless tunnels crammed with gnomes whose favourite food is the blood and flesh of babies, and who are determined to have it.

The gnomes steal from the larder as well, and often milk the cows in the stables before the owners can get there.

This comparison gives some idea of the frightful conditions under which Wood ants live when their home is surrounded and invaded by a nest of Solenopsis. How does the association come about? Is it by chance? Does Solenopsis, building its extraordinarily long tunnels and going about its lawful affairs, happen occasionally to tunnel into a nest of Wood ants and then take advantage of an unexpected meeting? I am afraid not. I am afraid the whole thing is deliberate, for *Solenopsis fugax*, when established, is hardly ever found except in one of these compound nests. On the rare occasions when it is found alone there is generally evidence to show that it has driven another nest to desperation and flight, just as Pharaoh ants occasionally cause human beings to abandon *their* houses. Should this happen, the Solenopsis must find it very difficult to follow their victims, for, although minute themselves, their queens are comparatively enormous, and it would be difficult to carry them long distances, especially since they hardly ever travel on the surface.

The Solenopses make their openings into the other nest without secrecy, for it is quite impossible (and they know it) for the large ants to do anything with the long winding tunnels behind. The large ants can (and do) stop up the openings, but the Solenopses can easily un-stop them or make other openings. They come frequently into the big nest and select a cocoon. The tough silken bag is not easy for such small creatures to remove, but all combine and pierce it repeatedly with their mandibles until the tiny holes unite and the bag falls apart. The pupa inside is easier to tackle. There are legs and protuberances to hold on to and gnaw and pull. It is soon torn apart and cut into pieces, and as each ant gets a sizeable bit it hurries to a hole and safety. The grubs, strangely enough, take longer to dispose of, but at last they are pierced and rent, and their milky blood sucked up.

The large ants seem at a loss in attempting to cope with these baby-killers. Some naturalists think that the latter are so small that the larger ones cannot see them properly, but since the interior of a nest is dark one doubts if ants ever use their eyes much when inside. They go about their normal duties, however, just as if the place were flood-lit, so some other sense probably comes into play.

It is customary with us to admire and applaud the courage of something small attacking something big, but our sympathies quite often ought to be with the big one. Smallness can be an asset. A really small creature can dodge about between a large one's legs, keep out of sight, attack from sides and rear, sever arteries, ham-string, terrify. The smallness and agility of the weasel terrifies to impotence the larger and equally well-armed rat, who need not fear his lack of canines. Formidable Alsatians will flee from yapping Pekes. The big-game hunter who has just brought down a charging rhinoceros probably thinks himself more than a match for any animal on the veld, yet if a number of wild cats were to attack him simultaneously with the complete determination and lack of fear shown by, for instance, some ants, I do not see that he could do anything about it. He would soon die from loss of blood in spite of his rifle or revolver. But, luckily for the large ones, the small ones do not often realise the advantage they have. Their size gives them an inferiority complex; they carry the thought of escape at the back of their minds. The tiny *Solenopsis fugax*, in spite of its second name, has no such inhibition when cornered, so it is not surprising that the large ants put up rather a poor performance when they fight them. And remember, the Solenopses are armed with stings, weapons not possessed by most of their adversaries. They combine, too, in clever fashion; some cling to the large ants' legs while others sting them on the body.

But it is no part of the Solenopsis plan to kill off the Wood ants. They prefer them to live. Indeed they prefer them to be as prosperous as circumstances permit. Dead Wood ants are no use to them: they cannot eat such brittleness, nor feed their young on it. It is the succulent babies they want. And to get these, in the numbers they require, the adults must be allowed to breed and rear them. By going too far (as they sometimes do), the Solenopses defeat their own ends and land themselves in an awkward situation. Therefore, as far as possible, they keep to their stealthy raids and quick retreats and, though fighters to the core, earn their name of *fugax*.

2

We study now another colony of dwarfs that also penetrate into the galleries and chambers of a large species. But these dwarfs are not like the Solenopses. They are friendly dwarfs, almost as amiable as those that helped Snow White in the fairy tale—though not so altruistic. The large ants are just as good-tempered, if not more so—indeed, nothing ever seems to disturb their equanimity.

Both live in North America. The name of the large ant is *Myrmica canadensis*, the small one, *Leptothorax emersoni*. The association starts in a similar manner to the Solenopsis affair, Leptothorax running its narrow passage-ways up to and into the galleries of Myrmica. These tunnels, however, unlike those of Solenopses, are never very long, and after the Leptothorax have settled down they often make their chambers so close to those of the Myrmica that the hole connecting them with the other nest is like a service-hatch between two rooms with us. The dwarfs, of course, can pass freely through these holes, but the Myrmica cannot—unless they choose forcibly to smash and break down the wall surrounding the hole until it is of a size to admit them. At times some of them do this, and later on we shall see the reception they get on the other side when they do so.

Having made holes in the house of Myrmica, the Leptothorax enter without hesitation. They greet the surprised giants (on whom, henceforward, they propose to live) affably, and wander about. It is as if they said, "Nice place you've got here! We're neighbours now and will be seeing quite a lot of each other."

Although the Leptothorax would be greatly offended if their large neighbours refused them access to any part of their nest, including even the queen's chamber, they consider it bad form to a degree if these same neighbours try to invade *their* privacy. (Similar anomalies are not unknown with us!) That the food both of themselves and their young is obtained entirely from the "house next door" makes no difference to this attitude.

So the Leptothorax have their privacy, bring up their young, and get their food for nothing. In short, they are parasitic on their large friends. This, however, tells us nothing. Parasites cannot just decide to live on others and straightway go and do it. They have to have some scheme. Indeed parasitism is a difficult and specialised profession, often demanding more work than earning an honest living. In Solenopses we have seen one way, the aggressive way, of living on a host. In Leptothorax we see another.

The dwarfs use the exterior entrances of the nest equally with the large ants, and lounge about outside enjoying the fresh air but keeping their eyes open. The Myrmica keep and milk cows in the shape of greenfly; they also milk wild greenfly wherever they can find them. Anon comes a Myrmica worker straight from the cow-shed hurrying home with milk. A dwarf accosts it. What it says is not known but it might well be, "Shampoo and brush-up, sir?" Every minute spent in a barber's shop is agony to me, but I know those who enjoy it. They have all the trimmings—haircut, singe, shampoo, shave, massage, and the rest, and tell me they lean back in a state of drowsy content all the time. Myrmica is like that. So instead of hurrying on to deliver the milk, it crouches, and the dwarf climbs up and begins to scrub its back.

Ants do a lot of tickling. They tickle their stock to make them yield milk; they fondle and tickle their queen; they tickle beetles and caterpillars; but there is no tickling here. It is a vigorous scrub and massage. It is not because the ant is dirty; ants clean themselves and each other continually as a matter of routine; it is just some energetic rubbing that the large ant enjoys. It enjoys it so much that when the dwarf, having scrubbed its back, moves forward and begins to scrub its head, it slobbers at the mouth. The slobber is regurgitated honey-dew, "milk" recently drawn from greenflies, and the dwarf leans over and sucks it up. Soon the large ant is deliberately regurgitating this milk it has been to such pains to collect in order to keep the masseuse at work. Other dwarfs, when the first one is full, take its place, so that when Myrmica gets back to the nest it will probably find that it has no milk at all to give to the nurses and children waiting there. It is, in fact, rather in the position of a woman sent out to get the family rations who returns and says she has been unable to get any because she has spent all her money on a perm.

From time to time ants come back from work that is unconnected with getting food. They are empty and indeed in need of food themselves. Nevertheless, they always like a back-scrub, and do not protest when a dwarf accosts them. And they *do* get a bit of a scrub, but not much. The dwarf does not believe in flogging a dead horse. It leaves that unprofitable ant just as the ant is settling down to a nice session, and intercepts some other worker who may be able to pay.

In the case of Solenopsis, the tiny passage-ways were a complete barrier to the large ants, but the passages of Leptothorax, though small also, are, as we have said, very short. Therefore, from time to time a couple or so of loutish Myrmica, when in their own nest, may suddenly decide that they want a scrub and smash open a hole and enter a dwarf living-room.[1]

It is as if we broke through the walls of a small cottage and surprised the inmates as they were sitting down to tea. Our reception would be cold, to say the least. Politeness, how-

[1] Wheeler gives us this information, using Lubbock observation nests.

ever, is the rule in this dual nest, but all the same when the two Myrmica louts break into the chamber they receive no welcome. The inmates would seem to look at the damage done, and then at each other with this unspoken question, "How can we get rid of them?"

They are not rude, but go up to the intruders and begin to pull them gently towards the wrecked entrance and indicate the way out. If the louts are persistent they may even give them a very short and irritated back-scrub, but in the end the dwarfs almost push them out and immediately get busy blocking up the hole and making a new one in another place.

The Leptothorax, when established, live on the Myrmica. Does this insidious and persistent robbery wreck the economy of the Myrmica colony? It does not seem to. And there are worse things. Our own Income Tax officials do not scrub *our* backs when they take from us much more than the dwarfs take from Myrmica. Nor do they shampoo our heads or give us any pleasure whatsoever in return.

CHAPTER 6

THE RANCHERS

IN a bus the other day I found myself seated behind two stout women who, as women often do, were discussing their various ailments. Judging by their conversation, both were riddled with diseases, though to outward appearance they were almost rudely healthy. The talk passed from pains and dizzy feelings to doctors, and here disaffection reared its head. "What did he give you, dear?" asked one. "Some of those white pills," replied the other, "and they're no good." "He gave me white pills too," said the first, "and I threw the lot away. White pills don't help me. I've had 'em before."

As the talk proceeded it became obvious that to these two women all white pills from their doctor were the same. Ignorant, of course, but not more so than the ignorance of people who think that there are only two types of aphids— greenfly and blackfly. There are hundreds of species, for aphids are very specialised, and one species lives on one type of vegetation, another or another. The aphids that are smothering the roses are different species from those on the peach tree close by, while those on the plum and apple trees and cucumber plants are also different. To make it still more difficult, aphids have a different host in summer from their autumn and spring hosts. Thus the bean aphid (which is also the sugar-beet and dock aphid) goes to the spindle tree in autumn and lays its eggs there, and its progeny breed and live on the spindle tree until summer is well advanced, while the hop aphid goes to plum and damson trees for autumn and spring, and the peach tree aphid to plants of the potato tribe. And so on. It all becomes very confusing, and we still have a lot to learn.

Like submarines in war-time, aphids attack our food supplies. Our methods of dealing with submarines were, in the long run, fairly effective. Our methods of dealing with aphids are completely inadequate, and if we relied on our own efforts we should, after a period, have to capitulate and give up growing the fruit and vegetables they attack. They themselves would eventually destroy the plants they favoured, and would then no doubt learn to accommodate themselves to other sources of food—which they are already doing. The outlook for us would be poor. The time would come when there was no bread, grain, fruit or vegetables, no sugar or sweets, no poultry or eggs, and not even a glass of wine, whisky, or beer to help us face the dreadful situation.

"Nonsense!" you may say. "We can spray and kill them off that way. And even when we do not spray, the things disappear. They come, at times, in large numbers, then they go. The cherries that were a mass of blackfly last year are clear this year. You exaggerate. The menace could never become as great as you suggest."

So? Let us first see how they breed, and let us keep in our minds the whole time the simple rules of multiplication.

We start, naturally, with the eggs in winter. They are probably on the twigs of some tree, and only to be seen with a pocket lens. There will be a fair number of them, and one soon learns to recognise them. They are not eggs one can pick up or brush off. They seem to be engrained in the bark. They are unaffected by cold, and be the winter never so severe it will not damage them. These eggs were laid by fertilised females, and in the spring they hatch out into wingless aphids.

It is a hen party that gets together in the spring on the young leaves and shoots. There are no males, and there will be no males for a long time. These females will never know even of the existence of the opposite sex, nor will their daughters, nor their grand-daughters, nor great grand-daughters, nor great great grand-daughters, nor daughters that follow even after these. Generation after generation of virgins will breed such a mass of greenfly as—if unchecked— would cover the earth. All these spinsters are busy the whole season, spring, summer, autumn, doing two things, both with great thoroughness, eating and breeding. Hardly has a daughter been born than *she* starts breeding too, and *her* daughters lose no time. All without male help. A female

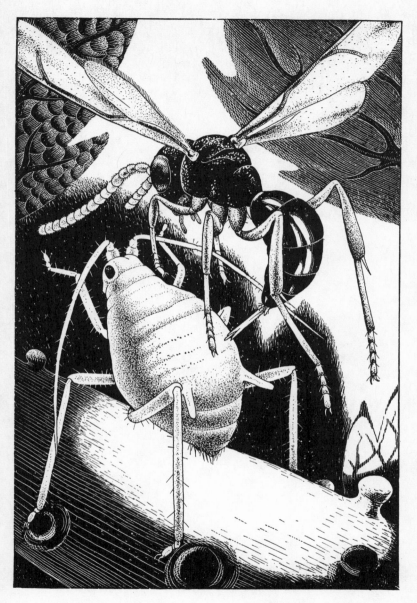

Ichneumon about to deposit an egg in the body of a Greenfly

millennium seems to have arrived. How long they can go on breeding from one generation to another without males we do not know, but under artificial conditions, such as a hot greenhouse, females will breed females for four years—which would amount to many thousand years with us.

I told you to keep multiplication in mind. Do you wonder now at the masses of green or blackfly you find? . . . or do you wonder why there are not more?

After the first batch not all the aphids are wingless. A wingless virgin will often give birth to a winged daughter, and vice versa. So the thickening crowd soon consists of both winged and wingless aphids. These winged forms are bred so that the breed may spread itself elsewhere. They fly in a casual way every day, always resting at night and taking off, if they feel like it, in the morning. This, however, is of little consequence; it is like sheep straying from one meadow to another, or a man taking a walk. Their other flights are more purposeful, and during the season in England there are three of them. Accustomed as we are to regard greenfly as static clustering masses, it is difficult to conceive them flying for as far as a hundred miles (as far as 800 miles when carried by the wind) in great flocks at high altitudes—1,000 to 2,000 feet. Yet such is the case, and, as I have said, there are roughly three flights per year, as has been shown by workers at the experimental stations at Rothamsted and Cardington recently.[1] These flights are what one would expect. The first flight occurs about May and consists of aphids reared on their winter host flora travelling to the trees, vegetables or plants that are to be their hosts for the summer, and which, as we know, are different in most cases. For obvious reasons, this is not a very large flight: the aphids have hardly started breeding winged forms yet. The second (and most deadly) flight is about the end of July, when the aphids, now bred into vast numbers, take to the air to redistribute themselves over all available flora of a similar type (but not necessarily the same) to that they have just left—in other words, their "summer" flora. (These creatures have everything mapped out for their proposed conquest of the vegetable world.) The last flight is

[1] These insects flights and others have been most thoroughly described in the light of recent knowledge by C. G. Johnson in *New Biology*, issue No. 9.

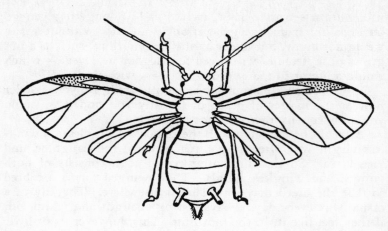

Winged Aphid

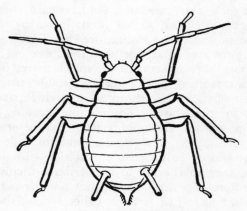

Wingless Aphid

about October, or earlier in a hard season, when the aphids, flying high again, go from their summer vegetation to their winter vegetation, where they will lay their eggs . . . in some far-away spot perhaps, but not so far away as to prevent their children coming back in early summer to our orchards and vegetable gardens.

At the end of the season males are bred out of this long, long female line. They fertilise the females and the females do not then produce living young but eggs—the eggs we started with on the twigs of some tree. By arithmetical rules these eggs should outnumber the eggs of the previous year by billions upon billions. A *single* female aphid, according to Buckton—who went into the matter carefully—should in one season (and given the food, of course) produce the fifteenth power of 210 aphids, which works out at 68,080,000,000,000, 000,000,000,000,000,000,000 aphids—sufficient, according to Huxley, to outweigh the total human population of China. The average garden, however, starts not with one but with thousands of females, so there is more multiplication to be done! Therefore, if aphids bred quietly and normally and without interference and could get the food, man would be out of a job as an agriculturalist—and indeed dead—in one year.

Why is he not? Because of his spraying? No, rather in spite of it. In *Alice in Wonderland* the Carpenter wept like anything to see such quantities of sand. We, too, might well weep to see on our plants such quantities of greenfly. The Walrus's suggestion of employing seven maids to sweep up the sand over a period was considered impracticable by the Carpenter. Equal doubt arises as to the practicability of getting rid of greenfly by spraying. It is too local. It hardly even begins to tackle the problem. Were that all, no harm would be done, and even the few aphids destroyed would help, and leave certain trees clear that would have been covered else, but the matter is not quite so simple for the whole business of aphis control is in other, more efficient hands than ours, and we do not co-operate with them.

Justifiably on the whole many of us dislike insects. We think of flies, mosquitoes, bluebottles, fleas, lice, bed-bugs, weevils, cockroaches, and others of the formidable gang that

seem so set on making our lives uncomfortable and even
hazardous in various ways. Insects, we say (possibly remem-
bering to exclude the bee), have declared war against us. So
be it. As regards those that attack our crops and fruit we
know a thing or two now. We have scientists and chemists
and apparatus-makers and other cunning artificers who can
poison and otherwise destroy the teeming hordes that have
been rash enough to pit their puny wits against ours. Let
these hordes look out, for they are in for such a massacre as
they have never known before!

So mankind brought out his latest weapon, the Spray,
often operated by engines powerful enough to drive tanks.
And the massacre *was* great. Even unhealthy, weak, non-
resistant fruit-trees were freed from the enemies that had
been busy exterminating them and allowed to continue a life
that nature had thought inadvisable. Great was the rejoicing,
and orchards presented the pleasing spectacle of clean trees
and fresh, uninjured leaves. We are at the beginning of that
rejoicing now, but even thus early, the broad smiles of some
have given place to pursed lips. A few even shake their heads
—slowly, but significantly.

At the beginning it all seemed so obvious, so reasonable,
so certain, so simple. True, man had tried to interfere
with nature before almost invariably with disastrous results;
but this was different. What, then, has happened to
wipe the smiles from certain faces. Here are *some* of the
answers:

(1) A drug-addict can become accustomed to doses of
morphia that would kill others. By taking arsenic and other
poisons in increasing doses, the human body can become
immune to normally lethal quantities. Similarly, fruit-tree
and other pests gradually (though possibly "rapidly" is the
better word) become immune to sprays and their young inherit
their resistance.

(2) Natural pest resistance in the trees themselves is being
bred out by the survival and promulgation of the unfit. A tree
may not appear to be unhealthy to us, but if it is attacked by
unusual numbers of aphids and other pests it indicates a
fundamental weakness. Such a strain is better dead.

(3) Since spraying began aphids are increasing in numbers.

(4) Sprays kill the enemies of the pests even more efficiently than they kill the pests themselves.

So spraying evidently is not going to solve the problem. We must still depend on the natural aphid enemies. Light, however, *is* beginning to penetrate. Hop-growers at any rate have found a new preparation. Its name is *Bis(bisdimethylamino)-phosphonous anhydride*. This is absorbed by the plant and makes the sap poisonous to any biting insects. Greenfly are thus killed but the ladybirds and other non-plant-biting insects who prey on them are said to be unaffected. One wonders a little, for the bodies of greenflies still alive might be expected to be poisonous to those, such as ladybirds, that actually eat them, but it is a step in the right direction.

Where and who are these enemies? The greenfly are there, on that plum or apple tree, herded in packed masses, their fat bodies stuffed to bursting point with the plant's sap, and, if greenfly *can* register contentment with life and conditions, these seem to be doing so. But there is no sign of an enemy. We must not be so superficial. Get a lens and examine one of the rather oily bunches under one of the leaves. Under the lens you will find some aphids that do not look too prosperous. They have a collapsed appearance. Some have also (if you look still more carefully) a little hole, perfectly circular, neatly drilled into their bodies. It is through this hole that they have given birth, not to a greenfly, but to their greatest enemy, the Ichneumon.

I need hardly tell you what has happened. A mother ichneumon laid an egg inside a greenfly, the egg hatched into a grub, fed on the greenfly's juices, pupated, and a little later cut a hole and emerged as a fully developed "fly."

Even so, you may not be impressed. Putting the lens back in your pocket you may say, "Quite. There is no doubt about it: one or two of this lot are dead. But what odds does it make? For every dead one there are hundreds alive and fit."

Do not be too sure of this. Probably the bulk of them have been "treated" by an ichneumon. Whether they have or not, every single aphid that stays on that tree will be exterminated by enemies.

The ichneumon "fly" (there are many species) is neat, elegant, narrow-waisted, but drably coloured and possessing no claims to beauty. To many she will seem to be just another gnat flying vaguely about the trees. Others will not notice her at all. And how many, seeing her, will realise that they are in the presence of one of the saviours of mankind?

The careful watcher will soon see the ichneumon descend on to the back of one of the multitudinous aphids. For most of its life, and apart from the migrations of the winged forms, the aphid is not active. It has summed life up and decided that life consists of two things, eating and breeding, and that all the rest are frills. Therefore, while it can, it sits motionless in bloated ease. When the ichneumon descends on to its back however, it loses this detachment and bucks and rears in a most un-greenfly-like manner. The ichneumon, riding it like a jockey, waits until its untrained muscles tire. She then stabs it with her ovipositor, inserts her egg, and flies away and treats another.

Some wag once put an advertisement in a paper offering, for a fee, to give an infallible method of killing greenfly. Those foolish enough to send money for the instructions were directed to place the greenfly on a smooth block of wood and then hit it with a hammer. This method sounds absurd because it is complicated and individual, and yet the methods of the greatest of all aphid exterminators are just as individual and far more complicated.

The receipt of the egg, after the initial pain of being stabbed by the ovipositor, does not worry the aphid. It returns to its normal avocation, the sucking in of sap. The egg hatches in the belly of its host and a maggot emerges into what must be a sort of heaven. It lies bathed in food, and shows its appreciation by putting on weight rapidly; so much so that it soon occupies the whole of the aphid's abdomen (you may see it through the skin, curled up inside.) Needless to say, the aphid dies, and by this time must be glad to do so.

The wheat aphids in certain places and in comparatively small numbers, begin to feed on the green shoots in spring. In July they march up in their billions to attack the ear itself. All seems over: no more bread or sandwiches, or toast and marmalade for breakfast. *Must* we now live on potatoes? Will no one answer our cries for help? Someone has done so already. A small ichneumon, named *Ephedrus plagiator*, is falling upon the hordes that have outmanœuvred and defeated us. Already the bulk of the multitude that cover the ears of wheat are suffering internal pains and most of the others will have the same complaint shortly. Their rich food seems to do them no good. They suck but grow thin. When the corn begins to ripen there may be a few live aphids left, but most of them will be brown and empty sacks.

Ephedrus plagiator is often itself parasited whilst inside the body of the aphid by an insect of similar type called *Ceraphus carpenteri*. Wheels as it were within wheels, so that an aphid, having been injected with an egg from a mother *Ephedrus Plagiator*, may die in the usual way, but have emerge from its body not the expected *Ephedrus plagiator* but *Ceraphus carpenteri*.

The ichneumons do not fight alone in the war against aphids. Almost as formidable are the pretty brigades of Ladybirds in their colourful black-and-red spotted uniforms.

In China the frog is known as the " Protector of the Rice." To kill one in a paddy field is a crime. The Chinese are by no means "kind to animals," but they *do* recognise those animals that help them, and realise their commercial value. We in the West are singularly lacking in gratitude to those who help us. We will lavish affection on a useless toy dog, but all the ichneumon can expect from us is an angry swipe or a dose of lethal spray administered when it is in the very act of preserving for our use the kindly fruits of the earth. For ingratitude the British beer drinker is high up on the list. Swilling down his pints, he gives no thought at all to the "Protector of the Hops," the ladybird, which the French, more responsive, call the *Vache à Dieu*. Should I ever buy a pub its name will certainly be changed to "The Ladybird Inn" and the sign outside will bear a picture of that beetle —easier to paint by the way, and more colourful than a Royal Oak or a Marquis of Granby.

In the insect world young and old rarely eat the same food. The cabbage-white butterfly, is harmless in itself to the vegetable plot, yet her young are likely to strip it bare. The hunting wasp sips only nectar from flowers, while her babies eat nothing but living carcasses. The ladybird mother and larva, however, both eat aphids, and to such an extent that they would seem to consider aphid destruction their mission in life.

Although ladybirds (there are about 2,000 species) are very pleased to give us assistance in killing the greenfly in our gardens from time to time, it is the hop-aphis ladybirds that seem to take their duties most seriously. For at certain times, in certain years, and in such swarms that almost darken the sky, the hop ladybird army goes into battle, travelling long distances and going from one hop-field to another. Hops are a comparatively localised crop and these great armies have only been observed in Kent, Sussex and Surrey. Writing of ladybirds in a newspaper in 1829, a writer says: "In 1827 the shore at Brighton and all the watering-places on the South Coast were literally covered with them, to the great terror of the inhabitants; they being ignorant that these insects were emigrating after having cleared the neighbouring hop-grounds of the destructive aphis." When these migrations have been on a very large scale it has always been noticed that the hop crops the following year have been particularly good.

Nobody, especially a gardener or a hop-planter, is likely to worry much about the sufferings of aphids, yet when the lady-birds go into action millions of their prey suffer a dreadful fate. Again the usually static aphid rears and struggles, but the ladybird holds it down and eats it alive, beginning at the tip of the abdomen. Or rather, it eats half of it alive, for when it has eaten the belly, the ladybird leaves it for another victim, not bothering about the less satisfying thorax or head. The aphid is still alive and walks away and lives for some hours afterwards. Meanwhile the ladybird, after a clean and brush-up, has started on another aphid. For the ladybird has (and we must be thankful for it) one of the most voracious appetites ever known and can consume thirty greenflies in one hour—a greenfly every two minutes. Multiply this by the numbers in the vast hordes of ladybirds that from time to time almost darken the sky and one gets an idea of the scale on which Nature's Aphid-Destruction Companies work. Our own spraying efforts are futile by comparison. The six-footed, brownish larvae of the ladybird are equally efficient. They have mandibles well capable of holding down and sucking out the juices of aphids, and appetites just as voracious as those of their parents.

Does the aphid feel pain when the ladybird operates? Pain is one of those problems. We hear a lot of talk—and a lot of nonsense. Vivisectors say that their subjects never feel pain: any struggling or signs of agony is "reflex action." The fox, according to the huntsman, *likes* being hunted. The rabbit, according to trappers who have a large number of gin traps in store and are expert in setting them but unused to other ways, suffers practically no pain when caught by the leg in a pronged steel trap but *does* suffer when gassed by cyanide or caught by any other type of trap. A cottage woman, whose adored cat was a wicked catcher of, and player with, birds, told me that she thought cats injected an anæsthetic fluid into their victims so that it is impossible for them to suffer! According to experimenters, large spiders, frogs, toads and others die immediately if put into spirits of wine, despite the fact that they struggle for hours. Again that useful word, "reflex action." A well-known surgeon stated in a book that men are anatomically more sensitive to pain than women: a woman, referring to her unsympathetic husband, once said to me, "You see, *he* doesn't feel pain. I do." Where are we?

If we know so little about the feelings of ourselves and the larger animals, we are not likely to discover much about insects. The greenfly has had its abdomen eaten away. Did it feel pain? In reply, the wasp will probably be instanced. That creature, when pumping marmalade into its inside, can have its abdomen cut off smartly at the waist and continue with its meal. Obviously it has felt nothing. That seems to end the matter. But does it? I do not know, but I am inclined to think that a man suddenly cut in half would feel nothing either. His brain might work for a short period, but I doubt if there would be pain. Every hunter knows that an antelope, standing on the alert and shot in a vital spot, will often remain on the alert for a minute or so, obviously not knowing that anything at all has happened to it: then it suddenly bounds off and falls dead. And whilst on this subject, let me instance something that happened in a certain R.A.F. mess during the last war.

It was evening, and a few officers were in the ante-room having rather a session and drinking more whisky than was good for them. All were what is called "mellow." The mechanism of revolvers came under discussion. A flight lieutenant had his with him, and to illustrate some point, produced it, whereupon a pilot officer, with the inconsequence of insobriety, suggested that the flight lieutenant could not hit a haystack at fifteen yards. Responding to this bantering element in what had started as a serious discussion, the flight lieutenant swung his revolver round and said to the pilot officer, "I can hit *you*, anyway!" To the surprise of everybody, especially that of the flight lieutenant, who, of course, "did not know it was loaded," the weapon went off and the sound of the shot was followed (much to the relief of the flight lieutenant) by the mocking laughter of the pilot officer, who said his point was proved and the flight lieutenant could not hit anything at any distance.

More drinks were served, and then the pilot officer went to the lavatory. In the lavatory he found that the water he passed seemed to be red and that his hands were of the same colour. He then felt an uncomfortable wetness in his trousers, and, looking down, saw that blood was dripping from their ends. He looked back, saw a bloody trail the way he had come into the lavatory, and immediately fainted. The bullet had gone through his chest. It had struck no vital spot, but the point is that it had gone through without the man feeling any sensation. If the penetration had been slow, however, it would have been a very different matter.

My illustrations all boil down to nothing, and we are no wiser about the feelings of a greenfly when it is slowly eaten. Let us hope it feels no pain, for a greenfly cannot help being a greenfly. Like ourselves, it must conform to a strict routine from which there is no escape.

We have studied the aphid's enemies—at least the two chief enemies, for there are several others, with which we have not time to deal. Has it any friends? With the exception of ourselves and our sprays, it has only one other friend—but one by no means to be despised—the ant. Whether this friendship is responsible for much increase in aphis life I do not know;

the aphid is able to plague us quite sufficiently without the help of ants.

The aphid sucks the juice from the stems and leaves of plants; also from the roots, for many species live underground. It sucks with vigour, so that it becomes swollen out with sap. Why it feeds so voraciously is rather a mystery; its stomach cannot cope with all that is taken in so that the creature is continually voiding fæces of only partly digested matter. This excrement is practically colourless, and often shot out for a considerable distance. The semi-digestive process has also made it sweeter in taste than the sap of the plant.

The excreta is called honey-dew, and is much in demand with certain insects; many species of ants in particular prize it above all else. To human palates, however, the taste of honey-dew is not as nice as the name.

Actually there are two honey-dews, not one. The first is this same excrement of aphids and the other is a sweet substance exuded by the leaves of certain plants around the petioles where the leaves join the stem, particularly by willows, vetches, laurels, oaks. Damage by insects may also make leaves exude honey-dew. Both these honey-dews are collected by bees, but only when forced to do so by starvation. I remember one very bad honey season, which incidentally was my first season of bee-keeping. Cold winds persisted. The bees could get nothing from the clover or the lime trees. The nearest apiary to mine was about three miles off and the hives there contained no honey at the end of the season and the bees were being fed. Yet all the combs in my supers were sealed and heavy. I felt the same sort of pride in my bees as a father feels who has cleverer children than others. It was, of course, honey-dew they had collected, chiefly from oaks; sweet stuff but of a greenish colour and with a sulphury, lubricating-oil taste. I buried the lot in the ground, for bees that winter on such food often get dysentery and die—but ants adore it.

Ants "milk" aphids, and milk them expertly. It is not everyone who can milk an aphid. Darwin tried several times, using the finest hairs and doing his best to copy the methods of the ants, but not a drop of milk would the aphids give him. Since then, one or two experimenters have succeeded, but not many. The ant strokes and taps the belly of the aphid with her antennae on either side in a special way, and the aphid exudes a drop of liquid slowly from its anus. Note the word "slowly"; the diarrhoea-like squirt which characterises the normal discharge of the aphid does not occur under the manipulations of the ants. Instead, the drop issues at such regulated speed that the ant can imbibe it as it comes.

How did the ant learn to do this? The ant is a fierce creature. Its normal reaction to an insect weaker than itself is to kill and eat it. In the old days primitive ants mus have killed aphids and, like ladybirds, eaten their bellies, and probably the rest of them as well. Yet no species of ant to-day ever kills an aphid. We both milk and kill our cows, ants milk but never kill theirs.

If ants just went out and milked what greenflies they found on leaves, etc., no one could take objection to it. Unfortunately they go further and their methods with their "cows" are too much like our own with ours to be comfortable for us. Currency is poor stuff. It is valueless in itself and its value as a token may evaporate overnight when inflation and other disturbances set in. But cattle are always cattle. Disease, drought, etc., may bring loss, but cattle have an intrinsic value in themselves that currency has not. Consider only one part of them—their milk. It is an unnatural food and was made by nature only for the use of the young, but *how* we adults like it! Not all like to drink it neat, but there are puddings and sauces and tea and . . . There is no need, however, to go into its uses; all one need do is to find out how many people do *not* take in milk—the milk roundsman will supply you with this information. You might also call at the grocer's and ask how many of his customers do not require butter or cheese.

Milk, or rather honey-dew, is an unnatural food for ants also and there was undoubtedly a time when they never used it, but now a host of species live almost entirely on honey-dew, and keep herds of cattle, which they protect, care for, and pasture.

In the autumn these cow-keepers take aphid eggs into their nest, where they store them against the time they hatch out in spring. By doing so it is commonly said that they protect them against the rigours of winter, but, alas, few aphid *eggs* need any such protection. It is just that the ants wish to have them at hand. When they hatch, the young aphids are taken outside and "planted out" on whatever type of vegetation they require. They are then like cows in a field and are regarded by the ants as their special property. In cold weather all are taken back into the nest until conditions improve.

A rather extreme case is described by F. M. Webster in America, and concerns the ant, *Lasius americanus*, and the aphid, *Aphis maidiradicis*, the latter being a dreadful pest of maize, attacking and destroying not the foliage or cobs, but the roots. Furthermore (and this is a serious indictment against the ant), it appears to be a special breed raised by ants, for it is only found in the burrows of ants or under their control.

The eggs of this aphid hatch in the nest, and the young are carried out and placed on the roots of certain weeds that have sprung up in some ploughed field. (Even though stationed on the roots and so protected from the elements, all are taken back to the nest in bad weather.)

In due course the green corn shows above the surface of the soil—a pretty sight—and the ants gets busy. They transfer the aphids from the roots of the weeds to the roots of the corn. There cannot be very many aphids yet, but we know how aphids breed. With this particular species as many as sixteen generations may stretch between April and October, and the increase is carried by the ants from plant to plant and root to root. Sabotage, from our point of view, merely cattle-ranching from theirs.

To prove that the aphids *are* actually carried by the ants from infected roots to clean ones, Webster grew several plants of maize specially in plant-pots. These were placed between other plants in the field, and a number of infested plants pulled up. On the roots of these were colonies of aphids, attended by numbers of little brown ants, and the latter immediately began to remove their charges and carry them away.

Where? That became apparent next day, when the previously clean roots of the plant-pot corn were found to be covered with aphids.

By autumn things have got beyond the ants' control, but

there will be plenty of eggs for them to collect and store away for next year. And only those thus collected and stored by the ants will survive.

So the farmer's crop may well be a total loss. And let us not blame the aphids; it is the ants that are responsible.

This, as I say, is probably an extreme case. Our data is very incomplete yet. Exactly the same thing may be going on elsewhere. And even without such intensive cattle-ranching with selected breeds, the protection ants give to their charges is doing its small best to keep the scourge with us.

What sort of "protection" does the aphid get? What do ants do to the enemies of their beloved and almost holy cows? How do they deal with the ichneumons, the ladybirds, the wasps, and others? Ants build enclosures, or even complete cowsheds for their aphids and stay with them, passing the time by frequently fondling them. No enemy can get at them. Even those aphids on a chance leaf (whether they have been planted there by the ants or not) will often be found to be under police protection. There may be only one ant there when an enemy approaches, but this ant somehow manages to call reserves, and in a very short time a posse of ants comes rushing along. The ichneumon dare not tackle even one ant, the ladybird is soon hustled off, the wasp tackles the ant and knocks it right off the leaf, but the knocked-off one soon returns with friends and the wasp has no further chance. Its sting is useless against such tiny hard objects. All it can do is to fly about above, buzzing angrily. If it descends on to the leaf its legs will be seized by a number of small jaws, and it may find it difficult to get away. In any case it will have no further chance of grabbing a greenfly. Even man will be bitten and stung if he puts a finger near the leaf. In short, ant-protected aphids are more or less immune from their normal enemies.

To get their honey-dew ants adopt various devices. Some merely lick leaves on which honey-dew has been squirted. Others wander around and find "wild" aphids and milk them (getting nothing like the yield of that supplied by "domestic" aphids). Others go into the corrals of other ants, steal the milk of a few aphids and then try to make a quick get-away before the owners can catch them. Others "keep" aphids, enclosing them or not as the case may be.

The amount of excreta voided by aphids (or, more politely, the "yield of milk") is enormous. The drop itself is a large one, and Wheeler has shown that the maple aphid yields forty-eight of these drops in twenty-four hours. Indeed, one drove of greenfly will keep a large ant community amply supplied with food. An ant will milk four or five aphids at a sitting and then go back, very distended, to its nest. Aphids "kept" and milked by ants imbibe more sap from the plant than "wild" aphids.

Aphids are tended by ants in several different ways. To give a rough idea, the first and simplest method is by carrying aphids from leaf to leaf. This is like the cattle-keeping of several primitive tribes in Africa, such as the Masai, who merely drive their herds from one spot in the veld to another, making them no homes or enclosures, but carefully guarding them. (The ants often cut off the wings of winged aphids to prevent them straying.)

The second is the method we have noted already: keeping eggs in winter and planting them out on roots or foliage in spring.

The third is the permanent underground stable method. The ants clear away the soil from some roots and make galleries round them in which the aphids live and move and eat. Often the ants find a "wild" winged female about to lay eggs and clip off her wings and lead or carry her down to their nest where, in a special apartment, she lays her eggs in warmth and comfort.

The fourth is the outside stable method, used chiefly for foliage-sucking aphids. Special stables are erected on trees or plants, and the aphids kept inside. These stables are made of various materials—wood, mud, papier mâché, bark, etc. Often these cattle barns are some distance from the nest. The most elaborate in the latter class is the stable connected with the nest by a long, outdoor, covered-in corridor. Along this corridor the milkmaids trip to and fro continually.

The milkmaids returning to the nest seem to be willing to give milk away to all and sundry of their sisters who ask for some. The ant is a generous and often improvident insect, but probably these sisters will distribute the milk, or some of it, in the right quarters. At times, however, there are other sisters whose only thought is to fill their own bellies. We cannot really blame these particular ants for they suffer from a sort of disease. They are riddled with certain internal parasites that, rather like tapeworms in larger animals, consume the host's nourishment and, after a heavy meal, leave the host feeling as hungry as it did before. Such worm-infested ants do not occur by any means in every nest, but when they do occur they are an unmitigated nuisance. Chief of their crimes is that they never do any work. Their hunger occupies their thoughts to the exclusion of everything else. They relinquish all interest in the affairs of their nest, and just follow the milkmaids, begging them for food, getting in their way, and keeping up a stridulating whine of entreaty (for certain species of ants *do* whine and make similar noises that can be heard even with human ears). Worse than this, they often get out of hand, form themselves into gangs, attack milkmaids, force their heads down, and make them give them all the milk they carry.

Strangely enough, these beggars and gangsters are tolerated when things are going well, but in hard times it is a different matter. Probably, too, when starvation is affecting all, the importunities and rough stuff of the worm-ridden ones becomes worse than ever. At any rate the ants then put an abrupt stop to it and kill them off. This is yet another example of the improvidence of the ant: it cares little about waste until supplies get short.

The live-stock kept and milked by ants is not confined to aphids. In hot countries other types predominate. Chief amongst these are the scale insects and mealie bugs of the group Coccidae, which, like the Aphididae, belong to the order Hemiptera.

The order Hemiptera is the one of the twenty-three insect orders that man could best spare. A bold statement in view of the undesirability of most of the other orders, but, I think, a true one. Unchecked, this order could exterminate all life in a very short time.

The name means "Half a Wing," and was given by Linnaeus

Living Barrels

in spite of the fact that all the members of this order possess
either four wings or none. Its number of species is vast and
many of them breed almost as intensively and destructively as
greenfly. Practically every one of this great host lives by
biting into the skin and then sucking the blood of either
vegetables or animals. The order includes bed-bugs and many
of the blood-sucking insects of the tropics, as well as the
multitudinous kinds of blood-suckers found on bats and birds.
Amongst its few comparatively harmless members are the
water-boatman (if you wish to find out if a water-boatman
can bite, catch one by the head and see!), the Cicada or " Scissor-
Grinder," the Frog-hopper (Manufacturer of "Cuckoo-Spit"),
and the Cochineal. The last is the only member of this huge
order that does man any good, and that does not amount to
much in these days of synthetic dyes.

But annoying and dangerous as the various animal blood-
suckers are to man, the harm they do him fades to insig-
nificance besides the harm done to him by the plant-suckers
of the same order: the aphids, scale insects, mealie bugs, leaf-
hoppers, and the rest. Scale insects are so-called because the
females give out a secretion which sometimes forms a pro-
tective kind of scale. Mealie bugs do the same thing, but their
secretion is waxy and not hard. Neither of these types of
scales present any obstacle to the ant milkmaids, who milk
them as they milk aphids and get almost as large a yield. We
find these herds, too, kept in enclosures, stables, and the rest,
or, as with aphids, milked in the wild state, so we will not
waste time by going over ground that has been gone over
already.

The keeping of "cows" is routine work with ants. As with
ourselves, a portion of the community look after the cows
and milk them and deliver the milk daily to the rest of the
community. And the whole lot of aphid-keepers could live—
and many of them do—entirely on aphid milk. But—again
like ourselves—they like sweets and tit-bits in addition to their
normal sustenance. This they often get by exciting the glands
of a variety of creatures, including beetles. Indeed hardly any
creature able to pay for such excitement has been overlooked
by ants. Amongst those able to pay are the caterpillars of

certain blue and beautiful Lycaena butterflies. These have a small aperture on their backs which, under the excitement which only the ant knows how to give, exudes a droplet of clear liquid. Whatever this liquid is—whether it is in the nature of a sweet or a drug—the ants love it.

And the caterpillars get as much pleasure as the ants. So keen are they on being expertly titillated that certain species will live only on trees patrolled by certain species of ants— those no doubt that understand their anatomical peculiarities the best. It is a sensual partnership though appealing to different senses in the two partners.

Many of these caterpillars are taken into ants' nests and live there. So, with some of course, do aphids. But this is not quite the same. The aphids are only taken there for temporary shelter in bad weather, or, if kept permanently, are stabled on roots on which they can feed, which is normal dairy routine. There is nothing normal in the keeping of blue butterfly caterpillars. It is abnormal and vicious. For there is no doubt that the caterpillars are fed on the eggs and grubs of ants. Strange food for caterpillars!

I shall have more to say about this in another chapter. At the moment I am chasing another hare, and am more concerned with the mind of the ant than with its treatment of blue caterpillars. But the treatment must be shown before we can arrive at any conclusion.

The caterpillars eventually pupate. They pupate in the nest, and are then of no further use to the ants. They will yield no more tit-bits. After a long period they will turn into blue butterflies which are also of no use to the ants, and which will die quickly in that underground nest. Yet the ants tend the chrysalises carefully; that is to say, they lay them out and keep them clean from mould; and later, when the butterflies emerge, the ants make holes through which they lead the beautiful things to the surface and the open air. And at the surface they watch them fly off and say good-bye to them —for ever.

It is the "for ever" that is important. Do ants see into the future and realise that, though of no use to them, these butterflies will eventually produce caterpillars, and the more butterflies that can be released, the better for their hunting grounds later on?

I have really finished for the time being with this subject of the ant-butterfly partnership, but there was an interesting account given many years ago by a Mrs. Wyllie and printed in the Bombay Journal.

There is in India a tree called *Zizyphus jujuba* on which feed the caterpillars of a blue butterfly, *Tarueus theophrastus*. And at the base of this tree is often to be found the nest of a certain large black ant. Mrs. Wyllie studied one such nest. Here, shortly, is the story.

The ants are very busy with the caterpillars throughout the season, exciting them and getting from them the drops they covet. But when autumn approaches most caterpillars must pupate, and many, including this particular variety, have then to descend from their trees and burrow in the ground. When, in this case, the event is due, the large black ants (evidently aware of coming events) get into a state of great excitement. Some begin digging holes in the earth, others rush about the tree above, searching for those caterpillars most afflicted by the pangs of coming partial dissolution. These they lead downwards, as men lead fainting women out of a crowded hall.

Soon all have been removed, and all have disappeared.

Remove now the earth at the base of the tree, and you will find a busy scene. It is as if, at the end of the season, a draper's assistants were storing away the dummies ready for next year, when they will be brought out again clad in spring finery. There they are—ranged neatly in rows, and tier upon tier. They are chrysalises, or semi-comatose caterpillars, all being propped up orderly by the ants against the tree-trunk.

Investigating this scene may interest us, but the ants do not like it, as Mrs. Wyllie found. The chrysalises of this butterfly species must have darkness and a covering of earth. So, after they have been exposed to the light, the ants dig again, and range them farther down. When the butterflies emerge they are led upwards and allowed to depart, just as the others we have mentioned.

So ants would seem to be interested in the preservation of

species, and able to take a long-term view. Granting this they have more foresight than man who has already, through sheer greed and inability to see into the future, exterminated a host of species that were very valuable to him, and is even now in the process of exterminating many more.

Or are the ants' methods just instinct? If so, we could do with some of that same "instinct" ourselves.

2

In Cellar Cool

Ants are clever, but in one or two ways they fall short of their social colleagues, the bees and the wasps. They are expert miners of earth and hollowers-out of wood and pith, and thus make serviceable homes, with rooms, corridors, galleries, and the rest. *But*, having made them, they put nothing inside. When we go into a house we put furniture in. If we cannot buy or hire the furniture we make it ourselves. We *have* to make it ourselves in many of the more isolated parts of the globe. Many a cupboard, shelf, and table have I nailed together in Africa from soap boxes and other old wood. I am not boasting about this because others in like circumstances did the same thing and did it much better than I. But we *did* do it, and thus showed ourselves superior in this respect to most ants.

The ant seems incapable of making anything like this. What it badly needs inside its home are receptacles—cradles, bins, tubs, and the like. It does not matter how rough, the ant need not try to imitate the superb and beautiful interior furniture of the honey-bees, but it ought to have something. As it is, it dumps its young in all stages on the bare floor, and stores its food on the floor also. It is in the position of a tidily-minded woman who has nowhere to put anything.

It may be argued that they get along without these receptacles, and they do, but they themselves realise their own deficiency. Being unable to "manufacture" anything, their invariable plan is to make living creatures perform the offices usually designated to inanimate material. Thus we find, amongst other things, certain large-headed workers spending most of their time as a living plug, blocking up entrances to the nest. (It is as if we, finding ourselves unable to make a door, selected a large, fat man and made him jam himself between the posts and stay there.) Some other improvisations made with living subjects are sun-proof corridors—though certain ants *can* make these of earth—boats, ropes, bridges, seed-crackers. These offices often inflict great discomfort on those called upon to play the part and I pity them, but I pity none so much as I pity those called upon to play the part of living barrels.

It will be remembered that an ant milks its four or five cows, and that its milk pail is inside. This pail is a sort of bladder and is called the crop, and though the ant can transfer some of the contents to its own stomach if it wishes, the contents are as a rule regarded as communal property. This crop is distendible, so that a milkmaid going out to milk cows is a very different creature from the same milkmaid when she comes back. She goes off in the energetic jerky way we associate with ants, but waddles heavily back, the reason of course being her distended crop.

Now, a long time ago certain ants in hot, dry places found themselves in danger of extermination by starvation. There were times when the leaf-hoppers, mealie-bugs, aphids, if they were there, yielded their food. There were also galls on plants that exuded saccharine liquor in great quantity. At these times the ants had more food by far than they needed or could cope with. There are two things insects can do with excess food (if they do anything at all): store it away for later use like the bees, or convert it into young and build up a large community. The bees do both if conditions warrant, but these ants could do neither. It was no use building up a large population, because half of them would die of starvation when the short-lived period of abundance came to an end. And, unlike bees, they had no place to store excess food. If only they had suitable containers—casks, barrels, anything! But they were unable to make them. So, like most ants, they turned their thoughts to the possibility of making what they wanted out of living members of their own community. They noticed the swollen stomachs of the returning milkmaids. *Those*, to a certain extent, were casks, but only temporary ones and no use when the galls, etc., had dried up. They were merely milk carts.

But if others . . . ?

I need hardly say that the ants did not consciously puzzle over this matter. They merely felt a need, and generation after generation strove for what it wanted. But it was as if an idea gradually came to them—to evolve workers possessing a stomach ten, twenty, fifty times larger than that of the most swollen of milkmaids; as if they visualised a worker that was *all* stomach and whose other body parts, head, thorax, legs, were mere appendages. That such a monstrosity would be unable to work or even move did not—even if they had been able to think about it—worry them at all. They did not want it to work or to move.

Eventually they got what they strove for and what enabled their species to bridge over the periods of dearth; they evolved a living barrel, whose usual designation is a "rotund" or a "replete."

They did not do it at once. The expansion capacity gradually increased in certain selected types of workers. We can see the process now in its various stages of development, where some species have, as it were, only just started, some have got halfway, and others have reached capacities beyond which, surely, there can be no further expansion—though one never knows.

These living barrels hang upside down in the nest, grasping the rafters, or rather the inequalities of the roof of the cellars with their feet.

If one slings laden barrels from a roof instead of storing them on the floor in the usual way, one must look to the strength of the ceiling, otherwise it will collapse. Sand is a favourite nesting place of ants, and sandy deserts and plains were the normal habitat of the barrel-makers before they made barrels. They still are, but it has been noticed that they now select places for their nests where the earth is hard, even though it is so much more difficult to excavate than sand. The reason, of course, is that sand would collapse under, or rather over, the weight of the barrels.

The living tubs, when filled to capacity, are slung from the ceiling, and there, in cellar cool, sometimes six feet beneath the surface, they stay, and can be tapped as required. "Let those," justly says Wheeler (I condense his words slightly), "who extoll the energy of ants, give a thought to the patience and self-sacrifice of the rotund as it hangs from the rafters of its nest, month in, month out—for years perhaps—a reservoir of temperamental as well as liquid sweetness."

Rotund-manufacturers are not common, yet they are widely distributed and are found here and there throughout the hotter and more desert-like places of the globe, particularly America, South Africa, and Australia. They are not confined to any one species or genus. The first to be properly studied (it was by McCook in 1879) was a Mexican ant (*Myrmecocystus mexicanus*) and this species is now regarded as the real "Honey Ant" (as the rotund-producers are called). But there are many other species, and many that produce even bigger tubs.

The existence of these underground swollen ants had been known to naturalists ever since 1830, following an account given by Dr. de Llave concerning the Mexican ant. His account was accepted with reserve, especially since others afterwards, writing from hearsay and imagination, grossly exaggerated the size of the swollen ants. (Actually the size of the largest of them is about half an inch in diameter—like a very small gooseberry or a large black-currant. That of an ordinary red-currant is the normal size—and this is much bigger in comparison than any cask that brewers produce for us.) Dr. Wetherill ascertained that, in the case of the Mexican ant, 1,160 rotunds contained one pound of honey.

Natives were in advance of scientists, and had known about rotunds long before scientists suspected their existence. Indeed it is from natives that our knowledge of them originated (the belly is often a keener investigator than the mind). Natives had been accustomed to dig up rotunds and eat them centuries before civilised investigators got on their track. Since then others have followed their example and have also found them good to eat. And so they ought to be: from analysis the contents of the crop are almost pure fruit sugar (which does not crystallise). The taste, says McCook, is very pleasant, of a peculiar aromatic flavour suggestive of bee honey. "Agreeable . . . slightly acid in summer from a taste of formic acid," says Dr. Loew, while Dr. Wetherill pronounced it also agreeable, with an odour that suggested syrup of squills.

Rotunds have to be specially trained, and the training has to start early—which, they tell me, is also the case with a human contortionist. The integument of an ant soon hardens after it emerges from the chrysalis, and an adult ant would be unable to swell to the desired proportions without previous exercise in its soft, baby, or "callow" stage. Therefore the rotunds (there are about 600 of them in a fair-sized nest) are selected from the callows and put into training at once. The plates on the abdomen will harden in the usual way later, but the membranes between them (normally imperceptible) will stretch when called upon to do so like the rubber of a child's balloon, so that the plates themselves appear to be but slight and infrequent markings. According to Arnold, it is possible—at least with some species—that the future rotunds are selected and set, as it were, apart, even as early as the grub stage.

With many species the rotunds come from the large workers, and on assuming duty are fed by the small workers until fully distended. They are then (or before) hoisted on to the cellar roof. These cellars have smooth floors underneath, but rough ceilings above, the latter, of course, to enable the rotunds to have something to hold on to with their feet. Even so, how they manage to hang on supporting a huge weight, often for many years, is a mystery. And a fall is a serious thing. At the worst, the pumped-out body may burst. In any case it will be helpless and very difficult to get back into position again.

From henceforward the rotunds *are* no more than so many casks, and the small workers are the cellarmen, who keep the cellar and the casks clean and free from mould, and, in the frequently occurring times of scarcity draw from the barrels as required. (To tap a barrel, a worker puts her mouth to the mouth of a rotund, and the rotund obediently lets forth a drop of liquid, which is licked up by the worker.)

CHAPTER 7

HARVESTING

THE idea that things to eat were created specially for us seems rather presumptuous now. Yet until recently no one doubted it. Fruit, wheat, milk—a self-containing diet provided by beneficial Nature for *us*. Fish and meat too. With these things around us that are so good and essential for us, how could we fail to think that we were being "provided for"?

It was, however, tackling the subject from the wrong end. Porridge, bread, fruit, meat are good for us because they *have* to be good for us. When life came to earth it had to make do with what was there. Nature, that stern nurse, said, "Eat that—and like it." So life ate it—and liked it. Had man, for instance, never had corn, his Harvest Thanksgivings would now be for grass seeds. He would like grass seeds and call them the "staff of life." And they *would* be the staff of life, and just as good for him as wheat, because his system had grown accustomed to them and needed them, and consequently *liked* them. The same with all the other foods. They happened to be there, and only those forms of life that could persuade their insides to assimilate them survived.

One could go even further. Scientists, for instance, often say that life on various planets would be impossible because there is not enough oxygen, or because of this or that. But life on earth needs certain gases and liquids and temperatures only because they were there when life in its crude form originally came, and life had to accustom itself to them or cease to be life. Mars and Venus and the rest may be teeming with life. If they are, one thing is certain, that same life would be extinguished immediately if plunged into the conditions that obtain on earth.

But we need not go as far as the planets: we can see here how life accustoms itself to the obtaining conditions, and how

those conditions become the *necessary* conditions to the life
concerned. Thus we see a stranded fish gasping its life out in
the presence of a number of contented cows, or a cow gurgling
its last in the flood waters of a river full of contented fish.
We see (apart from a few exceptions) fresh water fishes dying
in salt water and vice versa. We see most land life, vegetable
and animal, quickly killed by conditions that exactly suit the
seal and the polar bear.

To get back to the subject, which was food; such animal
life as has survived has made itself eat one or more of the
dishes that happened to be on the table before which it was
made to sit. Some (like the caterpillar) are very choosy. Others,
like man, will take every course and try almost every dish.
This is not greed; it is wisdom, and partly explains man's rise
to his present position. He may not now be wise in certain
other respects, but he has been very wise about food. It may
have been forced on him earlier on when he was a rather
chivvied person and had to eat quickly anything he could find
or kill or pull off or dig up: however it happened, he has
learned one of the most important things in life—to make use
of existing food supplies to the greatest possible extent. Yet
even in man we still see traces of that stomach conservatism
that, throughout the ages, must have killed off so many
species. The caterpillar, having been brought in contact in
first instance with a certain leaf, has lived on that leaf for
millions of years and has got the idea into its head that only
that particular leaf—out of all the things on earth—provides
food. And it is not only an idea, it is a fact. So accustomed has
its stomach become to that leaf that it could not digest any
other leaf. As I said, even man shows traces of stomach conservatism. A thousand instances could be given. Three will
suffice. When tomatoes were first introduced nearly all who
tried them spat them out, and thereafter, for a long time,
they were used only as decorations. Home-grown tomatoes
here at the time of writing (April) are 7s. 6d. a pound, and at
that price customers are certainly not going to use them as
decorations. Matabele natives in Rhodesia, when I was there,
however hungry, would not eat fish, though they rushed like
maniacs to white ant-hills when flying termites were emerging.
During a famine, supplies of wheat were sent to starving

natives in India. It was not rice, so they would not eat it, and died.

The ant undoubtedly started life as a meat-eater pure and simple, and many of the more primitive forms still remain so. Exclusive meat-eating is a more chancy business than exclusive vegetable-eating. Man has found this out from time to time. If it was easy he has always had an inclination to revert to carnivorism. Primitive spears and bows-and-arrows gave him at long last a chance to deal with game that had so far eluded him or even destroyed him. Rich was the reward and man lived for a long time by travelling and hunting in parties and clans. The Bushmen of South Africa to-day (what few remain) are relics of these age-old parties. It did not pay in the long run, for man discovered a more certain li,elihood in planting and growing edible seeds. This gave him a more or less permanent home, time to think, time to breed, and time to build himself up into a gang much greater and more intelligent than any tribe of wandering hunters. Game, however, always represents "something for nothing." Corn means hard work—ploughing, sowing, hoeing, weeding, gathering, threshing. Domestic animals, like cows, mean hard work too. Wild creatures have been reared, brought up, and fed at nature's expense and labour, and nature sends in no butcher's bill to the man who kills and eats them. The rifle gave man a killing power he had never possessed before and he made the fullest use of it. Killing animals became easy. So certain members of the advanced and civilised corn-growers again took to living by hunting. They hunted in many parts of the world and nearly exterminated the great herds of bison in America. In South Africa particularly they found the veld teeming with massed herds of antelopes, and these provided an easy means of livelihood to hunters with rifles. These hunters and their families soon became, to all intents and purposes, purely carnivorous. And why not? There was the game in apparently inexhaustible numbers and easily killed. Why trouble to wait months for corn or vegetables? But arithmetic stepped in as it always does, somehow, in all our affairs. If you keep on subtracting something from something, however big the original figure was, you eventually arrive at nought. The South African hunters—much to their surprise and concern—found that this simple arithmetical rule applied even to them. The apparently inexhaustible herds that had held their own against spears and arrows for countless generations succumbed to the rifle and vanished for ever. So meat—at any rate free meat—was crossed off the hunter's menu, and he had to go back to seeds and vegetables and hard work. He was lucky to be able to do this; the primitive carnivorous ants, when meat got short, were for a very long time unable to find a substitute.

The seeds of vegetables are more satisfactory as food than meat in that they are more universal, cannot run away, contain concentrated nutriment, and can be stored for long periods. Now it is all very well to say how foolish of carnivorous ants not to have realised this before: the wonder is that they ever came to realise it at all. Their stomachs were not adapted to a vegetable diet, and seeds have to be cracked and husked. The day may come when lions take to nuts and corn as well as meat, but it is doubtful, though the lion is a highly intelligent creature.

The social insects, however, have a bigger urge than lions or any other mammal. The lion has only a few young to provide for: ants have many thousands. Such families need large supplies of food and the neighbouring game (especially when there are many other similar families living close by) soon get used up.

There are three answers to this problem for ants. (1) Go in for very small families as certain hunting species do. (This is not a complete answer for its success depends, as we have said, on the absence of other nests close by, and, furthermore, small nests are at the mercy of numerically stronger ant raiders). (2) Have no home, but follow the game, trekking on with all baggage and equipment from place to place, like the Driver Ants. (3) Become vegetarian as well as carnivorous, or purely vegetarian like the mushroom-growers and some cow-keepers (for milking aphids is merely an indirect way of living on the sap of plants).

Those species that realised that there was no future in pure carnivorism split up. Some became plant juice suckers (via aphids), some allotment mushroom-growers, some harvesters. It is the latter we are dealing with now.

It is to be doubted if *any* ant except a fungus-eater is purely vegetarian. There must be very few of them who, during their lifetimes, have not had at least a nibble or so at a dead insect. And even a live edible insect would be well advised not to be too trusting with even the most vegetarian of ants. Few of the harvesters, however, make any pretence of being solely seed-eating. They have learned in nature's hard school to eat seeds and to prefer them, but they will not refuse meat if it is put under their noses, so to speak. They are rather like a farmer who goes out to cut his ripened grain. His thoughts and activities are solely on the harvest, but he will not disdain to shoot and use as food such rabbits as bolt from the field. He would not care at all if there were no rabbits there, but if there are he feels he might just as well have them. And when the harvesting ants march out to get their corn they, too, are not thinking about insects but *will* eat any that happen to be there.

This refers to the majority. Others will go so far as to organise raids on termites, and others will seek with equal diligence both grain and meat.

Generally speaking, however, seeds are the chief thing. Few ants can resist honey. Moggridge once gave honey to some harvesting ants. They ate a bit, not much, soon left it, and when he came next day the honey was covered with soil and chaff thrown out from the nest. He also presented them with milk cows, aphids full of honey-dew. They paid not the slightest attention to them.

To sum up so far as we have gone, certain ants took to eating seeds. That was quite an advance, but the ant, being the ant, did not let it rest at that. Contrary to popular opinion the ant on the whole is not a storer of food. The bee puts it to shame. Yet the ant soon realised that the seeds it had now grown to like, kept. In the places harvesting ants preferred, the climate was hot and dry and the season short. Seeds came, and, in a few days, went. So the harvesting ants made granaries. It was just their line of country: no bins or other containers required (things they have never been able to make)—just empty rooms. The grain "sheds" of the typical harvesters are underground chambers, broadly oval, about six inches across and half an inch high, and the grain is dumped into them.

Thanks to patient investigators we know a lot now about harvesting ants. But our knowledge is recent. Until the nineteenth century no one believed that they existed. Who, then, had said they did?—for it takes more than one party to make a dispute. People who wish to know about natural science always try to get the latest books. But in natural science the most recent information is not always the most correct. In the early nineteenth century any student of ants would have been told that ants never ate seeds, let alone stored them, and to get at the truth he would have had to go back 2,000 years and more and to have studied the writings of Horace, Virgil, Ovid, Pliny, Plutarch, Æsop, Solomon and others.

All these said that ants stored seeds. It would be tedious to quote them, and I will not do so. Sufficient to remind you of King Solomon's words: "Go to the ant, thou sluggard: consider her ways and be wise, who . . . *gathereth her food in the harvest.*"

"In more recent times, however, and up to the beginning of the last century, no reliable observer ever discovered any ants that deliberately gathered seeds, so that scientists dismissed the idea as a myth." And apart from their own knowledge they had every reason for doubting the assertions of those by-gone writers. The ancients, as we know, were not lacking in imagination. Pliny, for instance, talks of an Indian ant as big as an Egyptian wolf, the colour of a cat, which entered the bowels of the earth in search of gold!

But King Solomon was in a rather different category. He was biblical and wise, and certain clerics and others felt it incumbent on them to explain away his apparent lapse. Thus they said (amongst other things) that the words were an addition grafted on to the Scriptures, and not Solomon's own: that the "seeds" seen were taken in as building material, not food: that the "seeds" seen had been pupa, not seeds. And so on. None of them thought of boldly doubting the modern scientists and suggesting that the Wise King might have been right and the scientists wrong. He gives the impression that *all* ants store seeds, which is far from correct, but Solomon definitely knew about harvesting ants. And if he did not study them himself, he certainly had contact with excellent observers. Indeed, it is now fairly certain what particular species he must have been referring to.

Though scientists are right not to accept any unproved assertion, some are often strangely sceptical when proof *is* forthcoming, especially if it contradicts something they have asserted. Their reply to the amateur investigator generally takes such a form as "For heaven's sake, don't try to revive that old myth!" This is natural, or at any rate human. We are most of us like that: doctors, scientists, politicians, soldiers, etc.—none of us like to have to eat our words.

With regard to harvesting ants, the first person, so far as we know, to upset the apple cart was a lieutenant-colonel named Sykes serving in India. This officer, when on the parade ground, found time to glance from the drill of his men to little mounds of seeds being brought out by ants from their nests. He may have been a brilliant soldier—I do not know—but his name would have been long ago forgotten had he kept to his duties and not let his attention wander to ants. As it is, he has a small back space amongst the immortals.

It was in Poona in June 1829, that this military man noticed the grass seeds being brought out by ants to dry in the sun. Each heap amounted to about a handful—a large quantity for creatures so small. He knew enough about natural history to be aware that entomologists had laid it down that ants never stored food. The piles of seeds soon disappeared, being taken down again into the nests after drying, and nothing much happened until October, when again, on the same parade ground, more heaps of seeds were brought out from the nests. And this time some of them were as large as two handfuls. All seemed to be over, bar—so to speak—the shouting. King Solomon had been right. Ants *did* store seeds.

But naturalists in general would not have it so. Probably they said to Sykes, "For heaven's sake, don't try to revive that old myth!" And they suggested again that the alleged seeds were building material, or this, or that. Truth, however, will out, though sometimes it takes a long time to emerge. Other naturalists were on their way. Between 1851 and 1880 many observers went into the matter and travelled far to find out about harvesting ants: Jerdon in India; Buckley, Lincecum, Norris, McCook, Mrs. Treat in America; the great Moggridge in the South of France.

With such distinguished investigators in the field, all doubt soon faded away. Harvesting ants existed. Not only that, their various methods were revealed and fully confirmed by still later investigators.

Harvesting ants are numerous in parts of America, Africa, Australia, India, and the Orient. The nests of some species are large—as much as twelve feet across and nine feet deep. Those of *Messor arenarius* of North Africa (probably the species King Solomon and others had in mind) sometimes measure ten yards in diameter and two yards in depth. The interior is honeycombed with oval granaries about (usually) six inches across and half an inch deep. There are many species, and the species are drawn from many genera—though all belong to the sub-family Myrmicinae. Naturally, methods vary with different species, but there *is* a similar scheme with most of the more advanced harvesters. Therefore, in describing their methods, it will, for the sake of brevity, be excusable to generalise.

The nest is situated in some hot, dry, though often grassy plain. Round the nest the ground is cleared for a distance of several feet. This entails much work. Each stem of grass has to be cut and carried away, and a stem of grass to an ant must be something like a pine tree to us. Worse in fact; for once cut right down, pines grow no more but grass does. So from time to time it all has to be done again.

This circular clearing round the nest, however, is insignificant compared with other country-planning schemes that the harvesting ants think necessary. From the circular patch radiate roads, not ant footpaths, but roads, six inches or so wide, that could be, and sometimes are, mistaken for human footpaths. But they are not caused, like human footpaths, by the passage of feet; they are deliberately made by cutting down the vegetation and keeping it cut down. And often

Harvesting Ant and Nest

they are as straight as Roman roads. They extend maybe a hundred feet or more from the clearing, like spokes from the hub of a wheel. The number of them varies—three or four, up to seven.

For some reason, when the ants go out to get seeds they think it necessary to do so in military formation. This, no doubt, originated in the past when the expeditions went out to fight and kill living prey (and, of course, with some this is still an important sideline). At any rate, at a certain time in the morning out pours an army from the nest and marches in formation down one of the roads. Never do ants of this kind go off individually to get seeds. They always have to do it *en masse*, and they always have to march down one of the roads! At a certain distance the army halts, breaks, and all its members run off to collect seeds.

"Which pillage they with merry march bring home." Shakespeare's lines seem more applicable to the ant than the honey-bee.

There is a certain amount of co-ordination in the seed-getting. At least, an ant will knock down, or detach and drop, seeds from some tall stem to friends waiting below—a great time-saver, for otherwise each separate ant would have had to climb that stem and then come down with one seed. Going home, as many as a dozen ants will combine to carry any particularly large seed. Sometimes they gather drin seed. This seed has a stalk with a long, feathered portion at the end. The ants carry this slung beneath them, grasping the stalk with their jaws and looking, as Wheeler says, like a lot of witches riding broomsticks.

Naturally, with such a varied assortment of loads, the march back is nothing like as orderly as the march out. (This was the case also with the slavers, if you remember.) They straggle home. Nearly all carry seeds, but some of them have not been able to get any. These seem to think that stigma attaches to those returning empty-handed, so they *pretend* they have a seed. They pick up anything, a tiny pebble, a bit of earth, a fallen petal, and march along with it. It will be discarded by the examiners when they get back, but in the meantime they probably feel happier and less conspicuous carrying *some*thing.

At the nest entrances, examiners await "the poor mechanic porters crowding in their heavy burdens at the narrow gate." The seeds are taken inside and husked, and the chaff is brought out and placed on the official rubbish heap, where the petals and other nonsense brought in by the pretenders have already been thrown.

Many species possess differently-sized workers, culminating with the huge-headed, huge-pincered "soldier"—often so large and unwieldy that, if turned over on a smooth surface, it can never get up again unless assisted. These soldiers march with the others, but their pincers are not adapted to collecting seeds, or carrying them. They are relics of the carnivorous age of these ants, and in their day, no doubt, were great warriors. The change-over from meat to grain left them without a job. They looked imposing and ornamental, but that was all. They were as out-dated as a guardsman with helmet, sword and cuirass is to-day.

The lack of a job is demoralising. The big soldiers of the harvest ants became demoralised, and consequently decadent. They lost even the will to fight, though harvesting ants are a fighting race and the smaller workers are to-day outstandingly brave and aggressive. They are what we call "vicious," and often punish intruders unmercifully. But not the big soldiers —*they* do not punish intruders. Nor do they dig, though to give them their due they are probably incapable of doing so. A nest of the breadth and depth already instanced, with innumerable granaries inside, and sometimes made even in solid sandstone, needs a lot of excavating and digging—but the soldiers give no help. And if the nest is attacked by an enemy army the soldiers think it no concern of theirs and stand aside.

Whether ants can deliberately rear to order large and small and smaller workers, I do not know. Is it due to feeding? Is it a special egg? *No* one knows. Perhaps another Huber will be born and find out. Anyway, the large-headed soldier became obsolete and would probably have been scrapped, but he came into his own when harvesting ants began to collect larger and harder seeds. Every seed stored has to be husked. The small workers can husk some, but not all. The jaws of the big soldier, that once broke into the shells of beetles, were found to be the only weapon that could tackle hard husks. He was retained, and now, though useless in most other ways, pays for his keep as a seed-cracker. And he still marches out into the fields with the seed-pickers though he is of no use to them at all.

Though the harvesting ants live mostly in hot dry places, these places, especially in India and Africa, have their seasons of heavy rainfall. The seeds then, being underground and stored in earthen granaries, are bound to get moist. They get moist in any case if stored immediately after picking. Our own farmers know this danger well, and if they propose to use a combine harvester (which sacks the corn at the same time it cuts it), the corn, if it is to keep, must soon come out of those sacks and be dried before it can be stored for any long period. The same problem presents itself to the ants, who invariably store their seeds immediately after gathering, and whose granaries, furthermore, are not entirely wet-proof. Therefore, in the rainy season every seed is brought out to dry on the first fine day, and taken back in the evening.

But there may not be a fine day for a long time, and under these conditions the seed would sprout and become useless. How is this avoided? One of the "Ancients," Pliny (he who told about wolf-sized ants going into the bowels of the earth to get gold), stated that ants bite out the radical, or growing point, of seeds to prevent germination. And Moggridge, and others, found that this was correct. (Evidently it is necessary to sift out the wheat from the chaff when dealing with the classical writers. And this does not only apply to the classical writers!) Ants *do* bite out the growing point of their seeds, but not invariably and not always at once. Often they wait until the seed has *just* begun to sprout. The seed is then more digestible and contains sugar as well as starch. The biting out of the radical does not absolve the ants from the necessity of keeping their grain dry, for damp seeds will heat up and rot even though they do not sprout.

But in the nests we speak of now there are many granaries and very many seeds. Ask any farmer how, in addition to all his other labour, he would like to have to remove the radical from each grain of wheat or barley he stored! So do not blame the ants because things quite frequently get beyond their control and in spite of all their efforts a large number of seeds sprout before they can be attended to. These too-far-gone sprouting seeds are brought out and thrown on the various rubbish heaps some distance from the nest. There they often take root and grow, until in due course the ants cut them down.

This brings us to a dispute that has been in progress for some little time, and has entailed a certain amount of bitterness and more talk about "myths." "Ant-rice" is the seed of a plant of the Aristida genus, and seed-eating ants are particularly fond of it. So much so that a Texan harvesting ant, called *Pogonomyrmex molefaciens*, is supposed to *sow* it near its nest. Now there is no argument about the sowing. These particular ants certainly sow it in a plantation that encircles the nest, and gather the seeds when they are ripe. They also keep this plantation clear of weeds and any other plants, and cut the stubble down after the harvest. The question is, do they sow it deliberately? To get the answer one has to know what motives actuate the ants when they put the seeds down, and we can never know the motives of ants; only guess them and then quarrel.

The distinguished observer Lincecum is responsible for the so-called myth. He said the ants sowed the seed deliberately. McCook went out and made a special study, and confirmed what Lincecum had said. At least, he stated that Lincecum might well be right. Which is all he *could* state, being unable to read the mind of an ant. Some of you may ask, "Have the ants been *seen* to sow the seeds? If so, that is proof and the matter is finished." That is not so, it all depends on what construction you put on their actions. "A" would say that they had *planted* the seeds; "B" would say that they had merely brought them out to dry and then forgotten them. If the seeds had begun to sprout when brought out, "A" would say they had been deliberately sprouted in the nest, and then taken out and planted, while "B" would say, no; the ants had found the seeds sprouting in the nest and thrown them out and they had happened to grow by chance. "B's" explanation in both cases is the simplest, but one wonders why the ant-rice is allowed to grow in such a large plantation, and why the plantation is kept free of other plants.

Wheeler pooh-poohs the idea that the ants sow the seeds deliberately. Indeed he gets somewhat wrought-up about it, which is unusual with this unbiased and level-headed writer. One can sense his vexation when he says that even the Texan schoolboy has come to regard the notion as a joke. Personally, having had some experience of them, I am not much impressed by what schoolboys regard as jokes, nor do I believe that the majority of them would get much amusement out of a wrong diagnosis of the habits of ants. But that is neither here nor there. Wheeler lists his objections to the theory. I will put them down and give my comments. I have never been to Texas and have never seen *Pogonomyrmex molefaciens*. I merely comment in a general way.

(1) Wheeler has found granaries containing sprouting "ant-rice." He thinks these are just carried out and thrown away on the cleared portion, where they take root.

As I have said before, there is no answer to this. It may be so. On the other hand, the ant is quite capable—over a period—of putting two and two together. A creature that has learned, as other species have, to make special compost and grow special strains of mushrooms ought to be able to come to realise that ant-rice grows and ripens if planted out. Moreover, according to the evidence, although ants store many kinds of seeds, which would also sprout, *only* ant-rice (their favourite food) is found in these plantations.

(2) He draws attention to the fact that not all nests of *Pogonomyrmex molefaciens* have ant-rice or any other crops growing round them.

Perhaps they *had* no ant-rice, or the weather was too dry and the seed would not germinate. But Wheeler maintains that plantations are caused by the casual throwing away of *any* seeds that sprout, so the absence of any plantation at all carries the argument no further.

(3) Wheeler points out (and there is no argument at all about it) that such circles of crops even as described by Lincecum could not supply all the grain necessary for a populous colony. They still make roads and go abroad. He concludes: "The

existence of these well-beaten paths, which are often found in connection with grass- (referring to ant-rice) encircled nests, is alone sufficient to disprove Lincecum's statements."

But is it? With us, most cottages have a garden around them where seeds are sown and vegetables raised. But the inhabitants of these cottages would fare badly if they had to depend entirely on their gardens and not go farther for extra supplies. Furthermore, the ant plantations in question are solely ant-rice, so that the ants are assured of at least a certain amount of a food they very much like and which they might have difficulty in finding amongst the wild vegetation wherein they gather their other seeds.

I may seem to have done so just now, but really I take no side in this dispute. I do not know and do not care whether ants sow seeds deliberately or not. It seems to me that since they have done far more remarkable things than that, the matter is not one of importance, especially since proof one way or the other is impossible to come by. Rest assured, *if* the seed-storers have not yet learned to sow seeds, they soon will. They have been dealing with seeds, sprouting and otherwise, for millions of years—and ants are no fools.

We usually associate bovine amiability with those engaged in agricultural pursuits. I do not quite know why. As a small boy given to trespassing, my early memories of farmers are of red-faced men who roared like lions. Even now I find that, given the necessary provocation, farmers can be the reverse of meek and mild. I was present recently when an erring member of the local hunt—a lady—took a short cut across a field of winter wheat. The farmer was present also, and his lung power and command of adjectives inspired most of us with awe. Farmers, however, are amiable enough until roused. The larger Agricultural ants are never amiable at any time. At least, no observer seems as yet to have encountered them when in an amiable mood. This has gone far towards making their study difficult. Their aggressiveness is combined with potent stinging power. Perhaps the two go together. Perhaps rabbits would be dangerous and "vicious" if armed like wild cats. Even amongst ourselves we realise now that the posses-

sion of a superior armament is often an incentive to aggressiveness. The ant Strongylognathus, mentioned in the chapter
on slave-making ants, is an example the other way round.
Possessing no armament at all, it wages continual war on
other ants. Such reversed cases, however, are rare for the
obvious reason that the species never lasts very long.

Heading the list for viciousness amongst much competition
is the large and powerful Agricultural (or "Harvesting")
ant *Pogonomyrmex barbatus* (practically identical with *Pogonomyrmex molefaciens*, the "Texan Harvester" and alleged sower
of "ant-rice.") It is supposed that this is the species used by
the ancient Mexicans to torture their victims, whom they
bound over the nests. From the accounts of those who have
been stung we learn that the pain is "Fiery and numbing"
(two adjectives that hardly seem to go together, but one
realises what is meant. Indeed, it is the best way of describing
a bee sting also.) The pain (which lasts for hours) shoots
along the limbs and then settles in the groin. Several men
have collapsed altogether under a number of these stings. One
gathers, however, that there is no permanent ill-effect and
no danger to life to a normal human being. It would be
interesting to know the effect of this sting on a small animal
such as a mouse or a sparrow, but we have no data on these
lines.

I said that the *large* harvesters were vicious: so are some
of the little ones. *Solenopsis geminata*, the small, notorious
"Fire Ant" of tropical America, is one of them. A tiny red
thing, it gets its name from its sting, not its colour, and its
name is justified. Incidentally, we have spoken of Solenopsis
before—the dwarf that made holes into the nests of larger
ants and lived on their young. The species *geminata* does
nothing like this and lives a completely independent existence.
It is a true harvester and husks and stores its seeds carefully.
It also eats almost anything else, including large quantities
of animal prey. It is, therefore, an example of a complete
vegetable *and* meat-eater, and as such ought to succeed. It does.
It gets on so well that it makes existence in many parts of
tropical America almost unendurable for others.

To illustrate this I can do no better than go to H. W. Bates,
who, in his book, *A Naturalist on the River Amazon*, has plenty

to say about fire-ants. I will quote a few of the remarks he makes.

"Aveyros may be called the headquarters of the fire-ant, which might be fittingly termed the scourge of this fine river. The Tapajos is nearly free from the insect pests of other parts, mosquitoes, sand-flies, motusas and piums; but the fire-ant is perhaps a greater plague than all the others put together. . . . Aveyros was deserted a few years before my visit on account of this little tormentor, and the inhabitants had only recently returned to their houses. . . . The houses are overrun with them; they dispute every fragment of food with the inhabitants, and destroy clothing for the sake of the starch. All eatables are obliged to be suspended in baskets from the rafters, and the cords well soaked with *copuaba* balsam, which is the only means known of preventing them from climbing. They seem to attack persons out of sheer malice: if we stood for a few moments in the street, even at a distance from their nests, we were sure to be overrun and severely punished, for the moment an ant touched the flesh he secured himself with his jaws, doubled in his tail, and stung with all his might. When we were seated on chairs in the evenings in front of the house to enjoy a chat with our neighbours, we had stools to support our feet, the legs of which, as well as those of the chairs, were well anointed with the balsam. The cords of hammocks are obliged to be smeared in the same way to prevent the ants from paying sleepers a visit."

So, with nests everywhere all containing immense populations that attack even man, the lives of smaller creatures in those parts must be a misery indeed.

To assess the degree of virulence of the stings of the various harvesters on man is hardly possible because men react so differently. Furthermore, observers go out to study the *habits* of ants, not to get stung, and any information of this kind they may acquire has usually been forced on them against their wish and in spite of their efforts to remain ignorant.

CHAPTER 8

MUSHROOM GROWING

FEW of the vegetables we eat are easy to grow: at least, we cannot just leave them to come up year after year without attention. This is singularly unfortunate for us, labour would be saved and the cost of living reduced if docks, daisies, dandelions and cow-parsley were as nutritious and palatable as cauliflowers and garden peas. And yet there would appear to be no reason why the plants that most succeed in life and are able to multiply without assistance should almost invariably be uneatable by mankind. More fortunately placed are those caterpillars and aphids that not only like but insist on dock-leaves or similar conquering types of vegetation for their sustenance.

In the last chapter we saw that ants, though never eating leaves, have at last accustomed themselves to a diet of seeds, eked out with occasional bits of meat. Where the ant differs from most other insects is in its ability to gain knowledge from experiments and in its readiness to apply this knowledge. So while certain ants were exploring the possibilities of seeds, others, also agriculturally inclined, were busy in another direction. They were making experiments that led to startling things and put them far in advance of mere seed-pickers—or seed-growers, if such exist.

These others grow mushrooms. What is more, they grow a special culture of their own which is found nowhere else.

Mushroom growing is not easy. When one tries to grow them oneself one wonders how on earth Nature manages to produce them so easily in ordinary pastures. I myself once tried to grow them. I got fresh strawy horse manure and, according to instructions, turned the steaming heap inside out every so often. I made the bed in a frame and sowed the spawn and covered it over with sifted earth.

I was so keen, so impatient, that it seemed to me that almost an evolutionary period went by before, one morning, I saw that something white had risen from the casing earth. The amateur gardener gets many thrills before he becomes *blasé*—the first emergence of seeds, the first fruit blossoms, the first rose—but I know of no thrill to compare with the first mushroom. Because it has been expected so long it is so unexpected. And the surprise it gives is complete. Fruit blossom, roses and the rest take so long in coming from the bud. It is as if one saw all the wearisome preparations for a pantomime tableau. Children, when dressing up at parties for some act of their own, will say to the adults, "Don't watch!" and eyes are averted until the "You may look!" is sounded. I feel that the first fruit blossoms and the first rose would also like us not to look while they are dressing up. But we do, and each day seems to bring very little change. We have grown almost tired of them before they appear in their glory. A mushroom cannot compare with a rose in looks, but it is far better at arranging a tableau. It does not let us see its preparations. It appears suddenly and thrills the waiting audience.

The first of my mushrooms appeared, and soon others, and in large numbers. Mushroom-growing seemed easy. Other amateur gardeners had told me they could never grow them. I felt superior. But the first flush was the last. Flies of various sorts took possession of my mushroom bed. A mushroom had only to show the apex of its white, bald head when it was riddled with maggots and made brown and horrid. I tried again another year, taking the precautions against flies advised by experts. A crop of toadstools was the result. Alien fungi had invaded my bed and killed off the mushrooms. I gave it up after that, for there was a field not far away where, in the season, I could get nearly all the mushrooms I wanted and with less trouble.

As all know, mushrooms, and similar fungi, start life in the shape of minute white threads which radiate in all directions. These threads *are* the fungus, and there is no need for the mushroom to poke its head above ground at all. But, luckily for the epicure, it feels that this underground style of increase is not enough; that it ought to spread itself a bit more than that. So it resorts to the haphazard methods of primitive vegetation and pushes up into the open the cumbersome erection that goes so well with stewed steak or bacon. The gills open and shed their millions of purplish spores, and the mushroom then decays—and, incidentally, when decay has begun, the mushroom can be dangerous food. Its method of propagation is not unlike that of the gardener's curse, couch-grass. That also radiates roots beneath the surface so effectively that couch-grass has no need to worry about any other ways of spreading. But it does, and produces seeds as well as travel-ling roots. The radical difference between couch-grass and the mushroom is that the former *has* to come above-ground in order to imbibe the source of all life, the rays of the sun. The mushroom needs no sun, indeed pitch darkness suits it better, for fungi get *their* sun rays second-hand by absorbing what was once created by the sun—rotting tree-stumps, straw manure and the rest. (This ability to grow in darkness is very important to us in this chapter.)

Mushrooms artificially grown need certain conditions and precautions. Let us make a list.

(1) There must be a suitable compost.

(2) The temperature must be right.

(3) The ventilation must be right.

(4) Flies and germs must be kept away.

(5) The spores of alien fungi must be kept away.

(6) The compost must have the right moisture content: it must be neither too wet nor too dry.

This is not a lecture on how to grow mushrooms, and I am far from qualified to give one: it is a list given me by an expert of the essential conditions for mushroom-growing, and I put the list down in order to illustrate what the ant mushroom-growers have to contend with. For ant mushrooms are just as difficult to grow as ours, probably more so, and the ants have to take the same precautions. And the penalties for failure are greater with them than with us: *we* do not *live* on mushrooms.

Of course, it was the old, old story: the idea that ants grew mushrooms was received with derision. Mushrooms indeed! What sort of mushrooms? Pinhead size, borne on flocculous mycelium, was the answer. The experts smiled: it was all so obvious, the ants had stored food and mould had got on to it. Mould is one of the ants' greatest enemies, and mould is a growth that bears spores like small fungi. Even so, tests were made by investigators. Nests many feet deep were dug up. The verdict was given. It was mould.

But the verdict was given in a hesitating sort of way. It was mould because it *must* be mould; all the same, something was going on in those deep underground nests that the investigators did not *quite* understand. The great McCook was one of these investigators and he went to great labour (and pain, for the mushroom-growers are almost as vicious as the harvesters) excavating nests. He found the alleged mushroom beds of the ants, but having started out to *dis*prove a theory, he got led away by preconception and decided it was mould he saw.

Bitterly did he regret this decision later, and he candidly laments that but for his preconceived idea he would have anticipated those who made their names famous by their discovery of the methods of the mushroom-growing ants.

Most mushroom-growing ants belong to the tribe Attii, foremost amongst which are the Atta or "Sauba" or "Leaf-cutting" ants of tropical America, one of the greatest ant pests the world has ever known. They live in colonies of millions and have ruined more flourishing estates than any locusts. When they (particularly *Atta toxana*) establish themselves in, for instance, a coffee or orange plantation, that is the end of the coffee or orange plantation. Now there are plenty of native trees in tropical America and no one would mind how much the Saubas used them. And the Saubas *do* use them and have used them for untold generations. But whenever new (and of course valuable) trees are imported, the Saubas forsake the trees they know for the new trees that they have never seen before. And in view of the conservative behaviour of most insects, this immediate acceptance of something new is worthy of note.

The *modus operandi* of the Saubas is as follows. They go out in long, almost endless columns from the nest to the trees along a hard, well-defined road trodden down by their passage (not cut, as with the harvesters). They climb the trees, and each ant cuts out a circular piece of leaf. It does this by cutting an almost complete circle and then wrenching the last bit off. Then they go back, taking their places in the return procession. All the ants in this return procession carry great circles of leaf as big as a sixpence high above their heads and look as if they were bearing banners. In a wind the leaves bend over and the ants look rather as if they were carrying parasols—hence another of their names, The Parasol Ants. The roads get longer and longer as the nearer trees are defoliated. In a short time whole plantations are stripped.

Now ants do not eat leaves. Even King Solomon never said they did. So what do they want all these leaves *for*? Bates (in that book of his we have mentioned before, *A Naturalist on the River Amazon*), thought he had solved the problem. " It has not hitherto been shown," he wrote, "to what use it applies the leaves. I discovered this only after much time spent in investigation. The leaves are used to thatch the domes which cover the entrances to their dwellings."

As a matter of fact, this was fairly well-known already, so that Bates had not quite brought off the scoop he thought. The leaves *are* used to thatch the domes—*some* of the leaves. But surely it is not necessary to strip whole plantations to thatch a dome! Many naturalists realised this, but did not bother much about it. Doubtless the rest were used to line the burrows and chambers inside, after the manner of that other leaf-cutter, The Leaf-Cutting Bee. *She* bites out circular bits of leaf to wallpaper the whole inside of her house. And *this* takes a lot of leaf, as many horticulturalists know. How much leaf, then, must it take to line the interiors of the huge cities of the Sauba ants?

In short, at that time there *was* no problem concerning the Sauba ants—except the problem of how to get rid of them. Various methods were tried. All failed: the nests were too large, too deep, too ramifying. Smoke blown down one hole would issue from other holes seventy yards away. It is said that Sauba ants excavated a tunnel under the bed of the River Parahyba at a spot where it is as wide as the Thames at London Bridge, though how this was proved we are not told. Anyway, fire and sulphur and other gases had no effect on them, nor had excavations of their nests, nor blowing them up with explosive.

To return to the leaves, a naturalist named Belt (author of *The Naturalist in Nicaragua*), after much observation, worked it out that what amounted to *shovel*-fuls of cut leaf were going into one nest every day. He thought this seemed rather a lot for wallpapering, but he only thought it in a vague way. It was certainly not in the spirit of scientific investigation that one morning he got a spade and began to dig into a nest close by. His garden had been stripped several times by Saubas and his patience was at an end. He was determined to get rid of them, and apparently did not realise that all the Labours of Hercules were as nothing to the one he proposed to tackle. He dug away with the determination of anger. Down and down he dug, opening up tunnels and chambers galore.

Oddly enough, none of these were lined with leaves, but the chambers, the majority of which were about the size of a man's head, were always about three parts full of a speckled, brown, spongy mass of something or other, and these spongy masses were riddled with white mycelium and spores. Ants were there, of course, busy at some work not at once apparent, and dispersed here and there over the queer surface were immature ants, cocoons and grubs. The ants that were busy were all of the small cast, a type of Sauba worker that never does any leaf-cutting or goes outside at all.

By now the spirit of anger and destruction had left Mr. Belt. He examined the sponge-like masses and found that they consisted of leaves chewed up into exceedingly minute fragments and held together by the white tangle of mycelium, from which sprouted "mushrooms"—white and semi-transparent like tiny drops of dew. He found also that when, having taken it up, he dropped any of this substance on to the ground, the ants gathered up every particle and took it back into their ravished nest with the same haste and anxiety that other ants give to unearthed cocoons.

Belt must have been as startled as everyone else when, after more investigation, he had to come to the conclusion that the ants used the cut leaves as a compost on which to grow a

minute species of fungus which supplied them at every stage
of their life with their only food.

Belt's theory, when it became known, was turned down.
Not perhaps so abruptly as it would have been at an earlier
date. It was the age of discovery generally, and of ant habits
amongst other things. People were getting intrigued by ants,
and anything new about them was "News." But this was
going too far. *Mushrooms!* And so we see McCook, with Belt's
full report before him and having actually examined ant
mushroom beds, joining—to his subsequent regret—those
who said that the sponges were due to some chance fungus
that spread in damp underground conditions to such an extent
that the poor ants were unable to cope with it.

It was about 1874 that Belt made his discovery, and he
had to wait twenty years before Moeller, Von Ihering, Goeldi,
J. Huber and others went into the matter with scientific
thoroughness and proved conclusively that these ants of the
Attii tribe *did* in truth make mushroom beds and grow mushrooms on them, and that they did it with the care and knowledge of experts.

Those who have time might turn back to page 123
and note the chief requirements for artificially growing
mushrooms. The same conditions must be provided by the
ants.

(1) The chewed leaves represent the straw of the manure
we use. It is often mixed with dung. Sometimes
caterpillar dung is used.

(2) and (3) Large shafts are made which are opened and
closed as required to regulate both ventilation and
temperature.

(4) and (5) Ants cannot sterilise by heat or chemicals, but
they do what is probably better by keeping the compost under strict and perpetual scrutiny, weeding and
coping directly with any germs or alien spores before
they have a chance to get established.

(6) If the leaves are too dry when brought to the nest
they are left outside until night, when they become
moister. If wet by rain they are also left outside
until they have become drier. If rain falls during

this treatment and soaks them hopelessly, they are abandoned altogether.

Several of the mushroom-growing ants have three sizes of workers. The largest would seem to act as policemen, or rather commissionaires, for they stalk about majestically but do little else. The middle-sized ones collect the leaves, bring them home, and mash them up. The smallest are the weeders, tenders and sterilisers. They allow nothing to appear on the beds but the pure ant mushroom culture. This work must be exacting, for the leaf-carriers are hairy and must bring many germs, etc., into the nest.

As the nest grows, additional chambers are hollowed out and filled with compost into which, when it is at the right stage, spawn, in the shape of bits of mycelium from other beds, is introduced.

The fungus used by ants is a special strain found nowhere but in their nests, though not all species grow the same culture. It is the mycellium that is used as food, and this is induced by some unknown treatment to form numerous small capsules, or swellings, called bromatia, which for simplicity are called "mushrooms." What we know as mushrooms could probably never be formed in the ants' chambers, and if they could would certainly never be allowed to. In deserted nests, however, the ant culture sometimes manages to send a thread to the surface of the ground above and form the fruiting stage in the familiar shape we are accustomed to. In such cases certain strains can produce a mushroom as large as twelve inches across. How they managed to raise it, or get hold of it, we do not know. Perhaps, like our penicillin, a chance spore once alighted and grew in some food of theirs and they liked its taste and realised its nutritive value and learned to cultivate it. Most food discoveries originated by chance, butter and cheese, for instance. We honour pioneers and those who die in a good cause, so we ought also to honour the pioneers who died in finding out what was good for us to eat —or rather what was not. And they are still at work. Hundreds of human beings die yearly in illustrating and emphasising what mushroom-like fungi are inedible. For instance, about thirty a year die in New York alone from eating the deadly

Parasol Ants in double Procession

Amanita or "Death Angel" (*Amanita phalloides*), a supremely poisonous fungus sometimes mistaken by the ignorant for the meadow mushroom. All the same, we are not taking a proper advantage from those who *fail* to die. We remain backward as regards fungi. We still stick to our rather insipid (and still more insipid when artificially grown) *Agaricus campestris* and *Psalliota campestris*, apparently not realising that there are hundreds of harmless fungus species with more flavour than these, including, particularly, the "Parasol" toadstool, the Blewit, and (best of all) the "Saffron Milk Cap" (*Lactarius deliciosus*). I foresee a time when many toadstools will come into general use and be cultivated, but for the present we are perhaps wise to imitate the ants and confine ourselves to the one kind.

Against the theory that ant mushrooms originated from some chance spore is the fact that so many different species have acquired spores and learned to cultivate them, including a creature that is not an ant at all, the Termite. A spreading of knowledge between these would hardly have been possible, though it *is* possible (though only *just*) that all of them took advantage at different times of chance spores. It must be borne in mind, too, as I have said before, that fungi are almost the only edible vegetables that can be grown in the darkness of a nest. Therefore such ants as wanted their own private vegetable allotments inside had no other choice but "mushrooms."

Mushroom-growing ants sometimes emigrate from their nests *en masse*. When they do, they take their eggs, grubs, cocoons and queen (or queens). They are very careful to do this, but they are still more careful to take plentiful supplies of their mushroom spawn for sowing in the new gardens they will make. This spawn is far more important to them than their young and just as important as their queen. Without a queen they would be exterminated slowly, without spawn they would be exterminated quickly. But "removing" is not expanding. It makes no difference to the increase of a race if it is in one place or another. To spread itself it has to split up, and we know how ants do this: how a single impregnated female digs a hole, lays eggs, and in due course raises a family and later a new colony. So it is with the mushroom ants. In some isolated spot a solitary fertile female, after the mating flight, makes a hole which, in time to come and with luck, will be the starting-place of a huge nest.

Were I lecturing, I would pause here, waiting for some signs of intelligence from my audience. I would appear to be fumbling with my papers, but really I would be hoping for some objection. " If," I would like to be asked," these mushroom-growers cannot live without mushrooms and cannot make a new nest unless they have carried to it adequate supplies of their special spawn, how about the females who fall to earth after the marriage flight and start new nests in virgin earth? Where are *their* mushrooms to come from?"

Well, this intelligent objector only echoed the question that the great observers put to themselves and each other when they studied the mushroom ants twenty to thirty years after Belt had put forward his thesis. As we know, they showed that Belt was right, and went into details that must have surprised even him, but the problem of the new nest remained. Ten thousand virgins fly out of the nest like steam from a valve, and males go with them. Twenty, perhaps, of these one-time virgins manage to escape their enemies and dig holes far away. Where indeed *do* such haphazard floating creatures get *any* mushroom culture, let alone a special brand? The investigators got the answer at last. Foremost amongst them were Von Ihering, Goeldi, and J. Huber (do not confuse the last with P. Huber, who taught us about ants at the beginning of the nineteenth century). They discovered, after patient work, that each princess that flies out from the nest carries, as a dowry, pouched in her cheek, a small piece of mushroom culture from her ancestral home.

Let us study a princess that has escaped the carnage, and mated, and alighted, and dug a hole in the earth. And in studying her let us always remember the investigators who have *enabled* us to study her like this, second-hand. She digs this hole, and after digging it closes up the entrance so that she is immured in her chamber. She then spits out on to the floor the pellet of spawn that she has retained in her cheek throughout so many diversions and excitements. It is about half a millimetre in diameter—a very small piece indeed, but enough, if properly looked after. It is warm and moist in the closed chamber, and in three days the pellet begins to send out white threads. By this time the princess has laid about six eggs. (From now on for a while we will call the princess "mother" and later on "queen.") In a day or so the white threads are stretching out in all directions and the mother, that hereditary gardener, for some no doubt adequate reason to which we have no key, separates the pellet into two parts. The fungus sends out flocculi like a cloud around the pellets, and the mother lays some ten eggs every day.

For ten or twelve days she keeps her growing pile of eggs well away from the precious mushroom culture, for of the two she values the culture most, but after a while she places some of the eggs amongst the flocculi. In eight or ten days the two half pellets have been joined together by a cotton-wool-like mass, and the mother makes a depression in the centre. And in this depression she now keeps her eggs. Grubs hatch some sixteen days after the laying of the eggs, and after a month (from the egg-laying) the grubs turn into cocoons.

Poor mites! they have had nothing much to eat; a bit of the flocculi perhaps, and certainly a few eggs—for the mother is not squeamish about using her eggs for food either for herself or her young. No wonder that the first workers that emerge from these cocoons are stunted.

When the first lot of grubs have turned into cocoons, mushrooms (bromatia) begin to poke up from the extreme outer circle of the woolly mass, that now measures about two centimetres across. When workers appear from the first cocoons the mushroom garden is flourishing in its small way.

I pause again, anticipating another intelligent objection. This spawn was deposited on the floor, a speck no larger than a grain of sand. It produced mycelium and increased until it was forty times its original size and then began to bear mushrooms. With us, all mushrooms have to be grown in manure, and even when plentiful supplies of manure are provided, that manure only lasts a short time, after which it is incapable of producing more mushrooms. In other words, mushrooms need food, and keep on needing food. So why does not the mycelium that comes from the mother's pellet of spawn soon die off from lack of sustenance?

Here was another problem for the investigators we have mentioned: an even bigger problem than the first.

Chief credit for the solution goes to Huber. In observation nests he kept a ceaseless watch on the mother. Hour after hour he watched. Said like that, it sounds easy; actually, it is most exhausting, a real trial of endurance. Try it yourself with a creature the size of an ant. It amounts almost to torture. There must be no relaxation of vigilance even for one minute. Anyway, let us forget Huber's discomforts and announce the result.

What happens is this; about once an hour, sometimes twice an hour, sometimes even more, the mother detaches a small piece from her "garden," and, holding this small piece in her jaws, places it against the tip of her abdomen. Then, through her vent, she evacuates her liquid faeces on to it—a clear yellowish or brownish droplet. The starved material she holds receives her excrement with gratitude. The mother does not put this manured portion back where it came from; she finds another place in the bed and inserts it there with all the care of a gardener planting a prized seedling. She then pats it down carefully, almost lovingly, with her forefeet.

Mushroom culture is never absolutely certain. Even with experts, things may go wrong—even with such an expert as the mushroom ant mother. Her pellet, for instance, may fail to germinate. Under natural conditions this is the end of her, but it is interesting to create such a situation artificially in an observation nest by taking away the pellet from the mother. Such experiments show that the raising of a new fungus bed in a new nest is not entirely automatic: in other words, it is not just a chain of unconscious processes. The pellet is taken away, and the mother, naturally, registers consternation. Then something quite different in appearance from the spawn she has lost, in the shape of a bit of culture from the nest she came from, is given to her. She examines it all over, her antennae quivering with excitement. She begins to dance about with joy. But there is little time for dancing; every moment is precious. Soon she is dividing up the culture and drenching each part with excrement.

We are not finished with problems even yet, and I am sure you will have noticed the next. There are two of them. First: since there are no mushrooms when the first grubs appear, and none during the whole of their grub life, on what do they feed? Second: where does the mother get all that manure from? We know that a queen can live for months on her tissues alone, but that does not give her gastric organs much work. There must be *some*thing in her stomach to enable her to pass copious faeces twice or so an hour.

The first question is easily answered: a few eggs, and a small portion of the mycelium, suffice to feed the grubs —sufficiently at any rate for the dwarfed shapes they will assume at maturity. The second question is easy also—now that observers have gone into the matter. Once it was thought that the mother, in addition to giving eggs to her young, also mashed up her eggs and spread them as manure on the mushroom bed. But fresh eggs are not manure. Nature's processes cannot be side-stepped like that. The manure *does* come from the eggs, but the mother has to eat them first, which is precisely the way *we* get *our* dung manure. With our mushrooms the horse usually does the eating for us. So, what with the mother eating them herself and also feeding her young on them, there must be a big egg consumption. There is: quite nine eggs out of ten are used as food in the early stages of the nest. Indeed, lucky is the egg that is allowed to hatch. Boiling it down, everything comes from the tissues of the queen, as everything must when a queen immures herself in a small hole. But in the case of the mushroom ant queen the process is more complicated and more thorough, for she uses even her own waste products, which other queens do not.

The first stunted workers appear and live on such mycelium and mushrooms as are available. But the new grubs are still fed mostly by eggs popped into their mouths by these workers —who have as little respect for the eggs of their mother as the mother has herself. Then the workers open up the chamber and make a passage to the surface, where a small crater appears. A shaft is now sunk from the original chamber, and a mushroom cave hollowed out below. The first leaf-cutters go off to work. A new nest has started which later on may destroy acres of plantations. All now live on mushrooms, and the mother, that once interesting creature, degenerates into an inert egg-laying machine.

Not all mushroom-growing ants work on the huge scale of the Saubas. There are about a hundred known species that grow mushrooms, and some have only one plot and the whole colony may comprise only twenty individuals. Some grow mushrooms upside down from the ceiling, or in little baskets. Different kinds of manure are used. Each species, however, keeps to one specialised kind of fungus, and to one only.

CHAPTER 9

BATTLE

WE have seen the slave-raiders at work and have studied their methods, but a slave-raiding expedition is not really a battle, it is a routine commercial undertaking. What happens when armies of equal strength meet on the field and when a quarrel, not a mere looting affair, is the cause of conflict? How do the Sanguin ants for instance, conduct themselves when, instead of pillaging wretched Negro villages, they are themselves attacked by vast armies of larger and more powerful ants? We propose to look into this.

Both ants and bees, the two leading members of the social insects, fight amongst themselves, and the fighting of bees is, to the casual onlooker, more awe-inspiring than the fighting of ants. When one hive attacks another the roar can be heard from a considerable distance, and the scene on the spot is shocking. But it is a crude affair really, with no generalship of any sort. It is a fight between normally well-conducted beings who have for the time being turned into primitive savages. I have never seen wasps, though normally fiercer than bees, fight amongst themselves—but then they never store food, so there is no incentive for one nest to fight against another.

A full-scale ant battle is not an affair one comes across every day. Indeed, even an observant man may never witness one in a lifetime; skirmishes and brawls, yes, but not the real thing. One can always *make* ants fight artificially by mixing nests up, but one learns little by doing that. Frequently the *casus belli* is unknown either by the observer or the ants themselves. It may originate in a quarrel over a bit of food, or even an exchange of glances between two ants of different houses: a sort of "Do you bite your thumb at me, sir?" In this case the matter may end in a duel and nothing else, but if friends are about it may assume more serious proportions. These friends may hurry to the houses of both Montague and Capulet, with the inevitable result that young bloods will come hurrying up from both places to support their colleagues. In these initial stages the combatants indulge in strife in a light-hearted manner as if they rather liked it, and passing ants will often halt and look on instead of attending to their own business. Indeed, these latter may join in, after, presumably, first asking if it is a private fight or not.

Here again, the affair may blow over and the brawlers may go home leaving only a dozen or so dead to mark the scene of the disturbance.

But it may go further. It is the mark of an advanced people to *combine* in war. It is one of the penalties of advancement. Anyway, ants combine, and are as put out as we are at the idea of the defeat of even a small number of their compatriots. They care nothing about the justice or injustice of the quarrel: if a party of their tribe are hard-pressed by others and they get intelligence of it, another party hurries out to help, and by so doing doubtless changes the tide of affairs. But this is only temporary. It is now the turn of the other side to send messages for help—an appeal that is never ignored. And once the ball has got really rolling it is impossible to stop it, and a full-scale battle develops.

We know the armaments of the ant armies. They suffer from what our generals would consider a serious disadvantage in having to rely on what weapons nature gave them. An erroneous view really, for artificial weapons can be copied, and he who invents a new weapon for the slaughter of others will soon find that same weapon in an improved form being used against himself—an endless business. Ants have progressed a lot, but have concentrated more on improving their standard of living rather than on evolving devices capable of exterminating both their opponents and themselves. They have three weapons, the sting, the formic acid squirt, and a pair of pincers, though none possess all three. It is impossible to say which of these weapons is the most formidable, so much depends on circumstances. The formic acid sprayers, however, are the only ants that can fight at long distance as well as short. The Germans are said to have been the first to use gas on the battlefield, but that doubtful honour really goes to the ants. For the formic acid sprayers, when faced by an army that refuses to come to close quarters, or when a stronger foe is charging down on them, raise themselves up on their hind feet and bringing their abdomens between their legs, spurt out their gas in the direction of the foe. A cloud of formic acid rises in the air which can be smelt as high as five feet by a human being. It has a slightly sulphurous as well as an acid odour. It is certainly disorganising to those it reaches, and in individual cases has a lethal effect. Normally, however, as we know, the formic acid ants prefer to make a wound first with their pincers and then inject the acid, and this they do when the battle comes to close quarters.

Huber has been both observant and lucky and has seen and described many battles. These may be divided into two sorts: (1) Between ants of different species; (2) Between ants of the same species. We are dealing now with full-scale set-to's. How they originated no longer concerns us.

When different species fight the affair is sometimes pre-meditated by one of the parties. Huber saw a battle between what he called the "Herculean" ants and the Sanguin ants. The Herculean ant is that common dweller in our woods, the largest British ant, *Formica rufa*, also called the Wood Ant, Hill Ant, Horse Ant, Fallow Ant, and other names, which shows the danger of popular nomenclature. It is a fine, strong ant (being one of the champion weight-lifters), courageous and often aggressive, but it lacks the cunning and the strategy of the somewhat smaller *Formica sanguinea* (whom we have met already as a slave-raider). Its methods, in fact, are the same as those employed by the British troops in the Boer War. It makes no flanking movements but attacks any enemy or position *en masse* and from in front, not infrequently with disastrous results. It makes another mistake. Having carried the position and overcome the enemy, it assumes that the battle is over and settles down to kill off all of the stricken foe that remain alive, ignoring the remaining troops now fleeing from the field and giving them time to form up anew and make fresh dispositions.

This is what happened in a battle Huber witnessed. The Herculeans (we will use his name) had decided to attack a large community of Sanguin ants that had established their city not very far away. (Possibly there had been friction for some time.) They had the advantage of surprise and appeared suddenly and in strength "at the very gates of the dwelling of the Sanguin ants."

The Sanguin ants rushed out gamely to give battle, but their case was hopeless. The large Herculeans indulged in an orgy of slaughter. The field was littered with dead.

The remaining Sanguins still in the citadel, ought now, one would have thought, to have poured the rest of their forces into the front line and perished gloriously to an ant. They did not do so. Leaving their front line to be massacred, and under cover of its temporary protection, all of them withdrew to a post fifty feet in the rear, posting detachments on either side to guard their retreat. When, later, the victorious Herculeans swept forward to deal with any Sanguins that might have escaped them, they met with an unpleasant surprise. Attacked on almost all sides, they were thrown into confusion. A large number were killed and many taken prisoner. The rest, presumably, went home.

Normally, however, the Sanguins are more or less ready for an attack by the Herculeans from indications given to them by workers afield. Forces in little troops are then stationed on either side, who fall upon the van of the advancing enemy and thus engage their attention and halt their progress. The main Sanguin army waits at home until the outposts see the Herculean troops approaching and send them word. Out then pour the Sanguins, but they do not march direct against the enemy. No Boer War tactics for them! They surround them and fall upon them from flank and rear, a scheme which in our own battles has generally paid good dividends.

When *Formica rufa*, the Herculean, fights against its own kind we get the sort of battle that Victorian artists loved to depict: lines of soldiers clashing against lines of soldiers, neither side knowing anything of tactics and caring less. Huber strikes the right crisp note in describing the beginning of one such affair:

"Both armies met half-way from their respective habitations, and the battle commenced."

The battle occupied all day. The ants fought in pairs and in mêlées. Prisoners were continually being led away to both camps, prisoners who "made several ineffectual endeavours to escape, as if aware that, upon reaching the camp, a cruel death awaited them." A penetrating odour filled the air. In fact, it was all very Crécy-like, with individual feats of heroism, and charges and rescues and counter-rescues.

And then night came and the armies retired each to its own city.

"On the following day, before dawn, the ants returned to the field of battle. The groups again formed and the carnage recommenced with greater fury than on the preceding evening."

All straightforward, with none of those outflanking movements which must appear not quite cricket to the Herculean, Wood, Hill, Fallow, or Horse Ant, call him which you will.

By midday about a dozen feet had been gained by one of the armies.

Meanwhile, "the ordinary operations of the two cities were not suspended." Prisoners were coming in and troops were marching out and a battle was being fought somewhere. That was all the ordinary citizens knew about it. The motto was "Business as usual."

"This battle terminated without any disastrous results to the two republics." The cause of the stoppage was long-continued rain.

Though battles are fought in this more or less sporting way, they are not child's play. One observer after a battle between these same two species found the ground covered an inch deep with corpses.

In Rhodesia I once saw a battlefield as big as a tennis court. Matabele and other ants were fighting and the operations were on at remendous scale, but there were no military formations that I could see: individual combats and scrum fighting were going on all over the place and at times I could hear faint hisses. I said that the battlefield was as big as a tennis court;

it must have been quite that, but unfortunately the surface was not that of a tennis court. The grass was far too long to enable me to view operations as a whole. Still more unfortunate was the fact that I could not stay for I was on a job that the authorities considered urgent. My feelings on departure must have been like those of a football fan who unexpectedly stumbles on to a football field where Newcastle United are playing some equally famous team and who finds he cannot wait to see the end of it, or even learn the present score.

The other day, in connection with an article I had written, I received a letter from a man in Devon describing what he had witnessed of a fight between " Large Black " and " Small Black " ants. I hazard a guess that these were the two we have just been talking about—*Formica rufa* and *Formica sanguinea*, who both appear more or less black until more closely examined. Unfortunately he did not witness much, but his letter is of such interest that I propose to quote it in full, and as he wrote it, in spite of the fact that it is not concerned entirely with ants. The writer is obviously a born naturalist and his letter is like a breath of air from the country. I have his permission:

" DEAR MR. CROMPTON,
     . . . Now about ants. I have always been interested in all kinds of insects, in fact birds and wild animals. Born in the country, I have been Gardener, Keeper, Policeman and have had every chance of seeing nature in the Raw. This war with the two sorts of black ants occurred when I was a boy gardener of fifteen at a place called —— in Somerset, the little Black was one side of the road, the large Black or Horse ant we used to call them was in an old Wall with Laurel and other shrubs growing on top. If ever there was a sight that was it, the little black doing the attacking and I will try to show you on paper just how they did it, the way they were formed up, the messengers going all along the line, the carrier ant returning with the dead and wounded, the awful slow motion in which they were advancing. There were simply thousands, yet every one in his place and doing their own particular job. Of course

I was going to spoil everything because the head gardener came along and after (my) asking if I should get the Tutor and the three sons to look at it he said "No, put the brush into them," but I think if those boys had seen it they would have watched for hours, as one, like myself, liked anything like that. Birds nests, Door Mice, that sleep so long through the winter, he used to come and talk to me alone when he had chance.

I gave him a sleeping mouse one day he kept a long time until the Lady companion found it in her sponge whilst having a bath. You can just imagine the scream that went up when she saw the mouse swimming around, the warm water soon woke him up.

My job was to sweep the back drive about half-mile on Saturdays, so that was why the gardener would not let me go and fetch the sons. But if he had not come along for a few minutes I should have done it on my own for it was as good a lesson as the tutor could have given them that morning. I expect it had been on for quite a day or two by the dead and wounded been carried back, and by the number ready to go into action it was going to last quite awhile.

The Horse ant always gives me the shivers, they smell awful and seem to send a fear greater than anything I have ever felt unless its Mosquitoes. They I hate the hum or buzz of. If I pass where they (Horse Ants) are I smell them at once and a queer sort of shiver goes down my back. They like dry walls or old trees with rotten centres. An old Poplar blew over where I was once on duty so I had to inspect and report it, and it did not take me long to tell the one who was with me that there were Horse ants in it, and sure enough they were there. I asked if he could smell them, but before he could answer me I was moving back. I have a strong sense of taste and smell. I often refuse my food because my nose does its duty. My wife often gets cross but it's no use for I should taste it if I ate it, but of course I should not eat much.

I have destroyed hundreds of wasp nests, but never until the end of August when they rather eat fruit than insect. They do a marvellous lot of good in their first month or six weeks full strength.

I am a police pensioner, 25 years Metropolitan, and have done 10 years market gardening up during the war 5 a.m. to 11 p.m. and now am suffering for it. Two acres of fruit veg. and Flowers. I have rheumatoid arthritis, cannot walk a step without sticks. Now, Mr. Crompton I will close with best wishes.

Yours very truly,

Enclosed with this letter was a rough sketch depicting in diagram a shrubby stone wall held by an army of "Large Blacks" on one side of the drive, and lines of "Small Blacks" attacking from a wood on the other side. The bare drive, of course, was an ideal place to see the formation and the operations. Rare as it is to see a "natural" battle at all, it is a hundred times rarer to see it on such an ideal stage.

I greatly prize letters like this from keen naturalists; and do not apologise for quoting another from the same source; even though it contains no reference to ants.

"DEAR MR. CROMPTON,

. . . As a boy I collected nearly every one of our English bird eggs, often climbing very high trees. In one evening I got 160 rook eggs, and within a week I got 70 more from the same trees. The local doctor came along the first time to watch, also to save an inquest, he said, if I broke my neck. I gave him two dozen eggs to eat on toast. He had a large family at the time which I was collecting for, then my employer, —— Esq. who also had seven in the dining room. They liked them very much. Better some of the people who are causing so much talk about the rook did the same. From observations this year I can tell you that the Crow, Magpie, and Jay, which is increasing much too fast, has done a tremendous lot of harm to our insect-eating birds by robbing the nest of eggs and young, and unless there is something done to keep them down food crops is bound to suffer in due course. No one use to really like the keeper, not even the farmers, but as the Estates are fast breaking up and the keepers no longer about to keep those birds down, they are beginning to talk of egg robbers. I never saw anyone pigeon-shooting try to get then, but they are our worst enemy. Of course they are very easily done if the proper people knowing was allowed. There is certain things they cannot resist and a little of the right stuff with it soon clears a wood of them.

The Sparrow Hawk is another the real keeper does not like. He is one of the smartest birds of prey. In the nest he even plays tricks: if you go near he never flies clear away but comes tumbling down the tree like a piece of brown paper and before you get a chance he is clear away in a bush or tree thicket. Lots are shot in lanes and by waiting under the hedge you know them to be using by the feathers of small birds killed and eaten by them. The number of young partridges and Pheasants that are destroyed by these birds can never be really estimated. I once saw a crow take five young birds (partridges) a few days old in less than an hour. The farmer was cutting the grass and disturbed the old one, the young unable to fly. I ask the farmer if I could blow the crow's nest out, as it was not on our ground. But he said no. He said ' I'll put a little salt on their tails.' I pass on very disappointed. But when he said he had foxes (not long after, about six weeks) taking his chickens and ducks—what could I do about it? I said some-body had to feed the foxes, why not you?—like the crows—you fed *them*. He said no more but went his way, but I later heard he wished he had allowed me to get the crows, and after tried to be much nicer to me. He had his own farm and did not like anyone running over it, but he got over it and we became quite good friends. He often told me how I got my own back.

A fox is easier cleared than the Badger. Brock can throw up his food quite easy, but the fox dies very easy with poison. I have seen 14 foxes in one earth, and I have seen fox and Badger in the same earth with only 5 Holes. During the war there were as many foxes in some cornfields as rabbits so how could a keeper hold other game like that. We have foxes and Badgers close to where I live now and the first meet is in 14 days from to-day but its so thick they never kill. They saw 5 last time but not one left the woods or one killed. Just a run round for horses and dogs. Can you wonder at the keeper killing a few of them if he is expect to produce pheasants etc.

Now I had better close this. And let me know what the caterpillar was. I hope this finds you quite well.

From Yours Truly,

_____"

This village naturalist is a born describer as well as a born observer. Who could have bettered "The awful slow motion" (of the attacking ants) or "comes tumbling down the tree like a piece of brown paper" (of the tricky Sparrow Hawk)?

CHAPTER 10

THE DRIVER ANT

In two previous chapters we have admired the adaptability of
certain types of ants in changing over from meat-eating to
seed- and mushroom-eating. It is of course only assumed that
they started as pure meat-eaters—Man was not present at the
time—but there is evidence enough that this was the case.
The meat-eaters are therefore regarded as primitive types of
ants. These primitive types are still with us and belong to
the sub-families Ponerinae and Dorylinae. We are apt to be
misled by the term "primitive." Even amongst ourselves we
are apt to class primitive people as ignorant and undeveloped
people. This is a mistake. Primitive people had the same
brain capacity as ourselves who have descended from them,
but they had the advantage that they could concentrate that
brain on a few problems instead of on the network of puzzles
which their descendants have manufactured for themselves.
Make an impossible test: transfer the two. Put Stone-age
men (in Stone-age numbers) back in their own country but
in our time. They would survive. Aeroplanes, charabancs,
motor-cycles, etc., would lie and rust away. A great quiet
would descend. But primitive man would soon untie the
multitude of knots that so bewilder us. We, on the other hand,
transferred to primitive times would perish. A lump of flint
would never enable us to make a living. We could not live
without our masters, the steam- etc. engine and the furnace,
from which all that we consider good things come.

So with the ants, we must not put down the primitive types
as ignorant and undeveloped. Some of them are very far from
being ignorant. Some of them bewilder us by their intelligence
and by their power of concerted action. They have made the
mistake of keeping to one type of food and have thus made
life difficult for themselves, but this very difficulty has

developed in them discipline and intelligence of a high order.

Roughly speaking, as we have said before, there are two ways of living on prey: to hunt singly or in small parties, or to form great mobile armies. It is the latter class to which the Driver ants belong. Their ways are none too pleasant and the trail they leave is stained with blood, but few of us, if we are honest, can say that we object to hearing of the shedding of blood, providing the blood is sufficiently remote. That is why so many novelists make fortunes by dwelling on the unsavoury side of war, and why Madame Tussaud can charge us more for seeing murderers than for seeing archbishops.

When I was in the interior of Africa I occasionally went out hunting with Boer farmers. There was a refreshing, child-like simplicity about these men. Round the camp-fire in the evenings they would argue as to which is the most dangerous animal to encounter, or which animal is the true "Lord of the Wild." Agreement was rarely reached. Several candidates would be put forward for the first qualification, for the second the issue was narrowed to two—the lion and the elephant.

I cannot say which is the most dangerous animal to encounter—it depends too much on circumstances—but the "Lord of the Wild" in Africa is, beyond doubt or question, the Driver Ant.

"The dread of them," says Savage, "is on every living thing."

Some time ago, browsing in a library, I glanced through an illustrated book on natural history. The chapter on ants contained no mention of Driver ants, but the artist had evidently decided to remedy this deficiency on his own, for one of his pictures depicted three gorillas, two elephants, a lion, a rhinoceros, two gazelles and a giraffe plunging out of a forest at break-neck speed, their mouths open and their eyes wide with horror. The title of this stirring picture was "Pursued by Driver Ants." Well, things are not quite so bad as *that*, though any animal is well advised to get out of the way of a column of marching Drivers. There was no need, however, for this rather unusual mixture of animals to do so at such speed or in such panic. The word "pursued" also was out of place. The ant that can "pursue" a gazelle through long grass has yet to be born. But I must be fair: perhaps that picture was not quite as ridiculous as might appear, for Savage, who has studied Driver ants more thoroughly than anyone else, used to ride about on a donkey and he always knew when a column of Drivers was near because the donkey would throw him over its head and bolt madly in the opposite direction.

"I know of no insect," says the same Savage (referring to *Dorylusni gricans*), "more ferocious and determined upon victory. ' Conquer or die ' is their motto. I have known a live coal of fire held before them at which they rushed with indescribable ferocity, releasing their hold only in death." Smeathman, another observer, writes: "By being furnished with very strong jaws they can attack any animal whatever that impedes their progress, and there is no escape but by immediate flight or instant retreat to water. The inhabitants of native villages are frequently obliged to abandon their dwellings taking with them their children, etc., and wait until the ants have passed."

The Driver ants are entirely carnivorous. Should they invade a farmstead they will rifle it from top to bottom but will leave untouched any butter, honey, sugar, bread, cheese, cake, pudding—anything but meat, living or dead,. Even the bacon will be left alone for they do not like salted meat.

Driver ants are nomadic: they make temporary halts or bivouacs, but mainly their great armies are for ever on the move. During these marches any animal that cannot get out of their way is doomed. A full-grown caged leopard in South Africa was killed by them and picked clean in a single night.

Every member of the army is completely blind.

That summarises Driver ants. There is much to add and many tales to tell, but first we will examine them.

All ants belong to the family Formicidae, and this family is divided into five sub-families. One of these five is the blind sub-family Dorylinae, with three main genera, Dorylus, Aenictus, and Eciton.

The Drivers belong to the genus Dorylus, of which there are some two dozen species, all confined to Africa and S. Asia but most belonging to Africa, so that the Driver may be put down as an African ant. In addition to the males and females there are three working types. The first is the soldier, an ant about half an inch long with a head and pincers as big as the rest of its body. "Officer" is a better name than soldier, for this so-called worker seems to be the brains of the community. Observation makes it fairly clear that it organises the marches, maintains discipline, and leads attacks. The second worker is about a quarter-inch long. Compared with the officers, it looks insignificant. It is not: one of its chief duties is to tear flesh from living prey. It cannot tear out such large chunks as the officers but in its smaller way it is just as good a butcher. The third worker (not present in all armies) is a minute creature that functions chiefly as a porter. The queen, the source and nominal head of this formidable people, is, to outward appearance, just a cylinder. A head and thorax and legs are tacked on at one end just as a bit of tied-up skin is tacked at the end of a sausage. She is bloated and eyeless and over two inches long.

That these four so widely different forms can come from the same mother is remarkable, but that the *male* is also their own flesh and blood is more remarkable still. For the male in appearance is not an ant at all but a hornet—two inches long with magnificent wings and a splendid array of eyes. Can inconsequence in nature go further than this? The females are not only blind but they have lost all traces of eyes: where eyes, presumably, once were is now smooth and solid skull. It must have taken a long time for this reverse development to take place and yet the female still breeds males with eyes surpassing those of most other insects. Evolution plays strange tricks. With social insects it is able to discriminate between one sex and the other. Actually this is quite logical—though one wonders how it comes about—for any development, one way or the other, with the male would be a waste of time. He is purely a stud animal. His mission in life is accomplished in a few seconds, and he may not be called upon even for that short effort. But the females have to work and provide food, and to this end, over periods, must change their ways and forms to suit changing conditions and their own ambitions.

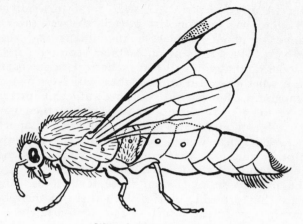

Winged Male Driver Ant

This absence of interference by evolution with the males of some species gives us a valuable insight into the past. In the case of the Driver ant it endorses the theory that ants are descended from wasps, a theory strengthened by the comparatively late appearance of ants in the evolutionary scale. So the present Driver ant male may be more valuable to us than any rock record (which with insects is hard to come by). He may, in fact, be a living fossil, a breathing Missing Link.

In Africa, this male Driver appears sometimes in numbers, to the alarm of some who think they are being attacked by hornets. But in spite of his appearance, this brother of the most blood-thirsty females the world knows is as harmless as a piece of thistle-down.

Knowledgeable folk sometimes smile when others mistake this male for an outsize hornet. But they need not feel too superior. The most eminent scientists have made the same mistake. Even the great classifier, Linnaeus, put this insect amongst the genus *Vespa*, or Wasp, and a hundred years went by before anyone thought of questioning his classification, or thought that this male had any connection with ants.

Since practically nothing is known about the breeding habits of Driver ants, we will pass on from this big-eyed handsome sire to the monstrous regiment of his sisters.

If you are up-country in Africa, in some store, or hut, or farm, or camp, you may one day possibly notice a few reddish ants wandering about the place in the aimless way ants have —or seem to have. Ants of all sorts are common in Africa and it is odds on that you will take no notice of these particular few. And whether you do or not they will have disappeared by the morning. But should you have sufficient interest and knowledge to identify these ants as Dorylus, then you will have cause for thought and—in spite of their disappearance —anxiety. For these were scouts of some Driver army, and though other ants may visit houses to pick up odds and ends and scraps, scouts of the Dorylus clan do not. They go with a particular purpose, and when those few reddish ants left your place they probably carried with them in their heads— or wherever they do carry such knowledge—a fairly accurate inventory of your possessions in the meat line. They also knew better than you yourself what vermin you were harbouring.

On returning to the headquarters of the army (which is probably not very far away) these scouts will "report," and on this information and under their guidance an army of millions may invest your house the next night, enter it, and slaughter every living thing that cannot get away, including, if you happen to be bed-ridden and alone, yourself.

On the other hand, they may not. Other scouts went forth to other places and may have noted booty richer than yours, or your house may be inconveniently distant from their line of march. Moreover, they do not specially seek human habitations; the country itself usually provides them with sufficient food so long as they keep moving, for an army of millions living on fresh game cannot afford rest.

When the scouts return to the grand army there is no sign that there is any army there at all: no challenges of sentries, nothing except apparently deserted country. The millions are hiding and resting in fissures, holes, crannies, hollows, the branches of trees, under stones, logs—anywhere. The scouts, too, disappear and make their reports to—whoever they *do* make their reports to.

This returning and reporting of the scouts is pure assumption, of course, but it is assumption based on what we know.

What we know, admittedly, is very little: there may be other explanations for the conduct and movements of Driver ants. We do not know, for instance, whether a preliminary survey is made of human habitations in all cases: most men pay no attention to a few ants wandering about the place, and after an invasion cannot say whether scouts had visited them previously or not. And of course there are bound to be dwellings invaded simply because they happen to be in the line of march. Often, also, the scouts are noticed only an hour or so before the actual attack so that they are obviously precursors of an army that is already advancing in that direction. Nevertheless, there is reason to suppose that a very complicated system of spying and reporting goes on amongst these Drivers in their every-day affairs.

I have never seen the assembly of the army. I have seen Driver ants on the march and I have been in a hut when they began to occupy it, but I have never seen the "start." I have, however, met eye-witnesses—a native chief in Portuguese East Africa and a Mashona in Rhodesia. Their accounts are more or less the same. Both were in apparently deserted country after sundown and both saw the earth suddenly belch forth ants. That was really as far as it got. They say they saw the ants forming into line of march almost at once, but admit they did not pursue the matter further. Driver ants are Driver ants and it is not healthy to be in the thick of them. But it is quite well-known that these ants after a bivouac come from their various hiding-places almost simultaneously and form their column. What is not known, and never will be, is who sounds the "Fall-In," and how? But that is a mere detail; what we must admire is the celerity with which they get under way. Try to imagine the fuss and bother and noise and chaos if a human army of several millions had to get on the march in a matter of about five minutes, especially if, like the Drivers, they had to take nurses and young as well!

Following the scouts, the army marches in more or less regular formation and roughly five or six abreast. (*Dorylus helvolus* never attains the complete military precision of some of the Ecitons in South America.) Stationed on the flanks are the big officers, at times rigid and motionless like mounted guardsmen lining a procession (I have to "mount" them to

give a true picture of their towering height, and quite frequently they *are* mounted by standing on the body of a brother
officer), facing outwards, their great mandibles lifted on high,
at other times moving along on the flanks of the marching
ranks. From time to time these moving flanking officers
become nervously alert; they run together into groups as if
discussing further plans, then run back to their stations again.
Anon, some of them rush away from the column, scenting
prey, perhaps, or danger. Meanwhile the army plods on.

Unless the affair is just a foraging expedition, somewhere
in the procession will come the queen carried by a large number
of her diminutive subjects. She must find it an uncomfortable
journey for she is as much dragged as carried. The bodies of
all Driver queens are scarred from stem to stern by this rough
treatment.

Sometimes, though rarely, a circus appearance may be
given by a few males walking along, towering like elephants
above the rest.

From time to time the column splits into two channels
which reunite later, forming an island in between. Often
workers can be seen running down the centre of the line in
the opposite direction to the marchers. Are these messengers
with orders or communications from the van to the rear, or
do they carry bits of newly-gotten meat to their comrades
behind?

The column takes a definite direction and knows where it
is going, but it has to be fed, and Drivers have enormous
appetites. They live on the country and clear everything up
as they go. Forays are made from either side and nothing
edible is overlooked from (as Swynnerton says) a minute
beetle to a cow. Grasshoppers seem paralysed when the Drivers
come upon them and those powerful hindquarters that ought
to shoot them like stones from a catapult away from the ants
and into safety become apparently numbed with fear. Rats
and mice fare no better, they hesitate for that second too long
and they are doomed. Snakes ought to get away. The majority
are swift, their skins are hard, and they do not get paralysed by
fright—they leave that to their victims. But few *do* get away.
The fastest and deadliest snake in Africa is the Black Mamba.
It is said to be able to overtake a man on horseback. Nonsense,

of course, apart from the fact that it would never try to do so but would make off in the opposite direction, yet it can certainly move almost as fast as a galloping horse for a short distance. I have disturbed several and they whip past one like the crack of a lash (therein lies the danger, for they may give one a panic-stricken sideways bite as they pass). A Driver ant column once flushed one of these snakes in the presence of an observer. The creature streaked off with the usual crack-of-a-whip motion, then it turned, came back into the midst of its aggressors, threshed about wildly, and was finally despatched. The reason for its apparent idiocy was that the ants had destroyed its eyes at the moment of encounter, a favourite trick of theirs, blind though they are themselves.

A Mr. W. A. Lamborn, seeing that his place was about to be attacked, rushed to rescue a tame guinea-pig, but the Drivers had already eaten out its eyes and torn a large hole through the abdominal wall. This is their usual method with such animals as rabbits, poultry, tame monkeys, etc., and it is done with incredible rapidity and organised method.

The python, sometimes thirty feet long and weighing as much as a bullock, is not immune. Indeed "Python" figures fairly frequently on the Driver bill-of-fare. It has a hard and scaly skin, but that does not help it against the Driver pincers. As we have said, any large animal that can get away in time is safe from Driver ants, and the python, in spite of its bulk, can move fairly fast—two to three miles an hour is its normal pace—but like the rest of us it has to eat, and it is then that it is in danger. For its favourite prey is a small antelope—of any size up to that of a goat—and this is swallowed head first. "Swallowed" perhaps is not the right word, for the animal goes down slowly inch by inch. Once having started such a meal, the python is immobile and helpless. In this condition what a gift the python is to Driver ants, who make short work both of the diner and its dinner!

Even when the antelope is safely in its stomach the python is just as vulnerable. With a whole duiker or stembuck inside, it cannot move for many hours. Natives say that, having crushed its prey to death or impotence, the python leaves it where it is and goes on a long circular tour of inspection in order to make sure that there are no Driver ants in the vicinity. That is as may be.

Nothing, *nothing*, seems immune. A Mr. Loveridge kept a couple of crocodiles in a tank in Tanganyika and once heard a terrific commotion going on. He found that Driver ants had arrived and were attacking them. One was already killed and the other, by revolving its body under water, was evading death for the time being, though even under the water a number of ants were clinging to it and biting into it. A dry river-bed in Nigeria was full of large, thick-shelled crabs. In twenty-four hours a Driver army killed every one and left only empty shells.

All non-flying insects encountered are doomed, of course, including other ants. According to natives, when the ordinary ants around one's place get suddenly excited and begin bringing their cocoons out and rushing here and there, it means that a Driver army is approaching, and the natives then make preparations for evacuation. The only "insect"[1] that keeps its head in the presence of Drivers is the spider. This creature sums up the situation, and without showing signs of panic moves to the top of some long grass stem or other available high vegetation and suspends itself therefrom on a practically invisible thread and awaits events. Some millions of ants have to go by but the spider by this simple but cunning device usually escapes the fate of the others.

The dice would appear to be loaded against Driver ants; not only are they blind, but direct sunlight kills them in a matter of a few minutes; even diffused light of a strongish nature does away with them if they are subjected to it for long. It is as if nature had decided to exterminate them. They have, however, refused to be exterminated: they prefer to do any exterminating themselves. So if the skies are clear the army halts before dawn and seeks shelter until the evening. If the day is dull or wet they travel on. Often, even in fairly bright weather they can maintain their journey by keeping to the shade of trees (actually at times travelling in the thicker upper branches) or moving through thick grass. Should a bare patch have to be crossed, or should the sun catch them

[1] The word is used here of course in its original comprehensive sense.

unawares, the officers form an archway with their bodies under which the others pass in dark comfort. The officers must suffer in the process but they manage to survive by being continually reinforced. Nothing *really* stops them, and if it is decided that the army must press on whatever the conditions, and the sun shines, earth is hurriedly thrown up from either side to form a covered archway. "Hurriedly" is the right word: they can do it with the quickness of a mole burrowing.

These ants like best the rainy season, moist, low-lying country, and the propinquity of streams and rivers—just the season and type of country one would expect them to like least. It follows, therefore, that they often have to cross streams. A stream a yard wide must, to an ant, be something like the river Thames to us. Driver ants are not swimmers, any more than any other ants, and if they *could* swim, so large a force would be washed downstream and dispersed. Their method is to make a bridge. The *modus operandi* has been observed more than once. The leading files come to the stream and halt, and immediately afterwards something like a traffic block occurs as those behind come pouring up, and a jammed and ever-growing mass accumulates at the water's edge. Meanwhile workers are rushing through the ranks in the opposite direction. This is nothing new, of course, but doubtless they acquaint those behind with the state of affairs in front. Gradually the traffic stops. Bulges occur, but to all intents and purposes the column halts and waits. The seething mass in front simmer down, and soon a procession is seen going to some spot on the bank—an out-jutting root perhaps, a tree, a shrub—on which a blob of ants is forming. The blob grows and from it a rope begins to drop and lengthen. This rope is composed of ants, and ants continue to run down it and tack themselves on to the end until the rope reaches either (1) the opposite bank (which can only happen if it is attached to some overhanging tree-trunk or root), or (2) the water. In the latter case the ants, even in the water, continue to lengthen the rope with the addition of more bodies until it is swinging in the current. Some time, sooner or later, the end will touch the opposite bank, when instantly a number of pincers will grasp anything that happens to be there—

a stone, grass, a root, a lump of earth. Once a pincer-hold has been gained a firmer anchorage is soon made to a more suitable base and the living rope made fast. The bridge is made, the metaphorical signal lights change from red to green, and the army resumes its march.

Similar bridges are made when the ants are travelling (for purposes of shade) along the branches of trees.

The strain at both ends of the rope must be great and only the large soldiers, those we have called officers, with their powerful mandibles and unyielding hold, make up these two portions. The in-between section is composed partly and mostly of the smaller type of worker.

Streams mean only a slight delay, but an obvious danger threatens these primitive lords of creation in the low-lying terrain they so often frequent. In Africa, when rain comes it usually comes in quantity. In the morning one can cross a sandy river-bed that is as dry as the Sahara Desert and return in the evening to find, in place of the bed, a river quarter of a mile wide. This was caused, of course, by torrential rains farther up the river-bed. Now such a river will quickly cover any low-lying parts, turning dry land into lakes, and in these areas there may well be Driver ants at bivouac or on the march.

Submerged in a lake! That, one would think, would be the end of them. Not at all—though steps have to be taken, and quickly. Perhaps they are warned of the approaching waters by the out-riders. Perhaps they can smell water. In any case they form themselves into a ball with the queen, larvae, etc., in the centre and the smaller workers round them. The outside, the rind as it were, of this circular Noah's Ark consists of those long-suffering guardians and leaders, the officers, who always seem to get the sticky end whenever there are difficulties to surmount. Their close-packed bodies make the ball practically water-tight for those inside.

The rising waters float the ball and waft it away. It reaches land at last, or the floods subside, and the warriors, very hungry by now, sort themselves out.

No reliable observer has seen one of these ant balls in the process of formation, and the chances of anyone ever doing so are remote. Natives say that a large army forms itself into several balls and that these, when washed to land, will re-unite however far apart the landing-places may be. Kraal natives are, or at any rate were, keen students of natural history and good observers, but when questioned they used to mix up facts with a lot of guesswork. How *can* components of a blind army re-unite over distances? But then, how can they do a lot of other things?

The floating ball method of water transport is not just a desperate expedient in times of flood. It is also used, or so it would appear, deliberately on waters too broad to be bridged. At any rate, one should not think oneself immune from Drivers even when on an island. Stevenson-Hamilton, for instance, tells us of a missionary travelling along the Zambesi by canoe. He camped for the night on a small island in midstream and let his natives take the canoe and go off to sleep at a kraal on the mainland. During the night an expedition of Driver ants arrived on the island and proceeded to clean it up in the usual way. Preferring possible death from crocodiles to certain death from Driver ants, the missionary waded into the Zambesi and stood in the water for the rest of the night. At dawn his servants returned, by which time it was found that every ant had gone. Now to get to that island in midstream the Drivers must have used the floating ball method, though not necessarily deliberately. The Zambesi may have been on the flood and encircled a patch of land that contained a Driver army, and this army may have formed a ball and let itself loose on the waters and been wafted against the island. But to get *away* from the island the ants must have launched themselves into the water intentionally.

The ball is afloat in water often for long periods. One wonders, therefore, how long the big soldiers that constitute the outer rind can endure such submersion. Savage made experiments. He put one of the large soldiers into a tumbler of water and kept it submerged at the bottom. It struggled for three-quarters of an hour and then lay quiet, apparently drowned. Forked out, it recovered within ten minutes and was as full of vitality and ferocity as it had been before. It was re-submerged at 1 p.m. and left under water at the bottom of the tumbler until 6 p.m. Taken out, apparently dead for hours, it again recovered in ten minutes, as lively and even more bad-tempered than before, for which latter condition there was every excuse. It was submerged again, and this time left submerged for twelve hours. When taken out, it revived to the extent of being able to move about a little on one side. It continued in this state for twelve more hours, after which it died.

In these experiments the ant was kept completely submerged at the bottom. Ants left on the surface could endure for very much longer periods.

The bite of the large soldier is, mechanically, of quite exceptional power. The great pincers penetrate almost anything. And having penetrated and met, they stay fixed, bulldog fashion, until they have wrenched out the piece of meat or hide they enclose. If they relax, as they sometimes do, it is only to get a firmer and a deeper grip. There is a use for most things in this world if we can only find it, and natives have discovered a use for the bite of the Driver ant. It takes the place of the stitches of the surgeon. The edges of a cut are held together and, one after another, Driver ant soldiers are made to bite so that one of the pincers is above and the other below the cut. The heads, or rather the bodies, are then cut off, and the pincers retain their grip. I have always wanted to see the operation performed but have never been present at the right time, though I have seen many natives walking about with a row of ant heads holding a cut together very neatly. I may add that I would not recommend the treatment to a white man (with his smaller resistance to blood-poisoning) unless the pincers had been sterilised first!

In this connection let us glance at some more of Savage's experiments. He cut off the head of an "officer" and put a finger against it. The pincers immediately grasped the finger and bit so hard into it that blood flowed. The severed head was now "flung" (his own word, and it bears witness to the severity of the bite he had just received) into an empty tumbler and left there from 3 p.m. until 8 a.m. next day. It was then tipped out and the finger again applied. The finger was bitten as wickedly as before.

Lest the behaviour of this head might have been exceptional, another officer was beheaded at seven o'clock in the morning. At 9.30 a.m. next day ($26\frac{1}{2}$ hours after decapitation) the pincers grasped and tenaciously held a newspaper. Savage then offered it a finger: the points of the pincers met beneath the skin. The head then withdrew its pincers in order to bite again and again, each bite, says Savage, being extremely painful. This head lived—at least showed signs of movement —for 36 hours. The body lived longer and kept up movements for 48 hours.

This sounds remarkable, but beheading an insect is a different matter from beheading an air-breathing vertebrate. The head of a beheaded man, for instance, "dies" in a split second from lack of oxygen to the brain. This does not happen with an insect: its breathing arrangements are more widely distributed.   Reptiles, however, including such advanced forms as the crocodile, show vigorous movement for long periods after death. As an example, I once shot a crocodile through the brain. It was basking on a river bank with (as is their custom) its mouth wide open. My shot went through the eye into the centre of the brain—a lucky shot for the brain is not large. The only movement after the shot was the dropping of the upper jaw. (The moving part of the jaw in crocodiles is the upper one.) I had three native carriers with me and we went up. The creature was dead and I took photographs—for this crocodile was an outsize specimen. To show its size, I had the natives sit on it. Then, so that I might photograph the mouth and the formidable array of teeth, we wedged the mouth open and propped a stick between upper and lower jaw. Then we lit a fire and made tea. We were just finishing the tea when the crocodile lifted itself on its hind legs and urinated! The three natives gave one yell and bolted into the bush—and I felt inclined to follow them! They came back after a period looking rather ashamed, and even, later on, allowed themselves to help me cut the animal open (I wanted to examine the contents of its stomach). It needed almost the lot of us to turn its dead weight over, first taking the prop away from its mouth. We slit it open and I removed the stomach and the rest of the inside. Amongst the latter was the heart, still beating strongly, which I cut out and threw on to the sand. It was about the size of a coconut and lay there on the sand beating rhythmically as if unaware that anything out of the normal had happened to its owner.

Anatomy fascinates me, and before I had finished I had all the inside out of that crocodile and the carriers were bored; they did not remain bored long; my knife touched some part of the wall near the base of the tail and the tail lashed out, narrowly missing one of the carriers. Having found the spot, by touching it I could make the tail lash out whenever I wished. When I left, shortly afterwards, the heart was still beating as strongly as ever, on the sand.

There is something eerie about a Driver attack on a human dwelling: it is on so vast a scale, but so silent. It is generally at night they come, and before one knows it the whole place is theirs. Yet all are under control and working to plan. Every spot is systematically searched. If a sleeping man happens to be in the room, and if he continues to sleep, it is said (and the accounts of those who have undergone the experience, including one man I met personally, tend to confirm this) that he will be covered with ants who wait for the word of command before attacking him. When the order is given all those in a position to do so will attack at once, each plunging in its pincers and doubling itself up as it strains and pulls to tear out the piece of flesh it has gripped. Nostrils and ear-drums are also attacked though, strangely enough, I have never heard of a man losing his eyes. Of course, a man who remains asleep cannot say if he is first covered with ants and then attacked by all simultaneously nor could any onlooker possibly be present, so we must not take this belief too seriously.

Many of my friends in Africa, with Driver ants in mind, used to keep the legs of their beds standing in pans of water or paraffin. You and I know to what extent a few inches of water are likely to keep Driver ants away! Paraffin may keep them off for a time, but not for long. They will soon make ropes over the pans, or from the walls or ceiling. They will not be in any desperate hurry to do this, however, for there are probably other things in the room, and the sleeper, especially if the ceiling is one of uncovered thatch, will soon be awakened by half-killed squealing, struggling rats or mice, covered with bunches of ants falling on to his bed.

We have spoken about sleeping men who were able to dash away when awakened, it is better to say nothing about the fate of sick men or helpless infants who may happen to be unattended when an invasion takes place.

It is surprising what a meagre bait sometimes (presumably) suffices to bring Driver ants. Stevenson-Hamilton in his *Wild Life in Africa* describes how his camp was attacked one night. He had previously seen one or two Drivers wandering about and returned at night to find Drivers in possession, covering the whole place in solid lumps. He had to spend a cold night outside without blankets or coat. The only thing that can have brought them, he says, was some animal fat with which he had smeared his cartridges. It may be so, but normally these ants do not like fat, and since we read that he had made his camp in the middle of a deserted native village it was more probably vermin that had attracted them.

In the morning (at least in the case of *Dorylus helvolus*) not an ant will remain. The millions that invaded the hut, house, or whatever it is and turned it into an abattoir a few hours ago will have departed as silently and mysteriously as they arrived. Nor, in all probability, will they ever come again. And they will have left the place very sweet and clean; de-vermined from top to bottom, from rats down to fleas and bugs.

If anyone has gathered from the above that Africa is over-run by Driver ants, I must hasten to correct that impression. There is no need for intending visitors to cancel their passages. Most of the inhabitants have never seen a Driver ant, and a good many have never even heard of them. There are exceptions to every rule, but normally Driver ants are confined to wild, "up-country" districts, and when they do visit human habitations visit only isolated dwellings. I spent many years "up-country" in Africa and have only seen them in bulk four times. And in seeing them that often I was exceptional. I might as well describe those meetings briefly, though they contain nothing of much interest and nothing new.

It was late afternoon on a dull, hot day. I had left my camp to look for something to shoot for the pot. Going along,

I saw a column of ants passing in front of me, marching about five abreast. I had, of course, seen ant columns before and took this to be such another. I had no idea that I was making the acquaintance of the " Lords of the Wild."

I was young and comparatively new to the country. To me at that time ants were just ants. Then I became more interested. What impressed me were the large ants, seemingly three times the size of the others, which were lining the route. Other large ants were running, halting, then running again along the flanks. It impressed me as it impresses everyone who sees the marching Drivers, for the large ones *are* so obviously officers. Another surprising thing was that there seemed to be no beginning and no end to this column. It stretched away on either side.

My growing interest was rewarded by a sharp pain just above my ankle over the sock. An ant was there and I tore it off. That it might be advisable to remove myself from the vicinity of these insects never occurred to me. By now I was fascinated by the whole military set-out.

I then saw that a little rivulet had detached itself from the main body and was coming in my direction, was, in fact, already pouring over my boots. The next second I felt them. I did then what wiser creatures, such as Savage's donkey, would have done long ago, and ran away. I brushed and pulled off ants as I ran, and then, at a distance, sat down to get rid of the rest. It was one of the most painful operations I have known.

My next meeting took place in similar country and under more or less similar circumstances. This time the ants were marching through fairly thick grass and I did not notice them and trod right on the column. I had enough sense this time to dash away as soon as I saw what I had done. Even so, they were coming up my leg and I felt quite frightened, knowing the punishment I was shortly to receive. I am told the best way is to crunch them with your finger-nails or to cut their heads off; never to try to pull them out straight away. The head still continues biting but without the body lacks the purchase to pull at the skin. I do not know. I got mine off as quickly as I could and was not in the frame of mind to use any particular method.

My third meeting with Drivers was a more serious affair and needs a little preliminary explanation. Whilst at a rather remote out-station in Rhodesia, I had occasion to go to a kraal about twenty miles away. I did not know the country, but according to a map made by my predecessor the route was easy. (Routes *do* look easy on maps, even on accurate ones, and this map was very far from accurate.) I went on horse-back, got lost, spent the night in the veld, and by afternoon next day was still riding about in deserted country. At last I struck a path, and this led me to a pole-and-mud hut, untidily thatched with old grass about three feet thick. Inside there was a bed and the place was furnished with a few bits of home-made furniture. Incidentally, the bed was home-made too—four posts let into the ground with lengths of bark forming the spring mattress. There were a couple of smaller huts behind, obviously the native quarters. All were deserted.

I had arrived *some*where at any rate and that night would have a roof over my head. In the meantime I had only some tea and a tin of condensed milk left of my provisions. I went off with the rifle and managed to shoot a duiker. It was dusk when I got back. I tethered the horse to a tree, gave him what remained of the mealies, cooked a piece of the duiker over a wood fire outside, unstrapped my greatcoat and blanket from the saddle and went to bed. I was not alone in that hut—squeaks and rustles in the thatch above showed that rats were present.

I came upon a couple of natives the next day and they were able to direct me to the kraal I sought. It was not very far away. In my wanderings I had evidently travelled in a semicircle. I did my business, by which time it was too late to make the journey back to camp. I definitely wanted daylight for that. So I returned to the hut. Everything was as I had left it, including the carcass of the duiker hanging under the eaves outside. I tethered the horse to the same tree and gave him some mealies I had got at the kraal, grilled another steak of duiker, stuck a candle on the table inside, lit it, sorted my things out, blew the candle out, and again to bed.

I awoke about midnight. The horse outside was restless. It was stamping and snorting. I thought it must have caught the scent of some prowling leopard. I was doizng off again when something soft and heavy fell on to my bed and then on to the floor. I got up quickly and lit the candle, for I am allergic to rats. The candle's light showed five rats, three running out of the door, and two half slithering, half falling down the wall from the roof. A second later a shrill scream came from the horse, followed by the crack of a broken *reim* and the thudding of hoofs galloping away.

This was bad. Without a horse I was in for an unpleasant time next day. I put on my boots, grabbed my rifle, and ran out. There had been rain, but it was moonlight now. I had heard the direction the horse had taken and ran, so far as I could judge, after him. He was a quiet, good-natured lazy animal normally and I did not expect him to go far. I thought I saw him once and went on hopefully for some distance, but in the end I had to give it up and return to the hut.

The candle was still burning, and I was going to walk in when the duiker carcass hanging outside made me pause. It seemed to move. Through the open door I saw that the walls inside the hut were moving and shimmering too. The table seemed to be covered with a tablecloth.

It sank home at last. Drivers had come!

I retired carefully and without injury, spent the rest of the night sleeping against a hillock, and when daylight came found the spoor of the horse and followed it and found him grazing placidly. I took him back, tied him up and re-entered the hut with quite unnecessary caution. Except for a few dead bodies round an extinguished candle there was not a sign of an ant. The skin partly remained but the inside of the duiker was mostly a skeleton.

Now will come the awkward question: did I see Driver scouts about the place before the invasion? Well, I *did* see ants in the hut more or less all the time I was there but I had much on my mind and I am afraid I did not examine their species. If the ants I saw, or some of them, were Driver scouts, which is exceedingly probable, the question arises, did they bring the army there for the sake of the duiker or the vermin? Or both?—for either alone might have been judged insufficient to cause a large army to make a special journey. Or did the hut just happen to be in their line of march?

I said I met Driver ants four times and I have put these meetings down in chronological order. The fourth meeting was anti-climax—just another column after nightfall in Portuguese East Africa within a hundred yards of a temporary camp. This meeting has, however, an interesting, and possibly instructive, side to it, for the day before I had shot a hippo for meat for the carriers and myself so that we had a lot of meat with us, yet that Driver column, though passing so close, never paid us a visit. For which, I may add, I am devoutly thankful for we were camped in a march alive with mosquitoes and I should have hated to have had to spend the night without my mosquito net.

We come now to the remarkable tale of a man who fought back against Driver ants.[1] Mr. Arthur Loveridge's house in Tanganyika was a substantial stone-built dwelling, but at 8 a.m. one day (an unusual time) Drivers in several lines of march were seen to be converging upon it. Officers with widely open jaws were stationed two inches apart along these lines. Some began to enter the stonework base and others climbed to the roof. Now Mr. Loveridge was well aware that from a spring-cleaning point of view a visit by Drivers is no bad thing, but he had valuable entomological collections in the house and did not wish to run the risk of losing them, so he decided to defy the ants, and rallied his natives and got busy with fire and strychnine. They worked to such effect that, in a short time, only a few individuals wandering aimlessly about were left of all that ordered host. "I congratulated myself," says Mr. Loveridge, "on having punished them so severely that the survivors would avoid such an unhealthy locality."

That evening, still feeling pleased with himself, he relaxed in an easy chair with a book. His reading was interrupted by faint noises coming from his bedroom. He went to investigate. The whitewashed walls were a dark, moving mass of Driver ants—so was the furniture. Struggling insects, covered with ants, were falling continually from the ceiling, and the penetrating odour of a well-known species of bug that often invades houses filled the air. Mr. Loveridge had congratulated himself

[1] Taken from an account given by Mr. Loveridge to the Entomological Society of London in 1922.

too soon. Apparently the masses he had so discomfited had been merely an advance column.

Mr. Loveridge admits that until that time he had no idea of the amount of vermin he possessed, hiding in cracks, under boxes, amongst clothes. All were being destroyed. In spite of this, the ungrateful man decided to continue the war. He had won the first skirmish; he would win this main battle. He could not do anything yet, so went to another room where he put each leg of his bed in a bowl of paraffin and water, hung a closely-woven mosquito net over it, tucked the sides in carefully, and slept in the house.

The ants evidently had plenty of work on hand that night and did not bother him—or else, as well they might, they found the mosquito net impregnable.

At daybreak all the natives were rallied and the attack was resumed. Ants were killed by every possible means and shovel-fuls of bodies heaped into pails of paraffin and water. After hours of this strenuous work scarcely an ant was to be seen. The second round also went to Mr. Loveridge.

There are some unusual features about this attack. One of them is its duration. But the fact that the ants met resistance, a very uncommon thing to happen to them, and were seriously impeded in their work, may account for the protracted nature of their siege. Also the house was a large one with many rooms difficult of access, and this in itself would delay their operations.

Still, Mr. Loveridge would appear to have been justified. He had fought for two days and now the ants were exter-minated and all his butterflies and other entomological specimens saved.

Alas, that evening several long lines of Drivers were seen investigating chinks in the stonework of the house in an ominously business-like way, and two hours later, after dark, a very broad column was seen moving up the wall to the roof.

Having full confidence now in the moats cᶠ paraffin round his bed legs, and in his mosquito net, Mr. Loveridge retired. If the ants *did* invade, then he would kill them off next day just as he had done before.

That night, for the first time, the Drivers turned their attention to him. They made ropes from the ceiling down to his mosquito net. When dangerously large masses had accumulated on top of it his nerve snapped. He dived from under the net, rushed out of the house, and fled to a barn 300 yards away. There those who do not know Driver ants might say that he had jumped from the frying pan into the fire, for he was attacked continuously all night by battalions of fleas.

One is not surprised at the frenzy of his onslaught on the ants next day. Sore all over from flea-bites and in danger of losing the battle that had begun so auspiciously for him, he and his natives worked like demons. Red-hot ashes were used wholesale (Insurance Companies, please note!) and the flesh of newly shot birds liberally garnished with strychnine spread everywhere. And the slaughter was on an even more gigantic scale than before.

The thing could not go on for ever; after getting rid of the ants for the third time and not wishing to sleep in the barn again, Mr. Loveridge slept in the house. But he was very careful indeed about his bed. He added a still finer-mesh net and made everything inside really ant-proof.

More ants arrived to replace the slaughtered ones, but this was the Drivers' last night inside the house. They had cleared the place up pretty well by now but there were still one or two things to be attended to. This final clearing-up went on throughout the night. Mr. Loveridge heard a rat fleeing on the roof above his bed, and heard it drop with a thud. Then he had to listen for some time to the pitiful squealing of its babies as the ants put them to death. The ants made bridges over his paraffin moats. Some even accomplished the impossible and got inside his nets. They —but for the sake of emphasis let us have a new paragraph for this.

They got into his safe and destroyed his entire collection of rare butterflies and other specimens, which, so far as Mr. Loveridge was concerned, was the only *casus belli*.

Next morning the ants had quitted the house but were massed outside, doing a systematic round-up of the garden. To do a quarter of the good those ants were doing to Mr. Loveridge's plants would have cost him a vast amount of labour and money: and yet, the vegetation being dry, he set fire to it and listened with glee to the sound of thousands of

Driver ants sizzling in the flames. That is typical of war—one gets carried away by hate.

At every stage, this Loveridge *v.* Driver ant campaign has ended with Loveridge thinking himself the winner and bowing, as it were, to an imaginary audience. It was so now. The last of the army had left the house, only to be destroyed in the open. True he had lost his butterflies, etc., and so might just as well not have declared war at all but gone off and stayed with friends. But he had won. The enemy was annihilated. Then—— But let me quote his own words: "Then came the shock. In every direction, from east and south, ants were arriving in countless thousands." Quite thirty columns were marching steadily towards the house.

These columns travelled partly above- but mostly underground (probably through earthen archways). Dry grass in quantity was burnt over them whenever they appeared above surface. It was useless. Their numbers were so great that they were indestructible. The house was theirs—but they never entered it. Loveridge was amazed; he knew that the place had been cleaned up by the various advance columns, but, he says (rather pathetically) "there were abundant meat-baits left for them." He added, giving, in spite of his discomfiture, credit where credit was due: "The discipline and organisation of the army were beyond reproach."

Why did they not enter the house? Had information been passed to them that the meat that lay there in quantities was poisoned?

And so, having fought their way to it, these massed legions were forbidden to enter the house and spent the time before they marched away destroying whatever living things they found outside. Mr. Loveridge was tempted to set fire to the vegetation again, but a wind was blowing which might have carried the flames to crops some distance away, so, doubtless with a sigh, he put his box of matches back in his pocket.

As I have said, there are unusual features about this attack on Mr. Loveridge's house: one, the duration, another, the arrival of reinforcements when such were needed. It proves, of course, that these ants convey intelligence (send messages, in other words), but we know that already, and in any case it does not take us any further. Where did the reinforcements come *from*? Is a human dwelling or similar place attacked only by a division told off for the purpose who can if need be call upon the main army for more troops? If so, where *is* the main army, what is it doing, and how far off is it? Driver ant armies do split up whilst on the march but they generally re-unite after a short distance. The most probable solution of the mystery (and Mr. Loveridge held this view) is that the ants had established a nest not far from the house. They have to breed and raise their winged males and therefore must establish semi-permanent quarters from time to time. They cannot *always* be on the march. Indeed, such nests have been found. It has been suggested that all of them have some permanent city tucked away somewhere and that armies operate from them for vast distances after the manner of the Roman legions. This is improbable for it would not benefit a city, to have the bulk of its population gorging themselves with food miles away while the city was starving—unless the armies returned frequently with provisions, and there is no evidence that they do. Furthermore, the scarred body of the queen shows that she is allowed but little rest and knows no really permanent home. It is a pity that we know so little of the breeding habits of these ants, but the very fact is significant: were any of them stay-at-homes we should know more.

There is one other small matter in the account that calls for comment. Mr. Loveridge and his natives destroyed whole armies of them in the house. I cannot understand how they escaped severe punishment, yet no mention of any retaliation by the Drivers is made. Natives, on the whole, are not as scared of Drivers as white men—they feel the pain less for one thing—yet they invariably (so far as my knowledge goes) evacuate their kraals when these ants arrive. Myself, I would not go *near* a house if I knew that Drivers were inside, much less fight them! The Ecitons of America (we are going to deal with them shortly) are quite as good vermin destroyers as the Drivers and are allied to them, but they seem, in the main, to respect the larger forms of life. "Respect" is the wrong word, they just do not go to the bother of attacking them so long as they themselves are not seriously interfered with. So we shall see in our next section an intelligent woman (more intelligent possibly than Mr. Loveridge) joining forces with a great army of ant invaders of her house and helping them and being apparently accepted by them as "one on their side." This could not happen with Drivers, but then Ecitons do not chew up full-grown live leopards in one night!

"Driver" ants, by the way, are so-called because they drive everything before them—except (and I say this not facetiously, but in real admiration) Mr. Loveridge.

2

The Ecitons

The "Legionary" or "Wandering" ants, as the Ecitons are often called, inhabit Central and South America. There are nearly seventy known species. To list a large number of species of a certain genus gives the impression that everything is very cut-and-dried and satisfactory. And so it is, to a point. Were you to catch a Legionary ant in America and send it to an expert for identification, that identification would be forthcoming. But were you to go further and ask the expert about the habits of that ant—how it lived, what it did, how it got its food—a shrug of the shoulders might well be the reply. It is rather like a telephone directory with us: there you will find *Homo sapiens* for a certain area listed from A to Z, but, even after making inquiries from those who compile the lists, you will learn nothing of the way of living or mating habits of the individuals catalogued. Observation is for ever toiling wearily after classification, and nowhere is observation so far behind as in the case of the sub-family Dorylinae.

In short, nothing much is known about most of them. It is the stay-at-homes that lend themselves to study, not the nest-less wanderers that seem to want half a continent for their activities. Not a small amount of our knowledge of ants has come from observation nests—small affairs that can be put on a table. An observation nest for Drivers or Legionaires would have to be about the size of an English county if they were to be expected to act normally.

Most of the Ecitons, too, are blind, affected by sunlight, and march in armies.

First let us think about this question of blindness. Some naturalists have stated that blindness is actually an asset to the Drivers. Had they eyes, they say, they would be uncontrollable; they would break rank and chase after game on all sides for long distances and probably get lost altogether. Even now, the workers often get involved in kills some distance from the marching column and have to be rounded up and brought back by officers, not infrequently under specially made archways. But even these excursions are all part of the plan and if they had eyes now they would never get out of control. For the Drivers, etc., *did* once have eyes and lost them probably because they did *not* run irresponsibly after game, and therefore rarely used them. A member little used begins to deteriorate and this deterioration makes it unreliable and therefore even less used than it was before, until, by a gradual process it is not used at all. Nature in her own good time removes any member not in employment. As a rule, it first shrinks; then it disappears. This process of removal is nicely illustrated by the eye vestiges of various species of the Ecitons—a further example of living fossils that are so much easier to examine and understand than awkward bits of stone. Some species have eyes but without any connecting optic nerve, some have sunken sockets only, others mere rims, down to the Drivers, who have no remains of eyes but show a clean surface where the eyes once, presumably, were. So it is legitimate to say that all these ants once had eyes, and to add that when they had them they did not let eyesight ever tempt them to disobedience. Had they done so they would not exist to-day as an example of the most perfect discipline ever attained by any army.

For the Eciton and Driver armies are not masters of the Wild by being particularly formidable in themselves. They know no fear and *are* strongly armed, but in single combat that is not enough. One has to be stronger than the other. A single Driver or Eciton soldier is no match for a Stink ant, or some of the harvesting ants. But when they appear as an army (and they never appear otherwise except when they are scouting) they are, by virtue of their numbers and their discipline, invincible.

The extreme sensitiveness of many of these ants to light cannot easily be explained. On the face of it, it seems obvious. Because they only (or mostly) travel at night and lie up in dark places by day, sunlight is dangerous to them. Even with us, city workers who spend a bank holiday sun-bathing on a broiling day have been known to have been killed by it. In any case it is questionable if a prolonged dose of the real thing does anybody much good. Sunlight is strong medicine, and amongst ourselves those who are most accustomed to it are generally those who take the greatest precautions against it. Men and women, for instance, do not travel in the interior of Africa in sun-bathing costumes and without hats. And during the midday hours all the game, though protected usually by hair, seek shade. So naturally Drivers, etc., who live so much in darkness, must avoid light, and the more they avoid it the more dangerous it becomes to them. But the question is, how did it start? Did these ants take to living in dark places because they were sensitive to light or did they become sensitive to light because they lived in dark places? It is on a par with the old question—which started first, the bird or the egg? Futile questions both, so let us get on with the Ecitons, first saying that certain species are not disturbed by light and will march in the open by day, even when the sun is shining.

Some Ecitons possess comparatively small armies, others very large ones. Let the mathematically-inclined try to work out the numbers of *this* Eciton army, species unrecorded, observed by Thurn in Guiana. The width of the column was 20 *yards* and it took nearly half an hour for the column to pass. The formation was so close that the whole ground was said to be covered by a black mass of moving ants. (Observers have said that in the case of many formations there is no room even to put a pin between the members.) I do not know the speed, but it is the usual thing for Eciton armies to travel at the double.

With some species the marches are purely insect-hunting expeditions, and not always successful ones at that. At least, Wheeler once found a nest of harvesters many of whose inhabitants were running about decorated with the heads of

Ecitons still clinging to them—evidence of a battle in which they had been victorious. This could only have happened, of course, if they had been attacked by one of the small Eciton bands. Indeed when Ecitons are called invincible it only applies to those who travel in adequate numbers. Species that choose to cut down the army strength must expect to suffer occasional reverses, however well disciplined they may be.

Eciton praedator (a smallish ant) is one of those species that are more or less indifferent to light. It is also purely an insect-hunter, though it has no qualms about entering human habitations. Belt, in Brazil, says that predator armies used occasionally to visit his house, "swarm over the walls and floors, searching every cranny and driving out the cockroaches and spiders, many of which were caught, bitten to pieces, and carried off."

He goes on to say that he saw many armies of this species in the forest. The twittering of birds usually drew his attention to the fact that an army of predators was in the vicinity. He says: "On approaching to ascertain the cause of the disturbance, a dense body of the ants, 3 or 4 yards wide and so numerous as to blacken the ground would be seen moving rapidly in one direction, examining every cranny and underneath every fallen leaf. On the flanks and in advance of the main army, smaller columns would be pushed out. These smaller columns would generally first flush the cockroaches, grasshoppers, and spiders. The pursued insects would rapidly make off, but many, in their confusion and terror, would bound right into the midst of the main body of ants."

Insects in numbers would crowd to the tops of the branches, only to be followed and made to leap from their perches into the midst of the ants crowding below. The only survivors apparently were spiders.

"... Many of the spiders would escape by hanging suspended by a thread of silk from the branches, safe from the foes that swarmed both above and below."

Ecitons have more respect than the Drivers for the larger forms of life. Many species will punish severely any human who interferes with them, but they will never, so far as is known, regard him as edible. A girl of about twelve was once alone in a house in South America when it was invaded by Ecitons. They poured in in dense volumes. Petrified by fright, she sat frozen in her chair while cockroaches and worse fled up to her shoulders and up to her head, followed by blood-thirsty masses of ants. The ants slaughtered every living pest in the house, including the rats and mice, and she formed part of the battleground. The ants departed in due course and the parents returned later. Whatever her mental condition may have been, she had received no physical hurt at all—not even the slightest bite or sting. Had those Ecitons been Drivers, one hates to think what the parents might have found on their return.

There are few women who would regard an invasion of their homes by carnivorous ants as a blessing. Most would view it as a major disaster and wring their hands and ask whoever was present what he or she was going to do about it. An exception was Mrs. Carmichael of Trinidad. She lived in a house called Laurel Hill, and this house was once invaded by Ecitons—which she called "Chasseur Ants."

It was in the last century, and she has left a vivid account of her experience. The ants poured in in broad columns, some of which ascended, in formation, to the rafters where they threw down all the cockroaches to the troops below, who dragged them out of the house and slaughtered them.

Instead of getting pans of boiling water and pails of red-hot ashes and quantities of poisoned meat, Mrs. Carmichael joined in whole-heartedly with the invaders. "I was deter-mined," she says, "to take every advantage of such able hunters." For, as is often the case in the tropics, her house was riddled with hosts of undesirable creatures whose elimina-tion was quite impossible in normal circumstances. She ran up to the bedrooms, but the ants were already there and busy at work. They took no notice whatever of the human intruder, and Mrs. Carmichael energetically opened her trunks and cases, including a large military chest full of linen. These she flung open and pulled the linen and other things out on to the floor. In the linen were hundreds of cockroaches, "not one of which escaped."

She went downstairs again and found that "the battle

Driver Ants on the march. (*Winged Male, Queen, "Officers",
and Workers*)

was now more hot than ever," for the ants had opened an attack on the rats and mice and were putting them to death and dragging them outside. "No one who has not watched such a scene," she says, "can comprehend the celerity and union of strength. I did not see one rat or mouse escape, and I am sure I saw a score carried off during a very short period."

The ants had entered the house about ten o'clock. The rat and mouse campaign started after one o'clock. By about three, the house was cleared. Quarter of an hour later, the army started to leave, and in a short time every ant had gone. They had other work, however, to do, and went in their broad columns to the negro quarters, which they cleared up in the same way. By sun-down this work, too, was finished and the ants departed for good.

We do not know how the Ecitons nest and breed. Probably they too have temporary bivouacs and also semi-permanent nests. Owing to their vast numbers they could stay nowhere very long without exhausting the food supplies. Normally, carnivorous animals are kept in check by food. Nature (if left alone) keeps a very nice balance this way. But the Drivers and Ecitons have no intention of having their numbers cut down by one of nature's laws. They are a law, they think, to themselves and they have decided they *need* large armies. So they have dodged nature by continually marching on and yet managing to breed. As we have said, their breeding habits are not known, but whatever they are they are obviously adequate.

A peculiar Eciton nest was once discovered by Belt. The species was *Eciton hamatum*, the "Hook-Jawed Ant," a peculiar-looking ant with hooked jaws of great length, the function of which, if any, is unknown. We have observed before how fond ants are of substituting living subjects for inanimate material. Belt now shows us a living nest. It was a large mass, about a cubic yard in bulk, with openings and exits and passage-ways exactly like a nest formed in a tree-trunk, or soil. The difference was that this nest was composed entirely of living ants, a jammed mass of them, yet full of corridors and holes. Foragers were bringing in supplies and others were pouring out in the usual way.

Eciton workers are said to emit a nauseous odour like that of rotten meat. This may be so, though the meat they eat is always fresh: they will not, for instance, eat entomological specimens as the Drivers did in the case of Loveridge. (So far as Drivers are concerned, I have never detected any particular smell in the workers and have met no one who has.) It is said also that, on the contrary, Eciton females and males possess a sweet and pleasant smell. Females have been so rarely encountered that few observers can be in a position to judge, though I can quite believe that the males have a pleasing scent. At least—though it is a *non sequitor*—male bumble-bees have a very sweet smell and leave this smell behind in places where they have foregathered for the night.

3
The Aenicti

The three genera touched on in this chapter seem to have parcelled out the tropical world between them, for Aenictus mostly inhabits India and South Asia. We shall not let Aenictus keep us long for it presents few new features. People from India have often described to me ants they have seen marching, some in phalanxes, some in columns. These, of course, were Aenicti. There are about thirty species, and none of the workers are large. Wroughton says of this ant that it has brought military organisation to perfection, and that an Aenictus column never shows the slightest irregularity. At times large bodies detach themselves, and, forming into rank, march off in other directions. "This manœuvre," Wroughton goes on to say, "seems to be in the nature of a flanking movement. I have seen a strong column marching on a white ant heap, detach in this way columns right and left, and the several detached columns enter the heap from different points of the compass. The notion irresistibly forced on anyone watching these manœuvres is that they are either the result of preconcerted arrangement, or are carried out by word of command."

Neither Eciton nor Aenictus, so far as we know, ever employ scouts, and in this their military genius would appear to be behind that of the all-conquering Drivers.

CHAPTER II

HOSPITALITY

FROM time to time I have spoken about certain guests of ants. I now propose to give them a chapter, though a small one, to themselves.

Those who uphold the ant as a model of all the virtues, particularly as regards its strict attention to duty, have to close their eyes to certain doubtful practices. One may judge a man, they say, by his friends: if we judge an ant by the same standard our verdict must be adverse. Hospitality normally is praiseworthy—and no creature is more hospitable to her friends than the ant—but when this hospitality results in debauched petting parties one can hardly class it as a virtue.

For weird and remarkable is the varied mob that accept the hospitality of the ant, and very questionable are some of the scenes that take place. Conspicuous amongst the guests are a thousand species of beetles and twice that number of species of grubs. Conspicuous, too, are the young of some of our rarest and most beautiful blue butterflies. (Needless to say, these many guests are distributed: some species will be found in one ants' nest, others in another, and none in yet another.)

Denied the pleasures of sex, some ant workers would appear to recompense themselves by indulgence in exotic gastronomic sensations. These sensations are gratified by tickling the glands of other insects so as to make them exude a minute edible secretion. So great is her desire for the glandular matter secreted by many of her guests that in order to obtain it the worker ant is prepared traitorously to sacrifice the children of whom she is the nurse and guardian. For the creature that pleases her appetite can do no wrong, and if it, too, develops an unnatural taste and gets a liking for ant grubs and eggs, the nurse seems unable to say no.

Who are these guests—those who seduce and are seduced by the ant? Shall we give a long list? I think not. So many are the guests that the subject now forms a separate branch of ant study and is called Myrmecophily (a *Myrmecophile* means an "Ant Guest"). If, however, you wish to go into the matter in detail you will be able to obtain treatises about it and learn the names of the guests. But be prepared. It is a formidable study containing no such homely names as beetles, grubs, caterpillars, but ectoparasite, synecthran, myrmecoxene, syneokete, and so on.

So we will avoid it and repeat that predominant amongst what one observer called the "Motley Crew" of guests are beetles, grubs, and caterpillars of the blue butterflies.

Many of these dine at the ant table, feast like ogres on ant children, and, far from being expelled, are fawned on and caressed by their besotted hosts. All for the sake of a tiny drop of something that must be extraordinarily good to make ants go to such lengths to obtain it. The beetle and its off-spring probably come first in popularity. Should the beetle get jaded with a diet of eggs and grubs, the ants feed it from their mouths. Should it wish a ride, they carry it about for hours. Why the beetle should want a ride we do not know, neither do the ants, but it often does, and what it wants—with ants—it gets. The beetle grub is in the same happy position, it has a voracious appetite but is allowed the run of the nursery and is fed by mouth when it desires.

The guest caterpillars are those of certain blue butterflies, the Chalkhill Blue, and other rarer and even more beautiful butterflies, but all—mark this strange fact—blue. These cater-pillars have a gland on their backs near the rear portion (the eleventh segment to be precise) and this gland secretes an oily matter. This oily matter, however, is not on tap normally. It stays in the gland until some ant gets to work. She tickles the caterpillar with her antennae, and in due course a drop of fluid appears from the centre of the gland and the ant goes into gastronomic ecstasies. Where the secret lies in the tickling no one knows. It must be simply that the ant knows a few tricks that have escaped us or else that the caterpillar is excited by the presence of the ant as well as by the ant's touch, for experimenters have tickled these caterpillars most patiently with the finest of sable hair brushes, but not one drop of oil have they ever got: the gland remains unexcited and unresponsive.

Normally caterpillars are vegetarians, but there is evidence that caterpillars of the blues, when guests of the ants, descend to the level of beetles and eat ant eggs and grubs.

The seduction of these "blue" caterpillars has now gone so far that certain rare blue butterflies would become still rarer, would in fact become extinct, without ants. Furthermore, it must be the right species of ant, for one species goes in for one species of caterpillar, and another, another. And vice versa, each caterpillar species must have the right species of ant to seduce it.

Those who collect butterflies are generally depicted as running about the countryside with a panama hat and a butterfly net. This is correct to a certain extent, at least as regards the net, but they have other methods, and the most usual is to get the eggs or caterpillars of the specimen required and wait in comfort until the butterfly emerges from the subsequent chrysalis. This method is almost foolproof, provided one knows what vegetation the caterpillar feeds on and provided one can maintain an adequate supply—for very often it will accept no substitute. But when, as with caterpillars of certain blues, one has to find the right *ant* as well as the right plant, rearing caterpillars to the pupa stage becomes difficult in the extreme. Yet this is what rearers have to do if they want to rear them, for some of the caterpillars of these rare blues will not eat even their own selected vegetation without the comforting presence of a particular species of ant. No wonder they are rare.

There is no doubt that these "blue" caterpillars not infrequently get amongst the ant cattle, the aphids, etc., and do damage there. It is as if, with us, the guests of a farmer strolled over to his Alderneys and maimed and killed them. Imagine the feelings of that farmer! Yet the farmer ants, though with a twisted smile no doubt, suffer it.

In Britain, ants tend the young of the Chalkhill Blue and the Adonis Blue. They rarely take them into their nests, but they know their proper plants as well as any entomologist or botanist and place them out on them. To a certain extent, therefore, these particular caterpillars are in the same category as ordinary ant cattle; but it is a different story with the Large Blue (*Maculinea arion*), that rare and handsome creature, the largest of the British Blues, found only in Cornwall, Devonshire and Gloucestershire, and one of the greatest prizes of butterfly-hunters, who have contributed in no small way to its rarity.

Naturally collectors tried in every way to get specimens of this coveted butterfly; on the wing if they could, and also by the normally simpler and more certain method of collecting the caterpillars and feeding them in captivity until they pupated. There ought to have been no difficulty about this. Their food was known: it was thyme, and a fair number of the caterpillars could always be found on thyme in the proper districts. These were taken every year by the collectors and fed on fresh thyme. But always, at their third moult, which with caterpillars in general is usually the last, they refused their food and died.

Yet under natural conditions they obviously did not die or there would have been no Large Blues flying about the following July and no Large Blues at all anywhere. Various explanations were given: problems are part of the fun of natural history, and giving explanations, however far-fetched, is part of the fun of problems.

Meanwhile collectors went on hopefully feeding Large Blue caterpillars on thyme and watching them die after their last moult instead of turning into chrysalises.

This particular problem was not solved until 1915, when a Dr. Chapman discovered a Large Blue caterpillar in a nest of red ants. And this caterpillar was much larger than any of those that had died when being tended by collectors. It followed, therefore, that the Large Blue caterpillar must have a *fourth* moult before it pupates, and there seemed to be a possibility that that moult was made not amongst the thyme but in an ants' nest.

We know now what happens. The Large Blue caterpillar lives on thyme until its third moult, when it descends to the ground and begins to wander about. After some hours an ant, of the species *Myrmica rubra*, comes along and accosts it. A kind of courtship ensues and finally the ant "milks" it. The ant then carries it off to her home. That the victim has no objections to being seduced and kidnapped is shown by the way it arches its back and stiffens itself so as to make it easier for the ant to seize it in her jaws and carry it off.

It is carried into the bowels of the nest and enters into a life of the utmost luxury. It is tended carefully and fed on newly hatched ant grubs. This diet, though so very different from its previous diet, obviously suits the caterpillar, for in six weeks it *trebles* its size. It also becomes of a pinky-white colour. The amount of ant grubs consumed must be enormous.

It is now given a small room, a cavity where it can settle down in comfort for the winter and spend that hard season in warmth and drowsy content. It awakens in the spring and is served again with newly hatched ant grubs to the point of surfeit. Finally it turns into a dark yellow chrysalis. In three weeks it emerges as a butterfly, still in the bowels of the nest. Escorted and assisted by the ants, it now makes its way through the winding corridors to the surface, where it unfolds and dries its wings and sails away.

So without ants we would have no Large Blue butterflies. On the other hand, had ants left them alone in the beginning they would probably have been content with their thyme and pupated on it and saved collectors much frustration.

Seduction is rarely one-sided. The seducer, without knowing it, is often being seduced herself. At any rate, there is no doubt that blue caterpillars entice the ants to excite them by erecting a pair of small tubercles situated just behind the coveted gland and which probably give off an odour. When the caterpillar realises that its aims have been achieved and that an ant is coming to tickle it, the tubercles are withdrawn.

Why is it that Large Blues in Britain exist to-day only in Cornwall, Devonshire and Gloucestershire? Have they naturally died off elsewhere or is it because only ants from those counties know how to find and look after the caterpillars? Or is wild thyme more common there? We do not know the reason, but it is certainly not because the Cornish, etc., ants know more about entomology than the ants of other counties, for the caterpillars of Large Blues taken to Kent (where they are now unknown) are greeted enthusiastically by the Kentish ants and taken into their nests. As it happens, these Blues were not always absent from Kent, for Lewin in 1795 states that they were found on high chalky lands in the neighbourhood of Dover. They were found also in Somerset and Buckinghamshire. But that was 150 years ago. So, in England at any rate, the ants appear to be fighting a losing battle in their efforts to preserve this species. For its increasing scarcity perhaps the ants blame the collectors, just as the collectors blame the ants.

Certain scavenger flies often lodge with ants. These are permitted to lay their eggs in the nest and the ensuing grubs keep the place clean by feeding on any waste matter—which cannot amount to much for ants are amongst the tidiest of creatures. Flies also act as cleaners and scavengers in wasps' nests. One envies insects the domestic help they receive without payment other than lodging.

Most ants kill and eat insects. In fact they might be described on the whole as a fierce race. Yet it is surprising how tolerant they can be. One can understand them harbouring beetles and caterpillars, they get something from them, but they harbour also many species of crickets, cockroaches, and woodlice. These live in warmth and security in the nest, though the ants get nothing from them and pay no attention to them. Some of these species are only found in ants' nests. A white woodlouse, for example, often lodges with the common garden ant. When you dig into an ants' nest your spade may turn over dozens of them, but you will find them nowhere else. Probably you will not notice them—they are very small —and probably you will not be interested in them in any case. Your lack of interest is fully shared by the ants themselves. This particular woodlouse, by the way, although so small itself, is called *Platyarthrus hoffmannseggii*. Spiders of the ant-mimicking kind are also sometimes found in ants' nests.

A highwayman is neither a guest nor a lodger, nevertheless the activities of certain mosquitoes must be mentioned in this chapter. These mosquitoes were studied by Jacobson in Java and Farquharson in Nigeria. They make a living out of ants by a knowledge of psychology. Ants hate being delayed when engaged in work and will take the easiest way to avoid such hindrance. The mosquitoes hover over the branches of trees where aphids or coccids are stabled by ants. When a milk-maid comes hurrying along, one of them alights in her path, barring her way and holding out its tongue. Much as we might toss a copper to an importunate beggar to get rid of him, the ant gives the mosquito a drop of food; the mosquito flies off and the ant hurries on to the cows. Not all milkmaids are so weak-minded, sooner or later comes one who thrusts the mosquito aside. This is part of the day's work to the mosquito and usually it goes away and waits for the next ant.

A full list of the creatures harboured by ants is very start-ling, but ants are not the only ones: were some gigantic naturalist from another sphere to dig up a human city he would find, in addition to the proper occupants, dogs, cats, rabbits, parrots, canaries, rats, mice, ants, cockroaches, and thousands more, and he would probably give them long names and say how tolerant human beings were.

CHAPTER 12

THE WHITE ANT

ABOUT two hundred years ago a startling discovery was made. It was an age of discoveries generally, and explorers in particular were bringing home tales of strange lands, peoples, and animals. These tales fired the imagination of romanticists, but even Haggard's Allan Quatermain never discovered so wonderful a people as the prosaic naturalist Smeathman did when he broke into a city of white ants. Make no mistake, white ants had been known before, only too well, but simply as destructive pests. Their cities, too, had been broken into, but only by angry men in futile efforts to destroy them. Smeathman was the first who broke into a city, not to destroy but carefully to investigate.

Now "The People of the Mist," and those dominated by the great *She* were easy enough to understand once the novelist's hero had reached them. White ants were fairly easy to reach but very difficult to understand. Break into their hills, and all one sees are masses of small objects running away as fast as their legs can carry them. To find out what goes on normally inside these vast cities calls for a lot more patience than most men possess. Patience and time. Smeathman had both and he used them well. What he thought he was going to find when he started off we do not know; what he *did* find surprised him. It surprised others also. For apparently an ordinary termite hill stretched for vast distances underground and was peopled by creatures of high intelligence who had a king and queen, armoured soldiers, policemen, and, amongst the civilians, chemists, water-diviners, well-borers, architects, engineers, surveyors, and other experts and skilled artisans. The city itself contained two-way traffic streets, bridges stretching over chasms, mean alleyways, and huge vaulted places like cathedrals.

This was rather a lot to swallow for people at home. They thought Smeathman must be letting his enthusiasm and imagination carry him away. But other naturalists were soon at work. They verified what he had said, and even went further.

The facts being established, that other question arose: How did mere insects manage to behave like super human beings? Who guided them? Many of the theorists brought out the old, well-worn pair of blinkers and said it was instinct or something similar, that white ants were acting as automatons, and therefore that there was nothing to inquire into at all. Others went to the opposite extreme, saw, as they thought, a civilisation higher than that of man and spoke of the "Soul" of the White Ant, and the "God" of the White Ant. Well, some species of white ants are certainly the most advanced of all the social insects, including real ants, and they may have a soul, which is a word hard to define. They may also have a god for all I know. Such matters are not for us here. Natives knew white ants ages before Europeans arrived on the scene, and they, at any rate, do not take kindly to the idea of their possessing anything of a spiritual nature. Witness Herbert Noyes, the author of *Man and the Termite*. He met a mission-educated native in Africa. This native boasted that by merely watering a white ants' nest he could make flying ants come out at any time. Said Noyes, "Not if their wings are undeveloped. Such a paltry subterfuge would scarcely deceive the God of the Termites, who has them in his keeping."

To which the Christian native replied, "What! Them dam insex got a soul like me? Not bloody likely!"

And this Shavian remark sums up, I think, the general reaction of many of us.

The name "White Ant" is to a biologist as a red rag is to a bull, for the white ant is not an ant but a termite, and furthermore is in the proud position of being the sole representative of an Order—the Order *Isoptera*. But it is no use biologists kicking against the pricks. In the old world at least, the ordinary man who lives in places where termites flourish calls termites "white ants." He found them first and so, really, has the right to name them. He knows by now that they are not real ants, just as he knows that sea-lions and sea-horses are not real lions and horses, but he does not greatly care what they are and is going to stick to the name he gave them. Even Government inspectors in Africa and Asia report on damage done by "White Ants," never by "Termites," or so it used to be when I was in those parts. After all, the chief function of names is to identify, not to classify. If you or I went to Africa to get further information about these creatures from those who lived amongst them we would save time by asking about "white ants," and not "termites." In this necessarily sketchy chapter I propose to use both names indifferently, so it must be understood that White Ant = Termite, and Termite = White Ant. And I apologise for bringing into a book on ants insects that are not ants at all, but whose nearest relatives are cockroaches.

In previous chapters we have had a lot to say about food and the bearing it has on success in life. An animal's brain is important but its stomach is more so. The brain functions only by permission of the stomach, and even then its chief duty is to think out ways of getting food for its master, the stomach. We have admired the ant for forcing itself to eat seeds as well as meat, to milk cows, and the rest. We have admired ourselves for doing more or less the same thing, and have pointed out that a large and varied diet makes for success in life. Another scheme which pays dividends is to eat something unusual. One thus eliminates competition. White ants are one of the successful forms of life that have adopted the latter method.

I take my daughter and some other girls, all about eight years old, to school every day. During the journey they talk a lot but the conversation, though animated, rarely merits much attention. The other day, however, they supplied me with a parallel. Food, as usual, was the main theme. "I wish," sighed one, looking out of the window at some cows that had got at a hay-rick, "that we could eat hay." That started things off with a vengeance. By the time they had come to the end of the journey they had eaten their house and most of the surrounding country. In the Utopia they visualised, the bricks of the house were candy, the woodwork chocolate, the furniture other confection. Having demolished the house, they went outside: the telegraph poles were Brighton rock, tree-trunks were solid nut, leaves were iced sugar, and mud, melting chocolate ice-cream.

This must have been the sort of dream that tantalised white ants in a remote period when they were unfitted to cope with ever increasing competition and had to do something about it or go under. And somehow their dream came true—which is more than the dream of those girls ever will. It became possible for them to eat and relish telegraph poles, trees, grass, hay, earth, sandstone, and other things, including, if need be, some of the material in their own home.

But wood (nearly always dead wood) became their chief food, and this was beneficial not only to themselves but to the tropical world at large which needed machinery for clearing away quickly and bringing back into circulation its many fallen trees. Millions of years later, however, this habit brought white ants into conflict with a new-comer called man, who also used dead wood, though not for eating. The conflict became still more embittered because, although previous to man's arrival white ants had lived almost entirely on wood, they now found such *bon mouches* as leather, canvas, oilcloth, paper, clothes, carpets, etc., very much to their liking. And if they did not altogether relish mortar and brick they were able to eat through them in search of something better. Man declared war.

We are, very naturally, self-centred and class an animal as good or bad according to what it eats. A "good" animal eats only things that are harmful to us or not wanted by us; a "bad" animal eats the kind of food we eat ourselves, or, if it is very bad, ourselves in person. About an animal's morals we care nothing. The exemplary family life of the fox, for instance, counts for nothing against the fact that it shares our taste for poultry. The sweet non-aggressive nature of the rabbit and its soft woolliness so beloved by children count for nothing against the fact that it is as fond of vegetables as we are. And this is a perfectly correct attitude. Whether we wish to or not, we cannot *afford* to be lenient to creatures that come into competition with us and whose sole idea seems to be to eat us out of house and home, which is literally true of white ants, who *do* eat our houses and homes as they stand and who

have destroyed more human property than even man himself
with all his bombs. But let us be honest about it and not
describe them (as they often are described) as "one of the
greatest pests the world[1] has known"; they are benefactors
to the *world*, but they are certainly one of the greatest pests
man has known.

Let us give a few examples for the benefit of those who
have not heard dozens already from travellers returning from
Africa or Asia or America. A friend of mine in Rhodesia had
a collection of books which he kept in a bookcase. He was
away from home for a week and when he returned white ants
had eaten practically every book and the whole of the bookcase. The same thing happened to a man's wardrobe. In a
week white ants ate all his suits and the wardrobe as well.
Indeed, in that land of (then) not very substantially built
dwelling-places men have gone on holiday and come back to
find practically their whole house eaten and needing little
more than a push to send it to the ground. A surveyor once
returned from a trip up-country. He put his trunk on the
table and went to bed. He deliberately put the trunk on the
table for safety: it contained all his surveying papers, notebooks, pencils, clothes, and the rest. When he arose in the
morning he found that white ants had consumed nearly
everything inside. They had not had time completely to eat
all the clothes, but there was no spot on them larger than a
shilling which was not riddled with small holes. The papers
and notebooks were completely consumed and so were the
pencils, together with the graphite in them. White ants can
manufacture corrosive substances which will eat into glass
and metal. In this surveyor's trunk were some silver coins
and most of these were found covered with black spots caused
by a corrosive agent so strong that not even vigorous rubbing
with sand would remove them.

From time to time white ants have made very expensive
meals out of bank notes, and, judging from the above, even
coinage is not safe from them. In India, at one time, white

---

[1] The greatest pest the "world" of land-dwellers has known is undoubtedly
man, dating from the time he invented the plough and axe and by laying bare
the soil to water erosion, and drought began to send the stored-up treasure of the
land into the sea by river and wind.

ants became a pest in an unusual way and figured largely in the law courts where it became the usual thing for absconders and debtors to claim that white ants had eaten bank notes. These particular white ants were evidently specialised, for they ate just the bank notes and nothing else.

Most termites are blind and as sensitive to light as the Drivers. Exposed to the sun, I have seen certain species shrivel up and die just as if they had been put on to a hot frying pan. Yet they travel long distances on the surface of baked terrain to get their food. Two questions arise: how do they find out where the food is? and how do they get to it? We do not know the answer to the first, but to *get* to the food they build enclosed mud runways (which dry outside almost instantaneously), often of great length. The inside of these runways must, to the termites, be very like the inside of the Blackwall or similar tunnels to us, including the ceaseless processions of two-way traffic. The traffic consists of empty vehicles (living ones) going to the food and full ones returning. (Incidentally the continental right-hand rule of the road is observed by termites.) Breakage of the tunnel at any point usually causes a traffic jam and work stopped until repairs have been affected.

The thing selected to be eaten—a large tree-trunk let us say—as soon as it is connected up with the nest by the runway, has to be enclosed in a layer of cement which is raised about half an inch from the surface of the wood and supported by pillars and walls. The outside of this earthen crust is rough and unfinished and gives the log the camouflaged appearance of having been dipped in mud which has dried on it: the inside is smoothly finished and (literally) varnished. Working inside this cement shell, the termites transfer the whole of the tree-trunk, via the two-way traffic tunnel, to their nest in a matter of a few days.

When the whole of the work is done and the termites have departed nothing has changed, externally. There lies the great muddy tree-trunk just as it lay before. But it is a hollow mockery. Its weight has changed from tons to pounds. The dainty foot of an antelope would go straight through it. You or I, if we tried to sit on it, would hit the ground with a thud in a cloud of dust, just as if some practical joker had pulled a chair away when we were about to sit down. But termites are not practical jokers, they are too busy for that. The shell was made to keep their workers in darkness and safety until the last bit of wood had been taken away and the fact that it did not collapse before then (nor, unless disturbed, for a long time afterwards) shows that considerable engineering skill was used.

How long do termites take over their various jobs? We generally find just the destruction and have no means of gauging the time taken to accomplish it. The instance of the surveyor's box (and other instances) show us that they can do a lot of damage in one night, but then they were on the spot and, since it was dark, had no need to build a complicated earthen rind. How long does it take them to build this preliminary outside covering? An experience of my own gives a good indication.

I was going on horseback from my camp to a native kraal about fifteen miles away. I rode till about midday and then, to give the horse a rest and to stretch my legs, off-saddled in dry isolated country. I knee-haltered the horse, put the saddle and bridle on the ground, and went for a walk with the rifle, hoping to get a small buck which I could strap to the saddle and eventually take home to the larder. I returned unsuccessful in not more than two hours (probably less, for being on a journey I had not much time to waste). The horse was there, a few yards from where I had left him, grazing half-heartedly on tufts of dry grass, but there were no signs of the saddle or bridle. It was one of those dreadful things which just can't be true yet which are. The saddle had gone! I hunted all over the place. One cannot ride a horse without a saddle and bridle—at least not the sort of horse I had. The authorities would not like it either; they would probably sooner have lost me than one of their saddles. A minor detail was that there was food in the wallets.

Then, as I strode about bewildered I noticed a small mound of earth. At first sight it did not differ from any of the many other bare dry mounds around, but on closer inspection it was shaped rather like a saddle. It was the sort of saddle a child might try to form out of mud with a wooden spade. I broke into it. Underneath was my saddle. The outside earthen covering was dry, but the inside, with the usual pillars and galleries, was still wet. Nearby, the reins and bridle could be seen faintly outlined under earth. Both saddle and bridle were unharmed except for one small patch on the seat of the saddle which the termites had just begun to gnaw. Those insects were there in numbers when I first broke open the crust but they left quickly.

I traced a covered-in runway for several yards along the ground, but it soon disappeared amongst grass roots and I had no time for further search. So how long a tunnel the termites had made to get to my saddle I do not know. What I *do* know is that if I had returned an hour later there would have been no saddle—except the metal parts.

As I rode away I remember that I pondered over two things. (1) How had the termites found the saddle so quickly? They do not have scouts running about on the surface like ants; they work in darkness and this was only just after mid-day. And the saddle had not been placed directly over a nest, as the runway I traced so inadequately proved. (2) I had a large water-bottle strung round me because this was the dry season and I knew I should get no water until I reached the kraal. The place where I had out-spanned had seemed bone dry. Where did the termites get the water to make the mud covering and the runway? (I shall have more to say about termites and water later.)

This covering with mud of what they have chosen to eat has been the method of most termites for many millions of years. Then—yesterday from their point of view—man came and built houses and put edible furniture inside. The termites took due notice. Now, coating an article with mud would appear to be a glaring preliminary advertisement of their intentions, yet it is surprising how rarely it is noticed. In the open veld, of course, it never is noticed, but even at one's doorstep, so to speak, it may escape detection. I remember a felled tree-trunk that I used to pass within a yard at least twice a day. Then the day came when I saw that termites had started work on it and covered it with mud. Immediate investigation, however, showed that that trunk was merely a piece of ancient history. It had been covered with mud and taken away long before. The operation had taken place under my eyes and I had never noticed it.

But this may easily happen outside: it is a different matter in a home. A house-proud woman, for instance, is hardly likely to fail to notice a raised mud tunnel coming in at the front door, proceeding along the polished hall to the drawing-room and there enveloping her prized escritoire in a shapeless mask of mud. The termites have come to realise this, either by experience or intuition or something else, and have altered their technique accordingly. Now they enter an occupied house (it is a different matter if it is unoccupied) by some unperceived chink, or bore a hole through mortar. The greatest care is then taken to conceal their runway. It will go under the foundations (if there are any), or use existing crevices such as the slight hollows between bricks. In the latter case the outside surface is made flush with the bricks so that it resembles mortar and is extremely hard to detect. In a room they will use the crevices between boards or at the sides. Nine times out of ten they will choose a piece of furniture near the wall and enter it from behind. They will discard the usual coat of mud and eat the furniture from inside but leave intact the outer shell. Yet had that same piece of furniture been found in the open they would have coated it first in the usual manner. (Different species, of course, are often concerned.) They are able undetected to destroy a table standing in the middle of a room by boring up from underneath through the floor directly into one of the legs, then up that leg, through the top and down the other legs. they will leave the table, too, a mere shell—which must involve very careful eating in the right spots at the right time, and a knowledge of the centre of gravity by the sappers responsible for the arrangements.

One is tempted to go on and give further instances of cunning concealment and bold yet undetected destruction of articles in apparently inaccessible spots, such as hanging frames, but perhaps enough has been said. One thing is certain; mankind has a very formidable list of offences against termites. Amongst these offences, you will be startled to hear, is the claim that white ants are responsible for the lack of intelligence of men living in the tropics. Most of us never knew that men

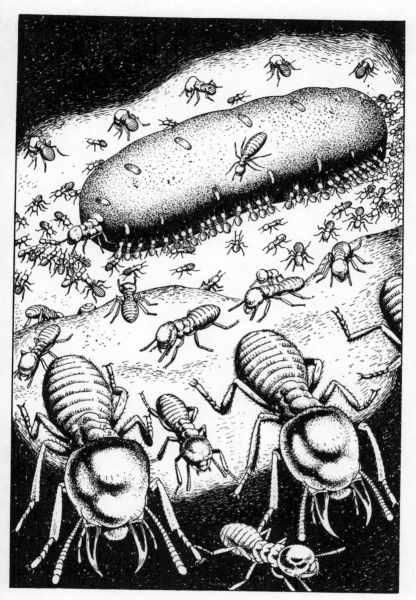

Court of the Queen (and King) Termite

living in the tropics *were* unintelligent, but apparently we were. Von Humbolt started the theory when, many years ago, he stated that he had never seen a book in tropical South America more than fifty years old and that the reason was that termites ate all the previous ones. So now it is said that the inhabitants of the tropics lack brains because they do not get a chance to read good books because the termites eat them too quickly.

This sounds nonsense but there may be a germ of truth in it. At least some of the inhabitants of the tropics may not be so well-read as others elsewhere because they do not like keeping books in their homes. Not only may the books be destroyed, but shelves of books form ideal bulwarks from which termites can operate. Furthermore, books seem to be definitely a bait for termites. (Paper saves them trouble for it is wood already pulped.) Public libraries are often long distances away, and in the past the books even there used to suffer great destruction. Probably these libraries are now termite-proof—if it *is* possible to be termite-proof.

Less conspicuous than African termites are the Asiatic "white ants" (also invariably known by that name). Their methods are more insidious. They make no hills (this is the case also with the more destructive of the African termites) and it is impossible to find their nests except by chance. One rarely sees the termites either. They come from no one knows where even into houses specially built to keep them out.

I lived in such a house once in China on the Yangtse in the town of Kiukiang. The house belonged to the firm I worked for, and every year a maintenance inspector used to come round. To us who lived in the house there were never any signs of white ants, but every year this inspector found extensive damage, chiefly in the cellars and foundations. They got through brick and cement and metal. It was uncanny; They were destructive ghosts that no one ever saw. The inspector would trace their channels and soon workmen would be busy with more cement and bricks and treated wood, and the white ants would be faced again with an apparently impenetrable barrier. But next year the inspector would find them back again. I should hate to own a house on the Yangtse;

the yearly white ant repair bill would be enormous. Fortunately they possessed none of the enterprise of their African relatives, they kept to the foundations and cellar beams, they made no lightning raids on our trunks or bookcases or wardrobes.

As I have said, my daughter and her friends have considered the possibility of eating wood. My Corgi pup is engaged in a more practical manner in the same research and has already eaten some sticks of firewood and part of the leg of a table, though as he grows older he will find that there is no virtue in this food and discontinue his experiments. Nevertheless a healthy primitive instinct is at work in both cases; a desire to investigate food supplies in general and not, like caterpillars, view with horror the idea of eating anything but one particular kind. Wood is everywhere, is comparatively easy to chew, even by human beings as the ends of countless pencils bear record, and is appetising in appearance, especially when smoothed and planed. Could we but tap this great source of supply we should solve one of the greatest of our problems to-day.

But we cannot assimilate wood; neither can any mammals, birds, or social insects—except termites. Dry wood is pure cellulose and, generally speaking, pure cellulose cannot be digested by animals. How then can termites digest it? The answer is they cannot. They live on it entirely, but cannot digest it. They get others to do it for them.

Amongst some crude forms of life that are able to assimilate cellulose are certain microscopic organisms called protozoa. Some of these exist in the bodies of white ants, though how they got there no one knows, for they "got" into the bodies of no other creatures: only white ants and only white ant *adult workers* possess them. They did not always have them and they did not always eat wood, but now they have so many that the protozoa in one termite account for nearly half its weight and must handicap its movements to an appreciable extent. Incidentally there are writers who think that termites deliberately by some unknown means introduced these protozoa into their systems. Certainly termites are expert chemists if not bacteriologists, but this theory, of course, is absurd.

Nevertheless, the last word about termites has still to be said, and those who ridicule the idea entirely ought perhaps first to tell us how the termites *did* get their protozoa. Anyway, if some of our research workers could manage to get *us* some cellulose-assimilating protozoa, they would be doing a great service to humanity who is already viewing the food situation of the future with dismay. I see no real reason why, in the long future, it should not come about; in which case we would be able to eat bread made of sawdust. There are those who say we do so already, but if so it is wasted effort on the part of the bakers who do not supply us with the protozoa to cope with it.

The termite-protozoa partnership is simple enough in execution. The termites chew and swallow the wood, at first for the sole benefit of the protozoa inside them who imbibe it and live on it. But amongst a large population there are always a number of deaths and in one termite protozoa are dying off continually. It is these corpses that give the termite its meal of pre-digested wood.

There is nothing unusual in this. We, who cannot eat grass, can eat and digest the corpses of bullocks, etc., who feed on it. Our digestion in general also depends to a certain extent on foreign organisms inside us. The only difference is that we possess no agent or intermediary that will give us the slightest assistance in eating *wood*. If we cannot acquire protozoa, then cannot we raise a domestic animal that will feed on cellulose and which we can kill and eat? The nearest answer so far is the goat, but actually the goat is no answer at all. It may, and does, eat paper and clothes hung out to dry, but it gets no more nutriment from them than the ostrich gets from nails, and pieces of glass. It can almost live on bark, but green bark contains little more cellulose than a cabbage, and its consumption kills the tree that is manufacturing the cellulose. The nearest man can get at present to having a satisfactory and filling meal of wood second-hand is to eat the termites themselves as they emerge in the flying form from the termite hills, or to eat toadstools, such as the "Oyster Toadstool" (*Pleurotus ostreatus*) that grow on dead trees or stumps and which (the Oyster Toadstool) is delicious when slowly cooked. And man does this whenever he has the opportunity, but it is, of course, only nibbling at the problem.

Cleveland of Harvard University made a special study of the protozoa in termites. Experimenting with certain American species, he found that these termites possessed in vast numbers four kinds of protozoa, none of which are to be found in any other animal. The first, and by far the most numerous, are *Trichonympha*, then come *Leidyopsis*, *Trichomonas*, and *Steblomastix* (it is hardly necessary here to give their second names). Only the first two (together or alone) are necessary to enable the termite to digest wood, and if one or both are present the termite can live happily and indefinitely on that diet. The third, *Trichomonas*, by itself, is by no means so helpful; its unaided activities only enable the termite to live for about sixty days. The fourth, *Streblomastix*, is no use at all. In fact, it is as incapable of assimilating wood as the termite is itself, and, like the termite, lives on the good offices of the other three.

All this has been shown by experiment. If its protozoa are taken away and the termite is still fed on wood, the termite dies in about fifteen days. If the protozoa are restored artificially before that time, the termite continues its normal existence. The elimination of all the protozoa is accomplished by heat— a temperature of just over 36° C. kills the protozoa but leaves the termite unhurt.

Dealing with the various protozoa separately, of course, needs other methods, and these methods are starvation and oxygenation. Six days' fasting kills *Trichonympha* and leaves the other three. Eight days' fasting kills *Leidyopsis* and leaves the other two. On the other hand, twenty-four hours' oxygenation (oxygen being a slow poison) kills *Trichomonas* first and leaves the other three. And so on. So that the experimenter can deal separately, or in any desired combinations, with these minute organisms.

Comparatively recently, a German chemist startled the world by "fixing" nitrogen from the air, thus paving the way for an inexhaustible supply of nitrogen fertiliser, and incidentally dealing a mortal blow to the guano industry in Chile. This fixing of nitrogen was a feat hitherto thought to have been accomplished only by the roots of certain plants; leguminous plants such as beans and peas. We know now that another animal had forestalled the German, that animal being the white ant. The credit really goes to the protozoa (or other organisms) inside the white ant who, by means entirely unknown, fix atmospheric nitrogen in its food, thus forming protein, without which the white ant could never live on a diet of unadulterated wood however well digested by its assistants.

Once in the middle of winter I had to take over an old and neglected orchard. They were mostly plum trees, many being of prized gage varieties. Half of them, however, I was told were dead. To save time I would have liked to cut all the dead ones down before the spring, but if there is a quick way of telling a dead old tree from a live or half-live old tree in the middle of winter I do not know it. I was, however, able to get busy to a certain extent by the help of toadstools, and all the trees with any toadstools on them got the axe forthwith and were carted away and sawn up before spring showed me which others must be dealt with in a similar manner.

For certain fungi, like certain termites, must have wood that is dead, wood that is pure cellulose. But they go one better than termites in that they are able to assimilate this cellulose direct. Some of these toadstools, as I have said, can be eaten by man, so it would be strange if such growths had escaped the attention of termites. They can be grown underground in darkness, and they can digest wood. Needless to say, termites being termites, they did *not* escape attention, and several of the more advanced species make beds of fungus after the manner of the mushroom-growing ants. The beds are composed of chewed and partially digested wood, and the fungus that is grown—again as with the ants—is a special kind, raised by them and found nowhere else. The same problems that confronted the ants confronted the termites: definite conditions of moisture and temperature, and the necessity of keeping the beds sterilised and clear of alien growths. There is one difference, however; the teeming millions of the large termite cities cannot all live on fungi, they could never raise enough to go round. So, with most species, the food is reserved for the young, for the king and queen, and for the pampered alates. (We shall meet the alates later.)

Workers, skilled workers who probably do little else, sow the beds and tend and raise the toadstools. Other workers carry the food to the rightful recipients. And delicious though this food is (judging by the way soldiers and others beg for some) the workers have never been observed to eat any themselves. Nature does not call for such self-sacrifice from the workers of the mushroom ants.

So much for a survey of the activities of termites; it is time now to enter a termite city and meet the inhabitants in person. This meeting ought to be preceded by some account of the different species, but that is impossible in a single chapter. There are 1,500 known species and probably an infinite number of unknown species. The latest list takes two large volumes. It is compiled by an American, Thomas E. Snyder.[1] America, is, in fact, the fountain-head of our present-day knowledge of termites, even the British Museum (Natural History) send their more difficult problems to America for elucidation by the experts there.

The various termite species do not vary much in general appearance, but they vary in habit and development. At the bottom of the scale we get species possessing nests of but a few individuals ekeing out a hazardous and primitive existence: at the top we get the great termitaries of highly developed insects whose internal economy so amazed the first investigators. Mankind, although he possesses but one species, is rather similarly differentiated: he has at the bottom of the scale *his* undeveloped types—his half-dozen or so Bushmen, for instance, living in a clearing in an African forest, and by progressive stages he has his Londoners and New Yorkers. This chapter deals with the more highly developed species of termites.

In London or New York or any city it would be impossible for any gigantic naturalist from a different sphere who was studying mankind as we are trying to study termites to make

[1] "A Catalogue of the Termites (Isoptera) of the World" by Thomas E. Snyder. Published by the Smithsonian Institute, U.S.A., in 1949.

a list of the types of humanity found therein. There would be too many of similar appearance engaged in different pursuits. Without a doubt it is the same in a termite city. We can, however, spot the main types, for termites, like ants, instead of issuing varying uniforms to their public servants, issue them with differently sized and shaped bodies.

Here is a list of the different castes in a termitary:

(1) The Queen.
(2) The King.
(3) The Large Soldier.
(4) The Small Soldier, or Policeman.
(5) The Worker.
(6) (Not always present.) The Alate, or "flying" termite.[1]

Let us examine the various castes.

(1) and (2). *The King and Queen.* Of all insects, indeed of all animals except man, only termites have a properly constituted king as well as queen. These two live together in a great royal apartment for from five to ten years. The king, however, is more of a consort than a king. He has no say in affairs of state. Neither has the queen, but the queen is the central figure and without her—even ignoring her breeding duties—the whole state would collapse.

It is a huge apartment with a majestic domed roof in which she lies. Any apartment that contained her would have need to be large for she is the size of a gherkin, four to five inches long, but her apartment gives ample further space. The workers compare with her in size as rabbits compare with an elephant. We have spoken of these gargantuan queens before when dealing with ants, but none of them can compare with the queen of the termites. She is a greasy yellow cylinder, so fat that she seems on the point of bursting, and she is, of course, incapable of movement. On her accession to the throne the queen is given a banquet. It is a prolonged banquet, for it lasts until her death. Day and night, year in, year out, the queen never stops eating. Oil runs down her

---

[1] It is interesting to note that the arrangement is rather similar to that of a chess-board. Leaving out the alates, who are not permanent residents, there is a King and a Queen; the Policeman represents the Bishop, the Large Soldier the Knight, the Termitary the Castle, while the Workers represent the row of Pawns in front. We even have the possibility of one of the "pawns" winning through and becoming a queen.

towering sides as, with us, perspiration runs down the face of a gross eater.

At one end, where the head, thorax and legs appear as a mere pimple on a balloon, relays of hundreds of workers are busy feeding pap into the small mouth. At the other end an equal number are engaged in collecting, cleaning, and taking away the eggs that issue with monotonous regularity. On either side workers are busy licking clean the bulging, oily flanks, and their eager attention to duty would seem to indicate that they are not averse to the taste of this royal sweat.

Nevertheless, by virtue of size and immobility alone, there is a certain amount of dignity in the mountainous, motionless form. There is no dignity about the king. It is hard for any male to look dignified when in the company of a female about a thousand times his size, and the termite king does not improve matters by spending his time lying beneath his wife's belly or prancing gaily about on her back in an "I'm the king of the castle" attitude. Yet these two started married life the same size, indistinguishable the one from the other, small, agile, svelt, and prettily winged. Even now, in spite of her changed appearance, he is a devoted consort and rears up in an attitude of defiance when any danger appears to threaten her. He, too, is fed on the fat of the land, so we may assume that he pays for his keep by fertilising at intervals the queen's eggs.

Let us take a look at the rest of the apartment. We are able to do so only through the infinite patience (combined with luck) of one or two observers. The royal apartment invariably lies deep down in the heart of the vast region made up of the towering hill above and the extensive galleries below. And all is made of cement. To dig out a queen is difficult enough and could never be done with an ordinary spade; to find her chamber, insert a glass window, and study what goes on under natural conditions is, you will appreciate, almost impossible. Yet it has been done.

We have the great vaulted apartment with, in the centre, the queen lying like a stranded whale attended by hundreds of workers. Farther away, a procession of ordinary citizens is circulating round her. It is evident that the queen is always "on view" to the public, who are allowed to file round just as with us the public are allowed to file round the body of a dead monarch lying in state. Keeping order, are numbers of police who jostle the crowd along and prevent them from drawing too close to the royal form. Even so, now and then, an individual from the moving throng will manage to break through and try to rush up and touch the queen's body.

Still farther off, beyond the perambulating sight-seers, motionless, heads down as if in silent reverence, pincers open at the ready, stand a detachment of the big guards, facing outwards. They form a circle, or rather an oval, and there is a space between each guard. Not a movement comes from any of them, and their statue-like immobility is in striking contrast to the restless crowd behind.

When, after many hours, the time comes for the changing of the watch, a fresh party of guards, about twenty in number, marches out from one of the apertures and its members take their positions and assume their postures in the spaces between the guards on duty. The latter then come to life and march off.

Because the queen never ceases to eat, it does not follow that she is a self-indulgent glutton. She has to turn out eggs continuously and she cannot do this without *food*. A sausage machine has to be fed continuously but one cannot compare the queen with a sausage machine which merely turns out in a different shape exactly what has been put into it. Eggs are concentrated and converted food. Even so, certain observers say that the queen termite lays an egg a second, or thirty million a year. Marais says he "knows" she lays "on an average" 150,000 eggs every twenty-four hours (nearly two a second), though *how* he knows he does not say. Escherich puts the output at 30,000 a day, which is about ten million a year. It is obvious that no one really knows, but we can safely say that she lays two or three million eggs a year.

The eggs, when cleaned, are carefully carried away to be incubated under special conditions of temperature and moisture. Whether the queen, or workers, can control the type of nymph that will emerge; whether, that is, they can decide what an egg is to become—a worker, a policeman, a soldier, or an alate—we do not know. Probably the workers *have* some control, by feeding.

The queen's life terminates as soon as her egg output begins to fail. Like some board of directors of a business firm studying a chart that shows a falling output and giving orders for the dismissal of the manager, the mysterious power that rules in the termitary notes the decline in the number of eggs produced and orders the execution of the queen. She is killed by starvation. Her food is cut off. That, one would think, would be sufficient to kill her by shock alone, and perhaps it is in some cases. Maeterlink suggests that termites starve their queen to death so that none need feel directly responsible for the dreadful deed of regicide. This is probably crediting termites with finer feelings than they actually possess. Starvation is the official method of execution. Surplus soldiers are killed off in this way. Efficiency, not sentimentality, is the termite's creed.

When the queen is dead she is eaten (and almost licked to death before she dies!). Nothing goes to waste in the termite city. All dead bodies, every scrap of excrement, is eaten. This need occasion no virtuous horror on our part. Most of us eat dead bodies every day and one of our major problems at the present time is that we cannot get enough of them. We dislike cannibalism but a number of our own species practise it as the ordinary thing even now. With the rest of us the taboo is partly self-protection and partly finnickiness, a finnickiness that time and time again has not stood the test of hard conditions. As for excrement, we should get very short supplies of bread, vegetables, milk and meat if we did not eat it second or third hand. Amongst termites excrement is eaten and re-eaten. This is not just a repulsive habit, it is a necessity. The protozoa do not complete the process of wood digestion in the body of one host: the intestines of a termite are not long enough. So the half-digested wood is passed on to another termite, and so on. This, as Haldane points out, is similar to what occurs in our own bodies and corresponds to the passage of food through our intestines where one segment of the intestine passes on its partially digested food to the next. The termite method, however, is far more thorough, and the final residue is sweet and clean and can be used in making mortar. Thus termites are able to live hygienically in a sealed-in castle and to operate the most efficient and economical sewage plant yet known.

Obviously termites do not kill off a queen without having another one ready to take her place. With ants, this successor is one who has flown and mated, and at one period of their history there is no doubt that this was the sole method of the termites too. But the hazards of the marriage flight are so great that the method is not dependable. With ants the flight, though uncontrolled, is adequate enough in spite of the losses, but termites are sinking as it were deeper into the ground and sealing themselves in and losing contact with open spaces. The termite city became so vast, so elaborate, so scientifically controlled that one is not surprised at the termite viewing with dismay the one and only factor that jeopardised this city's permanency. To have to trust to luck for the replacement every five years or so of the source of everything—the queen! *Some*thing had to be done if the termite was to continue with its underground plans. There are termite cities to-day which may well have been in existence in the days of Cleopatra. Such antiquity is not attained by a succession of lucky chances. We do not know when or how, but at some period termites succeeded in making reserve queens (and kings) out of termites that never left the nest. This, of course, was side-stepping nature, but termites are amongst those who thrive not so much in spite of but *because* of nature's apparent wish to exterminate them.

All we know about the process is that certain of the nymphs become substitute queens or kings, and there is evidence that even an ordinary worker can be so converted. About thirty of them as a rule are kept in one "room," ready at any time to be invested with the purple. Needless to say, the bulk of them never receive that honour.

The whole scheme sounds so ideal and simple that one wonders why termites go to the infinite trouble and expense of raising and dispatching into the air their multitudes of fattened alates, but perhaps these artificially manufactured substitutes cannot permanently replace the genuine article. Perhaps a queen and a king that have flighted naturally must be introduced from time to time. It is obvious in any case that termites are in the process of becoming a very underground people and would like to sever their connection with the clean, cold, fresh air above. But that is a matter we have earmarked for future discussion.

(3) *The Large Soldier*, or Guardsman, or, simply, "Soldier," is a giant compared with the workers or even the policemen. He is valiant in war and formidably armed. He has a huge armour-plated head which accounts for more than half his length and a great pair of pincers that can draw blood from a man's thigh, but, unfortunately for him, his behind part, the abdomen, is as defenceless as a ripe currant. So when, as often happens, the emergency call goes and he has to rush out to defend the city, he is in the position of a soldier who has hastily donned a helmet and a cuirass but has paraded still in his pyjama trousers. So if the termite guardsman turns and runs he is very vulnerable, but he rarely does turn and run, though he frequently beats an orderly retreat.

At home, in times of peace, he is treated rather like Kipling's "Tommy Atkins." He seems to have no functions to perform except for (with a few) the ceremonial guard duties in the royal palace, and mouches about begging busy workers for food and as often as not being refused. "*It's Tommy this, an' Tommy that, an' Tommy, go away. But it's ' please to walk in front, sir ' when——*"

Breaches in the cement walls of the city may be made by specially equipped mammals (such as the ant-bear and the scaley ant-eater), also by the termites themselves at flighting time. For such breaches the heredity foes of the termites, the ants, are always on the look-out. They try to swarm in, and the guards rush out to stop them. Behind the guards run massed bodies of masons, whose job it is to build a wall to close the gap before the enemy can get there. They are superintended by a small rearguard of the main body of guards, who act as overseers and see to it that the work is done at a pace that can only be described as frenzied. (In human circles such overseers would result in a nation-wide strike.) The number of masons that rush up and get to work is enormous. They resemble a football scrum. If men in such numbers tried to build a wall they would never be able to lay a single brick.

But social insects have learned to work in numbers and to co-ordinate, and the wall rises rapidly. Each mason carries a grain of sand and lays it in "mortar." The mortar is fluid which the mason ejects from its mouth or sometimes its anus.

Meanwhile the guards are engaging the enemy and fighting a delaying action. Soon they make a slow retreat and, fighting all the time, gradually approach the wall, which by now is all but completed: there is just a narrow gap at the top. The guards pour through it, the gap is sealed and the thwarted enemy left outside. That is what *should* happen if everything goes according to plan. The enemy now goes home, carrying the dead bodies of the guards they have killed.

Smeathman was very intrigued with the behaviour of these large soldiers, and often made breaches into termitaries himself to see what happened. I will quote his observations on one such occasion:

". . . The labourers who had fled on the first alarm, are now seen hastening to repair the breach, every one with a burden of ready-tempered mortar in its mouth. This they stick on to the breach with such wonderful celerity and order that, although thousands, nay, millions, seem employed, yet they never embarrass one another. While the labourers are thus engaged, the soldiers retire, save here and there one, who saunters about, never touching the mortar. One, in particular, places itself close to the part undergoing repair; it may be seen turning leisurely on all sides, and every now and then, at an interval of a minute or two, lifting up its head, and with its forceps beating upon the building and making a vibrating noise, on which a loud hiss, apparently from the whole body of labourers, issues from withinside the dome and all the subterranean passages: that it comes from the labourers is very evident, for all these may be seen hastening at every such signal, redoubling their pace, and working as fast again. Attack the nest again, and with a loud hiss the labourers disappear, and the soldiers rush out; so that the experiment yields constantly the same result, of labourers at work and soldiers rushing to battle, the duties of each being as distinct as night and day."

When the breach is very large or the attacking ants very numerous it may not be possible to build a wall in time. In this case the defending guards fight to the last termite without attempting to make the usual "according to plan" retreat. The masons too (under the soldier overseers) seal up the wall completely (if they have time), thus making the fate of the defending guards doubly certain. If this cannot be done the attackers, after killing the guards, swarm over the uncompleted rampart and slaughter the fleeing workers on the other side. But if the termitary is large and well established it is unlikely that any attack by ants will penetrate very far. Farther inside, other ramparts are being built and fresh guards coming forward. Also the attackers themselves can have no reason to go on, once they have enough corpses to carry home. They are concerned only with supplementing the larder; they are not in search of slaves or territorial expansion or honour or glory.

When a detachment of termite guards is overcome by ants not all the guards are killed. Some suffer a worse fate and are deliberately maimed and carried back alive to the ants' nest.

Many ants in Africa, particularly the Matabele and Stink ants, prey, when they can, almost entirely on termites, and so must be considered very useful to mankind. But they have no dealings with those cement erections popularly known as "ant-hills" unless a breach has been made first by some other agency. Their normal prey consists of those less advanced termites that nest in the ground and make no castles (and are generally far more destructive to man than the castle-building species). This is because they are quite incapable of penetrating an "ant-hill," whose cement defies even a spade and can withstand the direct fall of a massive tree. And rain makes little difference, for the cement is practically waterproof.

Both the Matabele and Stink ants are powerful and large (the workers are three-quarters of an inch long), but even they cannot overcome termite guards except in the open. It is known, and has been verified by experiments, that from behind long apertures a few guards can hold off strong attacks by ants for hours, and if necessary for days.

Some species do not make earthen tunnels but go out into the open at night in long processions to get their food—which is often not dead wood, but the seeds of trees, etc. The guards on these occasions are in full control and march on either side

and are on the alert for danger and give orders exactly after
the manner of the officers of the Driver ants.

Other species will sometimes emerge from their tunnels
even in daylight and proceed for a short distance in the open
before taking to earth again. Smeathman witnessed this with
the species *Termes viarum.* He saw (to his great surprise) the
head of a marching column of termites suddenly emerge from
the ground.

"Their march was orderly and very rapid, and their
numbers prodigious. They were divided into two columns
sixteen abreast, composed chiefly of labourers, with here and
there a huge soldier, that appeared like an ox among sheep.
Other soldiers kept a foot or two from the column, apparently
acting as videttes, appointed to guard against surprise. Others
mounted the plants or blades of grass which flanked the main
bodies, and, thus elevated a foot or more, looked over and
controlled the proceedings of the moving multitude. They
turned their heads in the different directions whence danger
might arise, and every now and then they struck their forceps
against the plant and produced the ticking sound already
mentioned, to which the whole army answered simultaneously
with a loud hiss and quickened their pace. After proceeding
thus for about fifteen paces, the two columns united and sunk
into the earth."

The stream continued to flow on for *more than an hour,*
during which time Smeathman watched their movements.
The rear was brought up by a large body of the big soldiers.

The number of guards to the rest of the community is
roughly in the proportion of 1 to 100. This proportion,
obviously, cannot always be maintained: a series of heavy
raids from outside for instance, may reduce it even to the
point of danger. Termites then seem able to breed guards
quickly, or rather in greater quantity. And so a period of
peace following a period of raids may result in there being
too many guards, for guards are non-productive and cost the
city not only food but labour, for each one of them has to be
specially fed by a worker.

More or less the same problem confronts *us.* Peace after
war leaves us with large bodies of non-productive troops on

our hands. There is this difference, however; surplus soldiers with us can be returned to civilian life and join the productive ranks, surplus termite soldiers cannot be so converted—except in a dreadful way, by killing them and then eating them. The eating, however, is merely an automatic process on the no-waste principle. Surplus guards are not killed for food, they are killed because they are surplus.

So when a colony finds itself in possession of a super-abundant army the edict goes out that (say) twenty per cent are to be destroyed. They are destroyed by starvation, and what is remarkable is that the powers must *select* the individuals that are to be thus destroyed. These, in the presence of their fellow guardsmen, are refused food.

How do we know this? Certainly not through studying termites in their natural surroundings: one could not dig into a termite hill and study so intricate and prolonged a process. It is artificial experiments that give us the answer and there is no reason to suppose that the answer is not correct.

These experiments have been made with small colonies of captive termites, and are conducted on the following lines. We have two colonies, colony "A" and colony "B." The colony "A" has so many guards, and these are in the right proportion of about 1 to 100 of the other inmates. These guards are all marked with, shall we say, red. An equal number of guards are then taken from colony "B," marked with green, and introduced to colony "A." The introduction consists of just dropping them in. The result is sometimes similar to mixing the grey and white packets of Sedlitz Powders, and several guards may be killed. On the other hand, the green guards may be accepted without much fuss. When they have been accepted they become part of the family and the workers feed both red and green guards without discrimination.

But soon the power that rules the termitary, even so small a one as this, discovers that there are too many guards; that the proportion is not right. The order is given that a certain number be eliminated, and eliminated they are.

We know all that, of course, and we also know that definite individuals are put on the proscribed list, but in an experiment like this an interesting point presents itself: which of the guards will the colony select for slaughter? In a normal nest the problem must be a difficult one; none of the guards have done any wrong, all are exemplary soldiers, yet *pro bono publicae* certain of them must be executed. Which to choose? But in the artificially created soldier superabundance of these experiments the choice would seem to be easy: kill off the alien guards. They were not asked to intrude and it is their presence that has caused the undesirable state of affairs that exists. And yet, strange to say, the unfortunates that are starved to death come from both the red and the green guards almost equally.

Of course, with the social insects, acceptance of aliens *means* acceptance. They indulge in massacres at the beginning— often very bloody massacres—but not afterwards. Accepted aliens are, as it were, Roman Citizens, with full rights. Subsequent retaliation, as so often happens with us, will never happen with them. So termites kill and preserve impartially their own guards and those of another clan. It may be that after acceptance the colony cannot distinguish the aliens from their own people; the same smell, or whatever sense they use for recognition purposes; but this is improbable, especially so soon after the union.

The pincers of the guards are strong and effective, yet certain species have evolved for their guards a different sort of apparatus and one working on a different principle. Life is like that; species must not relax, they must keep abreast with the times, or, preferably, ahead of them. The makers of this (presumably) new invention is a family called Eutermes and their guards are called Nasute soldiers. These, instead of the normal armoured thorax and big pincers, appear to have put on what looks to be a sort of elongated gasmask. They present an almost laughable appearance, though their enemy ants find nothing funny at all in the device. The mask ends in a nozzle through which a liquid is squirted. The nature of this liquid varies with different species. Some species squirt a pungent, acrid and corroding fluid, others a liquid gum which hardens and clogs the movements of any attacking ant and indeed puts that ant completely out of action for a long time, if not permanently. Even the powerful Matabele

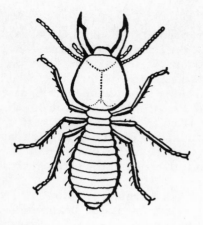

Termite Soldier

Termite Nasute Soldier

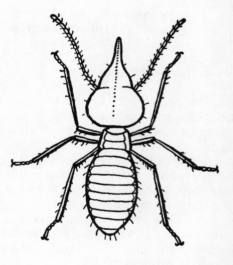

ants when confronted with such guards usually remember that they have other and more pressing business elsewhere.

(4) *The Policemen*, or Minor Soldiers. The functions of this caste are rather obscure. Some species do not possess police at all, others have two of different sizes. Admittedly they often join with the workers in doing ordinary routine work, but there is no sense in breeding differently-sized termites to help do jobs which the ordinary worker can do better. For the rest they run about in a fussy, officious way and probably *do* keep a certain amount of order amongst crowds; in fact, we have seen them doing so in the Royal Apartment. I cannot believe that there are any dangerous criminals amongst the workers, so these termite police must have an easier job than the police of *our* large towns. There *are* dangerous criminals in all termite cities, that beg, rob and murder in the streets, but these undesirables are not termites, but intruders. They live in the outskirts of the city and the police, so far as can be ascertained, never go near them. Their duty, they feel, lies amongst the more orderly inhabitants.

Still, these minor soldiers must be of *some* use or the authorities would not allow them to draw their rations.

(5) *The Workers.* Small, timid, blind, defenceless, these eaters of oak and sandstone are as fragile as boiled semolina. Everything except the fighting is done by them, the nursing, digging, house-building, well-boring, temperature-regulating, moisture-regulating, gardening, foraging, cleaning, and the other things. In addition, they get the food for and feed individually at frequent intervals the whole of the rest of the community, probably numbering millions: the alates, the young, the soldiers, the king and queen. Observation tends to show that no worker ever rests at any time, day or night.

These manifold duties performed by so many indicates the presence of a controlling and organising power. Everything *must* run with the precision of an intricate machine. Otherwise there would be chaos. Who controls and organises? We shall deal with that question shortly, and having dealt with it will be no wiser than we were before.

(6) *The Alates.* These are the young males and females that

in due course develop wings and fly off. We will say no more about them for they figure conspicuously in the next section, which, if we were using headings in this chapter, would be called *The Flight*.

As the rainy season approaches, White Ants prepare for their annual folly. These miserly creatures who would consider the throwing away of a burnt matchstick wicked waste, who will starve a portion of their army to death because of the little food they eat, now invite the whole neighbourhood to a banquet. Man, beast, bird, insect, all are welcome. There is no stint, and the meat has been specially fattened beforehand on rich food. There is something wrong here. The internal economy of the termites would appear to have gone out of gear.

Near the top of an ant-hill (as termitaries are always called in Africa) and sometimes at the side as well, an opening is made which bristles with the heads of guards on the alert, as always, for danger. The weather is close, the sky overcast. It is probably evening and it may be raining when the guards withdraw and the winged male and female battalions burst out. It is a kind of volcanic eruption, but a controlled one; more of a procession, in fact. It is not, for example, the kind of exit swarming bees make, who always come out of the hive in a jammed hysterical mass like the patrons of a crowded cinema when the place catches fire. Each termite delays for a fraction of a second before it unfolds its untried wings. They issue in vast numbers but there is an almost imperceptible note of hesitation throughout the whole proceeding. One feels that some of them are being given a push from inside. At a distance the scene *does* have some resemblance to a volcano, for faint blue smoke seems to be issuing from the crater at the top of the hill and a pall of blue smoke seems to hang above.

Maeterlinck (not from personal observation) states that the whole thing is over in a few minutes. Some other naturalists have laid down that it lasts ten minutes. I have seen many of these flights, but only one from the beginning to the end and that one lasted quite half an hour.

Very pretty the creatures look as they dance away on their

new, large, gauzy wings—rather like mayfly, but with even less than a mayfly's expectation of life.

There is no mating in the air, nor, physically, on the surface of the ground later. The promiscuous and lascivious copulation of flying ants has no place in the decorous code of termites. Some termites fly a long distance, some a short. All, sooner or later, come down to earth where, like spoilt children already tired of a new and expensive toy, they run about seeking to rid themselves of their wings.

Meanwhile almost every creature in the neighbourhood that is not entirely herbivorous has tucked in its bib, so to speak, and got busy on the *plat du jour*, White Ant. Birds in the air, on the ground, dragon-flies, spiders, lizards, shrews, mice, rats, bats, mongooses, monkeys, baboons, and a whole host of the smaller carnivorae—all make a point of being present at the feast if they get to know about it in time.

Mankind, if in the vicinity, and, again, if he gets to know about it in time, is in the forefront of this motley assortment of diners. I had camped in the veld once on a hot, clammy afternoon and dug a trench round my tent, expecting rain, when two natives shot past at speed. Their mouths were open and their faces had the drawn look of Olympic sprinters, and I waited to see who or what was pursuing them. Nothing appeared, however, so I told a native constable to follow them. He returned after an interval and reported that white ants were coming out of a hill and that the natives were sitting there eating them. I went back with him. A termite hill about four feet high was erupting, and three natives were squatting over it picking up the insects as they came out and popping them into their mouths. Already that glazed look that indicates ecstasy combined with vague stomach discomfort was in their eyes, but they went on steadily, automatically. As I went back I met other natives coming along with calabashes and pieces of cloth with which to collect and store the insects swarming on the ground, for, in spite of being tapped at the fountain head, plenty were getting through.

I regret now that I never tasted white ants while I was in Africa and when my digestion was younger. I knew a prospector, a Scot, who invariably collected all he could. He fried them. They were delicious, he said. Smeathman was very fond of them too. He had them roasted in an iron pot over a gentle fire. In his time (and now, for all I know) the maggot of the palm-tree snoutbeetle (*Curculio palmarum*) used to be served at the luxurious tables of West Indian epicures, particularly the French, as "the greatest dainty of the Western World." Smeathman says that white ants are even better: sweeter, and not so fat and cloying. Yes, I am sorry I did not sample them; perhaps I will, even yet.

The flight over, the termites—no longer flying termites—can be seen running about on the ground in a state of confusion, and the ground itself is covered with shorn wings. A houseboat I used in China had a large glass skylight and on two occasions I woke up and, finding it dark, went to sleep again, to find later that I was late for work. The darkness had been caused by a thick carpet of flying termite wings deposited on the skylight during the night.

The termites that fall some distance from the hill are fewer and more easily studied. A female (though one cannot distinguish the sexes superficially) will move about and from time to time stand and raise her abdomen. She is sending out a message calling for a mate. A male invariably arrives, though by what sense he is called we do not know. We can only think of our own senses. Let us call it scent. It is not scent, it is more akin to radio. But never mind, whatever it is, it is answered, and sooner or later, by air or on foot, a male arrives.

It is said that the female does not always approve of the first arrival and summons others until she gets one she likes. It may be so, for these flying termites seem quite unaware of the gravity of their position. Having paired up the two indulge in a certain amount of courting. There is no union as yet; that is reserved for a later period—if such a period ever arrives.

What happens now is apparently simple and straightforward. The two dig a hole in the ground, mate, the female lays eggs, the eggs hatch, and the young are fed and looked after by the parents until they are of an age to "take over." And so the little hole in the ground becomes the starting-point of another great termitary.

At least, it *ought* to be like that, and many natural history

writers say that it *is* like that. But is it? Or are we taking
too much for granted and assuming that termites behave
like average ants? Some species no doubt are exceptions, but
with most no one has ever seen a couple even beginning to
dig a hole, or ever found them in a hole they have dug.

Even if they *did* dig a hole, consider the difficulties. Neither
of the couple can feed themselves, and if they could they
possess no protozoa to enable them to digest their food. That
is not, of course, an insuperable problem; we have seen mother
ants living on their tissues for long periods, but there are
further snags in the case of termites. The period of gestation
is usually a long one and fertilised eggs will not appear for
some time; it is doubtful if the king and queen would survive
even to the time the first eggs were laid. And what is this
particularly helpless young couple going to do about the
eggs? Termite eggs have to be cleaned and have to be kept in
artificial conditions of temperature and moisture. Nymphs
emerge from them and *they* have to have artificial conditions
too. Furthermore, they grow up very slowly and have to
have several moults before they become adult, during which
time they have to be cosseted and fed continually. It would
be months and months from the *egg* before there were any
children capable of giving their parents the slightest help or
ceasing to be a continual drain on them. With termites there
is no cocoon period which, with ants, gives the young mother
such a needed rest.

And so we find naturalists who state that—what with one
thing and another—*all* the winged termites who fly from the
ant-hill inevitably perish; that that terrific effort is as much
use to the termitary as a firework display is to us, and far
more costly.

That is a rather sweeping statement. What is more feasible
is the theory that a few couples *do* survive and are taken in by
other termitaries and there properly looked after and held, as
it were, in store. The objection has been made that termites
are underground insects and do not run about on the surface
and so could never meet any of the survivors of a flight. But
since, in a very short time, termites found my saddle lying in
the open in daylight (a more difficult condition to them than
dark) it ought not to take them long to find, at night, a young

royal couple, who are probably sending out radio messages in any case.

This Marriage Flight, this *Dance of Death* as cinema captions would probably call it, is a relic of the past when termites were all winged and all had eyes and all flirted and mated in the open with the careless abandon of butterflies. Later they took to a subterranean existence to avoid their many enemies. To avoid the *great enemy*, the Ant, some naturalists have said. But the earth was just the one place where the ant could get at them—unless in those days the ant also was aerial. So it was probably *after* they had taken to earth that the ant became *the* enemy. Ants undoubtedly played a big part in the termites' evolution, and but for ants man might now find them more accessible and more easy to destroy. To avoid ants termites dug deeper and deeper and learned to make hills and cities of hard, specially manufactured cement. It may be, too, that it was because of ants that they selected a food which would not bring them into competition with ants. Indeed it is possible that termites owe their present very advanced position amongst insects entirely to ants. Enemies in the long run are sometimes more useful than friends.

Termites are probably in the course of severing their connection with the upper world altogether and becoming completely underground, except, of course, for their earthen tunnels to food. They can already breed kings and queens that never see the open and later on, no doubt, as we have said before, will dispense with the flight. There are indications even now: many termitaries do not make an annual affair of the flight; they postpone it for one, two or more years (and sometimes keep their alates waiting all that time!).

If it is asked how termites propose to start new colonies abroad if they abandon the flight, the answer is that the flight is ineffective for that purpose already. There are other ways of spreading. They often throw up new nests from underground that are connected for the time being by passage-ways to the mother city. And if they wished they could always carry a young couple through runways and plant them out, as it were, in a hole, together with an adequate number of workers to feed them and bring up and attend to their brood.

The flight in fact is an anachronism, but perhaps it introduces
a touch of colour and excitement into the drab round of
slavery, and perhaps on that account they feel loath to
abandon it.

When trekking in the dry season in Africa knowledge of
the direct route to one's objective is often a secondary con-
sideration. For as the dry season draws to its close it is unlikely
that one will be able to follow the direct route. At each stage
one must ascertain the locality of the "next water" and this
may entail a roundabout and zigzag journey. It is important,
too, that one's knowledge be up to date, for a pool that existed
a week ago may have become like a brick-kiln in seven days.
Carelessness in this respect may be fatal, for at that season one
is subjected to an atmosphere so dry that it seems to have
gone mad with thirst itself and tries savagely to suck from
living bodies the water it can no longer get from earth or
sky.

In such conditions travellers hurrying over the baked
terrain from one rare water source to another are unlikely
to give much attention to the great obelisks they pass that
mark the dwelling-places of White Ants. Still less are they
likely to wonder how the inhabitants inside are faring. If
they did give them a thought they would conclude that the
inhabitants must be dead and dried up long ago.

But the inhabitants are *not* dead. They ought to be, for no
insect needs water more than a termite. A large termitary
must use buckets-ful a day. Consider. The termites themselves
are little else than small bags of water. Their runways on the
surface are made of wet mud in the face of high evaporation,
they build continually with wet cement, their fungus gardens
die out if not kept moist, and the whole city, for some reason,
has to have an atmosphere so moisture-laden that it resembles
a kitchen on washing day and will dim a glass if the hill is
opened up.

Where do the inhabitants of these ant-hills *get* all this
water in such conditions?

Although many missionaries in Africa have been prominent
naturalists and have made important contributions to our
knowledge, the bulk of those I met were strangely indiffer-

ent to the wild life around them. Livingstone, however, the greatest missionary and the greatest explorer of this era, in spite of his many preoccupations, was also a naturalist and the problem of the white ants in the dry season did not escape his notice. Indeed he was the first, apparently, to realise that white ants, at certain times of the year, were doing the impossible and getting water in places where no water was. Eventually he came to the startling conclusion that, since there was no other explanation, white ants *must* possess the secret of combining the oxygen of the air with hydrogen and getting their water that way. Man, of course, can now do this, but only as an interesting experiment by an electric explosion in a bottle by which he gets about one drop of water, not at all a practical method. This theory of Livingstone's must not be entirely ruled out: termites, remember, can "fix" (indirectly) the nitrogen of the air. But there is an alternative solution which, although almost as incredible, has a certain amount of confirmation behind it.

The earth may be baked to a cinder in the dry season but cattle can be watered by sinking a well in the right spot. This well, however, will probably have to descend at least a hundred feet. Do termites get their water by sinking tunnels of that depth through hard and rocky soil? It seems unlikely. Surely it would take them years and every wet season might obliterate their efforts! And yet they *do* get water somewhere. That is the fact that has to be kept in mind.

Then why, someone once asked me, do not investigators find *out* if they *do* make these tunnels? Naturalists are expected to find out a lot of things but this is asking over-much. Consider the position of a naturalist who, in grilling sun, tried to follow a termite tunnel going down 100 feet in soil the consistency of brick! If he got as far as six feet he would have done remarkably well and would need a lot of water himself! And a straight shaft would be useless: any termite tunnel would be oblique and would curve and wind about to avoid stones and rock.

Even so, we have some data on the matter. In Bechuanaland, Wessels twice saw in wells canals made by termites to "incredible depths." Later, in Waterburg (definitely the wrong name on this occasion), another naturalist, Marais, obtained further evidence. It was the year of an exceptional drought. Long-established orange groves died out. Stock died. The earth had the appearance of having been put in a hot oven and forgotten. Marais was staying at the farm of a Mr. van Rooyen, and Mr. van Rooyen decided to sink another well to try and help relieve the situation.

Incidentally, Marais had been busy pottering about and opening up "ant-hills." In one case he had penetrated six feet and found the queen's chamber. In spite of the drought, everything was working smoothly. The queen was as bloated as ever, the air in the termitary was moist, the fungus gardens watered. Termites, apparently, were the only creatures in that district that were happy and normal.

On the farm there was a clump of bushes that remained green, in striking contrast to the dead vegetation everywhere else, and van Rooyen thought that this would be a good spot to sink his well. He called in a water diviner and the water diviner confirmed his opinion. There was water there, he said.

Of course, green bushes of certain kinds do not necessarily get their greenness from water in the earth; they may be living on their stored-up sap. There are several trees in the African veld for instance that, towards the end of the dry season when conditions are at their worst, burst unexpectedly into flower and perfume all the air around. In this they are unaided by any water, below or above. They accomplish the miracle on their sap and rely on the rains coming before that sap is exhausted. They are trees that have specialised themselves to a difficult environment.

Anyway, the water diviner said that there was water under the green bushes and that the water was only 25 feet down.

Digging started. But at 25 feet there was no water, and at 40 feet the earth was just as dry as it had been on the surface. The project was abandoned. But at the bottom of the pit Marais discovered a termite boring passing on an inclined plane to some place farther off and lower down.

The termitary responsible for this boring was about 30 feet away from the green bushes, which would make it about 50 feet from the bottom of the shaft van Rooyen had dug, though the actual runway would curve and probably be double that distance. The runway, or boring, was in use and crowded with traffic. By marking some of the workers with dye, Marais found that it took them half an hour to travel from the bottom of his shaft to farther depths for (presumably) water, and back again. Incidentally, he found that his marked workers worked not only all day but all night as well, and then all day and night after that; that, in fact, they never ceased to work. Though, of course, in that drought, getting water must have been an emergency job.

If that inclined shaft had been sunk by the termites to get water (and it is difficult to imagine what other purpose it could have had), then they knew where the nearest permanent underground water was. And it obviously was not under the green bushes, but much farther off and much lower down than 40 feet. And every bit of excavated soil would have to be taken to the top. It is almost incredible. But it is either that or Dr. Livingstone's theory.

It comes almost as a relief to know that even termites have their limitations. Some perhaps cannot sink a shaft deep enough, at any rate some termitaries *do* die out from lack of water.

It is obvious, as we have said before, that work in a termite city is co-ordinated. The millions work on their jobs, each knowing what it has to do and when it has to do it. While masons rush out to repair a breach in the outer walls, the changing of the guard goes on sedately in the palace far away, and somewhere else workers project a bridge over a chasm to make a short cut for increasing traffic.[1] And so on. Everything is under control. Therefore there is a controlling power, a governing body.

Who does govern?

That there is no visual sign of any governor or body of governors means nothing. How could there be? A monster

---

[1] The roads or galleries going from the bottom to the top of a termite hill are arranged spiral fashion to make the ascent easier for the workers. Across the chasm between, bridges are frequently made to provide short cuts. These are not excavated out of the earth, but projected from one side to the other. Smeathman measured one and found it to be 10 inches in length, half an inch in width, and quarter of an inch in thickness.

gazing at the crowds in London would hardly be likely to detect the Prime Minister or any of his Cabinet. He would see the soldiers and the policemen and the workers, and might. if lucky, see the Queen and her consort—which is just what *we* see in a termitary.

If there is a government, from what class does it come? Workers, soldiers, queen, king? Certainly not the last two. Soldiers? Well, they direct workers when assaults are made and take charge of expeditions, but it is a far step from this for a few of them to be the brains of the community. Workers? In a way they rule already; theirs is the hand that rocks the cradle and also holds the key of the pantry. There *might* be super-workers capable of directing affairs generally. What it amounts to is that we are just wasting our time trying to discover the nature of the power that rules.

But certain observers have not been content to leave it like that. Mankind hates a mystery and insists on explaining it. This is quite in order, and very creditable to man, but there are two sorts of explanations that are not explanations. The first is to give the phenomenon a long name, and the second is to compare it with something else even more mysterious. Marais of South Africa (who found the termite canal) took the latter course and announced that he had got the solution. *A termitary was like a human body except that it lacked locomotion.*

A human (or any other) body, as we know, works automatically. The owner has no say about his inside. The liver pours out bile when needed, the glands ditto with secretions, but they never consult him. The treatment of a cut finger involves complicated processes and the mustering of corpuscles and chemical agents which, if he knew about it, would make the owner of the cut finger gape with surprise. When he gets measles he has no say in the direction of his own troops of corpuscles that are waging a major battle inside him. When he swallows a mouthful of food *he* does not have to plan and execute all the shunting and changing of points that are necessary if that mouthful is to reach its right destination and not choke him to death. In fact, all the man is asked to do is to eat and drink, and he has to be told by the powers within him when to do even that.

For the human body is a complicated collection of different

organs, etc., giving and receiving orders and messages and working together in a co-ordinated way. Therefore Marais decided that he had at last solved the problem. *That* was how a termite nest functioned also.

He worked it all out—so far as he was able with the limited termite types at his disposal. The big soldiers were the white corpuscles, the workers the red corpuscles—also the mouth and the teeth. The queen was the brain. The fungus gardens were the digestive organs, and the flights of winged males and females were the discharging spermatozoa and ova of the human body.

I put it shortly. Marais went to a lot more detail. The earthen runways, for instance, were the arteries and the running workers the blood. Etc. He has it all in his book, *The Soul of the White Ant.* Incidentally, in evolving his thesis, he made the most extraordinary statements. Amongst other things he said that no individual termite ever feels pain, but any pain to an individual is felt by the nest as a whole; that when a colony's water supply disappears and the inmates are dying of thirst, any suffering is felt only in the queen's chamber!

Actually, Marais might just as well have compared his termite nest with a motor car and got himself just as far. A car, too, has an inside that runs by itself through the agency of its component parts. Its sparking plugs spark at a controlled time, its carburettor regulates the right supply of air and petrol, its pump feeds fuel, and a host of parts and gadgets are so co-ordinated that the whole works harmoniously. And here again, as often as not, the owner is ignorant of what is going on inside. All he has to do is to feed the thing with oil and petrol, and even then gauges tell him when to do it.

This "explanation by comparison" is really just a game and can go on endlessly. For instance, why should it be limited to the termites and social insects? What about ourselves? Our own cities are quite well organised and run with co-ordination. This organisation also might equally well be compared with our own insides. And the human inhabitants of these cities, with their more varied duties and functions, would provide a better analogy for anyone who cared to bother to work it all out.

Maeterlinck held the same theory—if a comparison can be called a theory—and I think he was the first to publish it. Marais's biographer, however, contends that Marais thought of it first and had it all worked out and written down. I do not think either of them need have worried. Their claim to fame rests on surer ground. It is not by means of remote analogies that we shall discover the nature of the power that rules in termitaries and hives.

But destructive criticism gets us nowhere. It is easy to knock down a sand castle but not so easy to build a new and better and firmer one. *Is* there any clue to the problem? Careful investigators claim to have found that messages and (presumably) orders are sent out by a sort of wireless from certain centres in a termite nest, and that these messages can penetrate stone and cement. They claim also to have found out the maximum distance for the reception of such messages. And this may be true. Certainly bees, when inside the hive, have a similar type of almost instant communication. I myself am sure that these investigators are right and that messages *are* sent out in this way, but, alas, it does not solve the problem. Granted that messages and orders are sent—who sends them? Who, indeed!

At the beginning of this chapter I explained that it would only be possible in the space of one chapter to deal with a representative termite of the higher type. Do not suppose, however, that the other so-called lower types are of less interest. Many of them are highly intelligent and much more destructive to man. They are not just dead wood eaters; they chop up and carry off the farmer's crops, his hay, and the thatch from his buildings. So that a farmer may have at the same time one species of termite removing the beam supports from his house, another carting away the thatch above, and another making off with his last year's harvest—all with that spectacular speed which is such a characteristic of termites. (It takes wood-worms and similar maggots, for instance, about twenty years to destroy a beam which termites could dispose of in a week.) Retaliation seems useless. Millions of termites may be destroyed, but the more the destruction the more they seem to increase and spread. Indeed, the humiliating thought arises that in spite of his modern agents of destruction termites may well regard man as their greatest friend.

An ominous sign for the future is that termites, blind as they are, seem to keep in touch with man and know what he is doing and what he is planting. It is as if they had him under a calculating scrutiny. They learn from experience quickly and adapt themselves quickly. There are instances innumerable. To select one or two; in untidy rubber plantations termites had food enough for their needs in the dead trees left lying about; under better management, when these trees were cleared away they attacked the living trees, a thing they had never done before, so that a measure calculated to get rid of termites only produced more destructive ones with different habits. Some termites deliberately "ring-bark" trees in order to kill them and make them edible (to themselves) in due course. (How did they find out this simple method of killing a tree?) In Australia, and elsewhere, farmers taking over new land would find certain portions covered with small "ant-hills." These would be all dug out and, when they reappeared, dug out again. What was the result? Extermination? No, in an amazingly short time those termites abandoned the practices of a line of forebears stretching from time immemorial and ceased to build the tell-tale sign-posts above their towns. In other parts of Australia large tracts of country have had to be abandoned altogether and handed over unconditionally to termites.

In Africa termites would appear to be changing their ways somewhat and, with the building of more solid houses, turning their attention to crops. Whatever damage termites do in that country, and it is a lot, one feels that one must attribute quite half of it to the original settlers, including the natives, the bulk of whom are settlers also but earlier ones than the whites. Nature, who has always been kindly to man and severe to termites, gave Africa (and other countries, too, but we are talking about Africa now) specially equipped termite-destroyers. Foremost amongst these, the heavy artillery so to speak, were two mammals, the Scaly Ant-Eater, or Pangolin (*Manis timmincki*), and the Ant-Bear (*Orycteropus afer*). Both are fairly large, the former looks like some bizarre remnant from the reptilian age, the latter like a pig in a distorting mirror; snout, legs and tail drawn out, it is also the size of a pig. These are nature's qualified and specially equipped termite-exterminators. They live on ants and termites and do no harm to any other living thing. Had they been protected and encouraged, the termite position in Africa would be very different to-day. Both have enormous strength,[1] can break into the cement of termite castles, and both can smell out and dig out those termites that live in unadvertised positions beneath the soil. But they are helpless, slow, and good to eat, and have therefore been slaughtered by man to the point of extermination. Whether termites *do* class man as their greatest friend we do not know, but they ought to!

Termites can only thrive in hot countries, but Pharaoh and other ants have shown us that heat-lovers can accustom themselves to cold. Ships now transport stowaways of every kind from rats to mosquitoes to every part of the globe. Already termites have got a footing in Europe. They are classed as low types, but low or not they once undermined two towns in France without the inhabitants having the faintest idea of what was happening. That termites will in due course invade the temperate regions seems certain.

So marvellous, complex and efficient is the social system of the termites that one is tempted to wonder what they get out of it. To what end have they been so clever? I confess I can see no gain—and this applies to the social insects generally. Individually the social insects seem to be far worse off than the "solitary" insects, the house-flies, spiders (which we will class with the insects for purposes of comparison), the solitary bees and wasps, and others, all very successful forms of life and having time for relaxation and enjoyment. With the social insects the workers, which comprise the bulk of the community, work like slaves in a salt mine, and the best they can hope for is premature death from exhaustion and over-work. "Many hands," says the proverb, "make light work," but with the social insects at any rate it is just the

[1] I have seen five men pulling on a rope attached to an ant-bear in a hole unable to drag it out, so strong were the latter's muscles and claws clinging to the sides. It was a popular idea with many in that country that a whole team of oxen are unable to drag an ant-bear from a hole, but this, I need hardly say, is incorrect.

reverse. If the workers do not die of over-work they are killed earlier by enemies or hunger.

So what gain *do* the social insects get from their socialism? Is it that they get satisfaction from sacrificing themselves for others (to the end that the others may lead similar hard lives also)? If so, we must change our outlook on these insects and grant them a god and a soul and, in justice, a hereafter. Or is socialism just a machine that once started cannot be stopped?

The net result of the efforts of the social insects is that tens of thousands are enabled to live in one place where only tens lived before, but I can see no advantage in mere numbers. With most animals, including men, large populations are fortuitous; the animals breed automatically and automatically fill up spaces when and where conditions permit, but the large populations of the social insects are deliberate, as deliberate as the manufacture of motor cars or other commodities with us.

However, it is too late for the social insects to do anything about it now: they are caught in the toils of their own systems and must go on producing continually their multitudes of slaves.

CHAPTER 13

INTELLIGENCE

I WAS discussing this subject with a man recently when he turned to me and snapped, "What right have you, or any human being, to set yourself up as a judge of the intelligence of ants or any other insects? Look at the mess man has got himself into, all by himself and without being able to blame any outside agency! Look how man has bungled things throughout recorded history!" He said a lot more (for this kind of defeatism is very popular nowadays), but what I have put down is enough. It does not matter whether man is competent to judge intelligence in insects, etc., or not. It is all a sort of game—a kind of jig-saw puzzle.

To call it a game, however, does not mean that it is simple. Half the pieces of the puzzle are missing and the rest are mixed up with pieces from other puzzles. The study of intelligence is mixed up *inter alia* with the study of instinct. Instinct is definable, being what is innate in an animal, but it is by no means so easy to identify and, as it were, separate out. For instance (amongst a number of other difficulties), an animal *learns* during its life, which means that investigators should know the age and experience of their subjects and should, in fact, follow them from the moment they were born.

An interesting example is the Cichlid fish. Tinbergen instances these experiments. The eggs of a young pair that had not bred before were taken away and the eggs of another species substituted. These eggs were accepted and the young raised. The first conclusion is that Cichlid fish will accept any substitutes for their children provided they are allowed to rear them from the egg—just as a hen will rear ducks, geese, turkeys, pheasants, etc., if given the eggs. Unlike the hen, however, our particular pair of young Cichlid fish have *learned* something from this first batch of theirs. What they have learned is wrong but that makes no difference: they have learned (as they think) to identify their young, so that at every breeding season afterwards they will kill off their own young under the mistaken impression that they are not the genuine article! But with pairs of fish that had bred before, it was found that they would never accept the young of species other than their own. They would accept the eggs, but once the eggs hatched, if the young were of a different species from their own they would be killed.

Many of the actions of man himself are instinctive but he is a difficult subject for experiment. The only way really to study him would be to put him alone on a desert island shortly after birth and leave him there to grow up with adequate food and a few observers entrenched in hide-outs. He would acquire no speech and would be unaided by the examples of others so that any tools, etc., he might make would show real intelligence.

Amongst the food provided for him might well be some in tins together with a tin-opener. Would he, one wonders, ever learn to use the tin-opener? And if so, at what age?

This would be an interesting experiment but, in spite of its thoroughness, inadequate in itself, for it is impossible to draw conclusions from one experiment. So we would have to put at least fifty infants on fifty different islands and combine the results of observations on them. Even then conclusions might be wrong, for the one who, for instance, used the tin-opener first might not be the most intelligent, though he would undoubtedly be classed as such by the observers. Some of the failures might have been absorbed by contemplation of the phenomena around. Most would take day and night, storm and rain, waves and tides for granted, but some might ponder over them in a vague way that was hampered by lack of mental speech. One or two (though it is exceedingly unlikely) might wonder why a ripe coconut always fell downwards. These types would probably never learn to use the tin-opener at all, and though the most intelligent of the fifty, would be put down by the observers as the least intelligent. (A classics master also may well have put down Newton as the least intelligent of his class—unless, that is, he had had a talk with the mathematics master.)

Man, by acquiring speech and the different mentality that speech gives, has isolated himself from the other animals. He can study them and draw conclusions, theorise about them, and even learn from them, but he cannot really understand them. That is not to say that he is fundamentally different from them (he was one of their humbler members not *very* long ago); to use a human analogy, he is rather in the position of one, coming from illiterate peasant stock, who leaves his home, has a successful university and business career, mixes with "high society," and then visits the old hamlet. Such a man would feel cut off from the inhabitants there that he once knew so well and would fail really to understand them, though no doubt he would make painstaking efforts to do so.

The older workers, intent on ethnology and physiology, more or less overlooked the psychology of animals. Laymen however have been studying this for a long time. The subject is usually their dog or their cat, because such are available in their homes at all times. From these studies we get *data* which is recorded in endless tales of the sagacity of dogs and cats. But the time we spend studying the psychology of dogs and cats is as nothing compared with the time these animals spend studying the psychology of human beings, and it is because of their more intensive study of us that they exhibit the psychology that furnishes *us* with such interesting study of *them*.

Many people are surprised at how much of their conversation dogs can understand. A dog will pick out such words as "walk," "rat," "gun," "sweet," "biscuit," etc., but this is merely associating sounds with ideas. Men react in the same way when, for instance, in camps or barracks the dinner call is sounded on a bugle. Indeed on such occasions I have seen dogs interpret the sound more quickly than their masters and get to the cook-house door before the men.

It used to be largely held that all the lower animals were motivated by instinct only. That idea has been abandoned, but there still exist those who (possibly because they were brought up on it) believe it. To such, of course, any remarks on intelligence in insects is a waste of time, for to them it does not exist. We are permitted to admire the astonishing feats of some insects but not to give them any credit for them. They become like one of our multiplying machines, that is marvellous and (when in order) infallable but of which nobody says that the machine itself is intelligent, the intelligence belonging to the maker. Similarly, while we admire the functioning of our own heart, liver, brain, lungs, etc., no one calls a man's inside "intelligent." The man himself will go through life doing from time to time clever things for which he will be labelled "intelligent," but none of the things he does will be as clever as the things his component parts do every second as a matter of routine. Where does the cleverness of *this* machine come from? It came about through evolution, but beyond that we know little. Yet it is the cleverness of these component parts that makes the man's intelligence. The over- or under-development of glands can turn a man into a creature with no more intelligence than a greenfly. That dictator, the stomach, too, rules over the man's intellect and not entirely in a negative sense. When in a good mood it stimulates its servant, the brain; when tired, as after a heavy meal, or annoyed, after no food at all, the man's intelligence declines and he would be ill-advised to sit for an examination with his stomach in either of those states. The tricky business of the battle of Waterloo was said by some to have been lost by Napoleon because his intellect was not what it had been in his earlier campaigns, but others put his defeat down simply to indigestion. Even the brain itself has its weaknesses, its almost "human" frailties. When a man is smothered he dies in about three minutes. Yet there is no need for him to die so quickly—he has enough oxygen in his blood to last him nearly twenty minutes—but the brain becomes panic-stricken; all it realises is that there is no oxygen coming in, and promptly resigns.

Instinct presents difficulties in itself. How was it acquired? Very clever traits that are now definitely instinctive would appear to denote intelligence at some previous time in the history of the species (it cannot *all* be put down to Natural Selection; nor must we imagine that a present generation is necessarily more advanced than its remote ancestors).

I started this argument by mentioning those who will

allow no intelligence to the lower animals, and would like to let Dr. Johnson sum up for me. (Not Dr. Samuel Johnson, he never discoursed on this subject, which is a pity for his remarks would have been entertaining at least.) This Dr. J. R. Johnson translated Huber's work from the French and was himself a keen entomologist. He wrote 130 years ago, but those who despise opinions so old should remember that neither ants nor men change much in 130 years.

"Man fondly" (writes Dr. Johnson), "arrogates to himself an active principle pervading his nature, denominated *mind*: that he should feel justly proud of this distinction, of that intellectual superiority which places him so high in the scale of animal existence, excites little surprise; but let him have the candour to imagine that he, perhaps, is not the only being thus gifted; let him but allow a small portion of the same influence upon the lower order of beings, and we shall then have a rational theory to account for those occasional deviations from their natural habits that are inexplicable on the ground of instinct alone."

The usual way of trying to gauge the intelligence of insects is to give them tests, and often this is the only method we have. But it is necessary to be fair, and half the tricks that observers play on insects under the name of "experiments" are not fair. They get their subjects thoroughly upset and then judge their intelligence by what they do immediately in situations never experienced before. Even when the tests are fair, and the subjects not hopelessly distracted . . . but Hobhouse puts it better than I could: "When comparative psychologists take occasional inconsistency as proving the utter absence of intelligence they are using an argument which would equally disprove the existence of intelligence in man."

Although I do not think it wise to take intelligence tests on insects (or on our own children if it comes to that) too seriously, yet they are interesting, and observers have recorded a large number. Almost every problem one could think of has been given to ants and to put them all down would take many books. Sufficient here just to give the general results of these examinations: some ants failed, some passed, some got credits, some distinctions. Which goes to show that ants, like ourselves, vary in their mental equipment. For instance, in many experiments, out of two marked workers from the same nest one would learn what for brevity's sake we will call a "trick" almost immediately, while the other could never learn it.

No one can have failed to notice ants doing apparently foolish things, such as two of them pulling at a load in opposite directions. This latter has been sneered at by Mark Twain, but had that famous writer had a little more patience, and waited, he would have found that the two soon adjusted their ideas and came to a working arrangement. The reason for the cross purpose we so often see in ants is, according to Wheeler, because there are leaders amongst the workers. These are not appointed leaders; they have no authority and certainly get no obedience; they are simply leaders in that they are more energetic and go-ahead. It is they who generally "start" things, even quite important things, and the others follow. When two of these energetic, strong-minded workers seize hold of the same bit of booty, building material, or whatever it is, a conflict of will ensues, and neither feels like giving in for the time being.

Stupid? Of course it is, and a waste of time. But have you ever seen a number of human amateur furniture removers in action? I have, and I have been one myself. What would any observer have said of *us*, I wonder—with our conflict of wills and our pulling in the wrong directions! It is the same old story: we deny intelligence to an insect if it ever behaves with the same stupidity we often exhibit ourselves. (Actually we learn from ants, etc., how stupid *we* are!) Were no inconsistences to be found amongst ants, then I think we *might* deny them intelligence and conclude that the individual units were mere automatic foolproof machines.

I brought up Mark Twain. It is impossible, of course, to quote all he says about the stupidity of ants, but I will cite his summing-up. "A pearl of witty inaccuracy," someone once called it.

"Science has recently discovered that the ant does not lay up anything for winter use. This will knock him out of literature to some extent. He does not work, except when people are looking, and only then when the observer has a green, naturalistic look, and seems to be taking notes. This amounts to deception, and will injure him for the Sunday Schools. He has not judgment to know what is good to eat from what isn't. This amounts to ignorance, and will impair the world's respect for him. He cannot stroll round a stump and find his way home again. This amounts to idiocy, and once the damaging fact is established thoughtful people will cease to look up to him, the sentimental will cease to fondle him. His vaunted industry is but a vanity, and of no effect, since he never gets home with anything he starts with. This disposes of the last remnant of his reputation, and wholly destroys his main usefulness as a moral agent, since it will make the sluggard hesitate to go to him any more. It is strange beyond comprehension that so manifest a humbug as the ant has been able to fool so many nations and keep it up so many ages without being found out."

Well . . . something has made Mark Twain annoyed with the ant. What? The ant has never *asked* us to admire it. All it wishes to do (if it *does* wish) is to conduct its affairs in its own way. So why did this man get so wrought up?—for he wrote pages and pages of quite false accusation. Others have followed suit; quite an anti-ant school exists to-day, not as regards the activities of ants but as regards their intelligence. The reason is not far to seek. Again that much-abused King Solomon started it by setting up the ant as a model. Countless writers since have been busy trying to make men lcok small compared with ants. Men do not mind being given a model (they need take no notice of it), but when they find that the model is not all it was made out to be they become indignant and imagine they have been hoaxed. In short, it is not always necessary to give a dog a bad name in order to hang him, or at any rate to destroy his reputation, giving him a very good name will do the same thing.

As we have said, it has been found by tests that (in the same nest) some ants are intelligent and some are not, and this has not helped us much. We have become a statistic-loving people and like to have things tabulated in percentages. We like summaries. We should like to be shown marks for the intelligence of the various insects set out before us: ants, such and such per cent, bees, so much per cent, and so on. I am afraid we cannot come to any such satisfactory conclusion. But is it ever of any use to try to gauge the intelligence of *social* insects by means of experiments on individuals? Indeed, to expect intelligence from any but a very small proportion of a social community is to ask more from ants than from human beings. We do not judge the intelligence of man from individuals. We say "man" invented electric light, the telephone, the aeroplane, etc., but apart from a *very* few individuals (few, that is, in proportion to the rest) man would still be living in the Stone Age and still worrying about the best way to tie a piece of stone to a stick. But these individuals, these "sports," as it were, crop up from time to time and give us improvements (or so they appear to be at the time!) that the bulk of jostling, shopping, football-watching, cinema-going, in short, the bulk of humanity could never even have begun to think out under any pressure or circumstance. And yet it is quite correct to attribute the ideas and inventions of the few to man as a whole, for man, like the ant, is a social animal even though he has not as yet been able to introduce the order or discipline of ants into his socialism. When ants pooled their resources in brain and sinew they did it in no uncertain way. They went into the furnace so to speak and fused themselves together. They arranged things so that a community worked as a *whole* and could not function otherwise.

Having done this, it seems to me that they are entitled to be *judged* as a whole, and in a community it is not necessary nor even desirable that all the members be brainy. *Some*one has to do the dirty work and the washing-up. Ants now need collective not individual intelligence. Have they got it? Tests, of course, can be made of collective intelligence, but ants are rather difficult subjects. Bees are easier, but again we cannot put down the various tests that have been made. Sufficient to give just one. Someone once thought of giving a hive sheets of wax on which were embossed hollows roughly corresponding to the bases of the cells made by bees. It was a far-fetched idea and the originator probably never thought that bees (whose comb-building was presumably instinctive) would have the intelligence to adopt this labour-saving device. It meant their working on an entirely different principle and in an entirely different way. It meant preliminary inspection and *realisation* of the possibilities. It meant also building sideways, a system new to them. In effect, it was like giving a squirrel a pair of nut-crackers and expecting it to use them.

One might have expected the bees to chew up the wax of the presented sheets and take advantage of the sheets that way. But no—they grasped the idea and built on to and completed the artificially prepared bases. (And if you had taken away one of the workers busy on this task and subjected it to tests, you would probably have found that it behaved with far less intelligence than any house-fly.)

But a better way of judging the intelligence of social insects collectively is simply to assess what they have accomplished up to date. Bees have solved surprisingly difficult chemical and mathematical problems. Ants . . . well, anyone who has read about them in this book or elsewhere knows what ants have accomplished and what they have not, and is as qualified to judge their intelligence as I am.

BIBLIOGRAPHY

APART from papers and journals, the following were amongst the works consulted:

BATES, H. W. (1891). *The Naturalist on the River Amazon*   London.

BELT, T. (1874). *The Naturalist in Nicaragua*. London.

DONISTHORPE, H. St. J. K. (1927). *British Ants*. London, Routledge.

FARREN-WHITE, W. (1895). *Ants and their Ways*. London.

HASKINS, C. P. (1945). *Of Ants and Men*. London, Allen and Unwin.

HUBER, M. P. (1820). *The Natural History of Ants*. London, Eng. trans. by J. R. Johnson.

HUXLEY, J. (1930). *Ants*. London, Benn.

LUBBOCK, J. (Lord Avebury) (1894). *Ants, Bees and Wasps*. New York.

MAETERLINCK, M. (1930). *The Life of the Ant*. London, Eng. trans. by B. Miali. Allen and Unwin; (1927) *The Life of the White Ant*. London, English translation by A. Sutro. Allen and Unwin.

MARAIS, E. N. (1937). *The Soul of the White Ant*. London, Eng. trans. by W. de Kok. Methuen.

McCOOK, H. (1907). *Nature's Craftsmen*. New York, Harper.

MOGGRIDGE, J. T. (1873). *Harvesting Ants and Trap-Door Spiders.*

MORLEY, D. WRAGGE (1953). *Ants*. London, Collins *New Naturalist*.

NOYES, H. (1937). *Man and the Termite*. London, Davies.

SMEATHMAN, H. (1781). *Some Account of the Termites which are found in Africa*, etc. Ray Society.

SNYDER, T. E. (1949). *Catalogue of the Termites (Isoptera) of the World*. Washington, Smithsonian Institute.

STEP, E. (1924). *Go to the Ant*. London, Hutchinson; (1946) *Bees, Wasps, Ants, and Allied Insects of the British Isles*. London, Warne & Co.

THOMAS, M. (1936). *La Notion de l'instinct et ses Bases Scientifiques*. Paris, Librairie Philosophique.

TINBERGEN, N. (1951). *The Study of Instinct*. Oxford, University Press.

WHEELER, W. M. (1910). *Ants*. U.S.A., The Columbia University Press; (1923) *Social Life among the Insects*. London, Constable.

INDEX